out & about
with kids
portland

fourth edition

Have some fun!
♡ willow

out & about
with kids
portland

the ultimate family guide for fun *and* learning

fourth edition

Nelle Nix
&
Shawn M. Jones

SASQUATCH BOOKS
SEATTLE

Printed in the United States of America
Published by Sasquatch Books
Distributed by PGW/Perseus
15 14 13 12 11 10   9 8 7 6 5 4 3 2

Cover illustration (rose): Bob Suh
Cover design: Rosebud Eustace
Interior design: Lesley Feldman
Interior maps: Lisa Brower/GreenEye Design
Interior icons: Jennifer Pearce
Interior composition: Sarah Plein

Library of Congress Cataloging-in-Publication Data
Nix, Nelle.
  Out & about with kids Portland : the ultimate family guide for fun and learning / Nelle Nix and Shawn Jones. -- 4th ed.
     p. cm. -- (Out & about with kids)
  Includes bibliographical references and index.
  ISBN-13: 978-1-57061-595-5 (alk. paper)
  ISBN-10: 1-57061-595-0 (alk. paper)
  1. Portland (Or.)--Guidebooks. 2. Family recreation--Oregon--Portland--Guidebooks. 3. Children--Travel--Oregon--Portland--Guidebooks. I. Jones, Shawn. II. Nix, Nelle. Out and about with kids in Portland. III. Title. IV. Title: Out and about with kids in Portland.
  F884.P83N595 2009
  917.95'490444--dc22
                         2009001563

Sasquatch Books
119 South Main Street, Suite 400
Seattle, WA 98104
(206) 467-4300
www.sasquatchbooks.com
custserv@sasquatchbooks.com

Contents

Acknowledgments

Any guidebook is an accumulation of research and opinion, and each edition builds on the last. This is our fourth edition of *Out & About with Kids: Portland*, and we have many writers to thank for contributing to make this work accurate, complete, and useful.

Elizabeth Hartzell Desimone was the author of the first edition in 1997, and we thank her for laying the foundation of this book with high standards and exceptionally thorough detail. The work of her researchers, Marilyn Soulas and Anina Bennett, is also appreciated.

Thanks to author Nelle Nix who managed and revised our second edition and thank you to contributors Michael Clapp and Sara Kirschenbaum.

For our third edition, thanks in particular to Anne Laufe for her extensive work updating and revising "Agricultural Adventures" and "Parks & Gardens."

For this, our fourth edition, we appreciate the extensive fact-checking. updating, and adding new and valuable information by author and tireless researcher Shawn Jones and her support team and fellow researcher, her husband Greg Coyle.

We all know that parent research requires children to tag along and we offer a special thanks to all the kids who put up with their parents asking one more question and who willingly got in the car for field work when they would have preferred to stay home.

Finally, the editing and production team at Sasquatch Books deserve recognition for their diligence and hard work in getting this sometimes unwieldy manuscript from rough draft to polished final form.

—*Ann Bergman*
Series Editor
Out and About with Kids

How to Use This Book

Our information was current at press time, but things change. Please confirm hours, prices, and location before setting out for your destination.

If you are looking for ideas about things to do with your kids around Portland, we suggest you start with our Quick Index on page 255. It is an easy way to narrow your search and get fresh ideas. Or, if you just want to learn more about all that the Rose City has to offer families, browse through the chapters.

The following icons appear throughout the book:

 Classes and/or workshops for kids

 Birthday parties

 Educational field trips

 Wheelchair/stroller accessible

 Recommended playground

 Free

Introduction: Portland at a Glance

Exploring Portland is like going on a treasure hunt. And truly, there are gems just waiting to be discovered around every corner by curious, adventurous families.

Some of these jewels—like the Oregon Museum of Science and Industry (OMSI), the Oregon Zoo, the Portland Children's Museum, and the World Forestry Center Discovery Museum—shimmer and shine from afar, attracting crowds to admire and explore them. Others—the parks, the fountains, the public art—can catch you by surprise, offering unexpected but glittering delights. Because a treasure hunt is always easier with a good map, that's what we've tried to create in this completely revised fourth edition of *Out & About with Kids: Portland*. We hope this book inspires you and makes it easier for you to chart your own adventures around the city!

The Lay of the Land

Whether you've just moved to Portland or are simply visiting, chances are it won't take long before you'll hear somebody call Portland the "Rose City," a reference to the city's ideal rose-growing climate. Or maybe you'll hear it called "Stumptown," a name reputedly coined in the mid-1800s when the city was growing so fast that tree stumps were left in the middle of roads because no one could take the time to remove them.

But as you're trying to get oriented here, it's helpful to remember that a river runs through the heart of Portland. The Willamette River serves as a natural divider between the city's west side and east side. Likewise, Burnside Street serves as the dividing line between the north and the south.

Downtown Portland is situated on the west side of the river. At its heart is the pedestrian-friendly **Cultural District**, which is where you'll find many of the major institutions for the fine and performing arts, including the Portland Art Museum, the Oregon Historical Society, and the Portland Center for the Performing Arts. Here you'll also see Portland State University, Pioneer Courthouse Square and Pioneer Place, as well as public art on nearly every corner, an abundance of fountains, plenty of sidewalk food vendors, and, of course, many fine restaurants (see chapter 1, Exploring Downtown).

Undoubtedly, it's fun to explore the downtown and its close-in environs, including **Old Town–Chinatown**, with such attractions as the Chinatown Gate and the Portland Classical Chinese Garden; the burgeoning **Pearl District**, with its boutiques, art galleries, and the much-loved Powell's City of Books; and **Nob Hill**, the blocks surrounding NW 21st and 23rd Avenues, a trendy place to shop and dine.

But one of the great things about Portland is that it has a wealth of neighborhoods to explore—more than 90, in fact—and each has its own distinct flavor. Just to name a few, there's the newly revitalized historic Mississippi District in North Portland; quaint Multnomah Village with its shops, cafes, and the well-loved Multnomah Arts Center in Southwest Portland; and the so-called bohemian Hawthorne District, known for its coffeehouses, bookstores, and resale shops, in Southeast Portland. The best way to learn about these neighborhoods and more is just to get out and explore!

Getting Around

Park It!

You can't count on finding vacant parking spaces when you need them in the downtown core. But when you do, a spot will cost you ($1.25/hour Mon–Sat 8 A.M.–7 P.M. unless otherwise posted; free in late evening, all day Sun, holidays). There are still individual parking meters, but where you don't immediately see a meter, you'll need to look for the electronic parking meters, which are replacing all the old-style meters. Usually they're located in the middle of the block. Deposit your money (or use a credit or debit card), wait for the ticket to print, and then stick it to the curbside window.

Can't find on-street parking? You'll find the city's most affordable short-term parking at any of the SmartPark locations downtown—look for their circular red-and-white signs ($1.25/hour for first 4 hours, about $3/additional hour; $2/entire evening after 6 P.M.; $5/daily maximum Sat–Sun 5 A.M.–6 P.M.).

When shopping downtown, remember to ask the merchants you patronize about parking validation. Hundreds of businesses, including many restaurants, validate parking tickets of customers who make purchases of $25 or more. Each stamp is good for two hours of free parking; the merchant picks up the tab. Go to *www.portlandonline.com/smartpark* for a list of participating businesses and for more information.

Portland Streetcar

The Portland Streetcar (*www.portlandstreetcar.org*) created quite a stir when it was inaugurated in July 2001. Hailed as the first modern streetcar in the United States, the city's fleet of seven streetcars run on an eight-mile continuous loop from Legacy Good Samaritan Hospital at NW 23rd Avenue, on Lovejoy and Northrup, through the Pearl District. It also runs on 10th and 11th Avenues near Portland State University and SW River Parkway, Moody (RiverPlace), and Gibbs in the South Waterfront District, where it connects with the Portland Aerial Tram to a terminus at SW Lowell and Bond.

The fares for streetcars are the same as TriMet's, and the streetcar system accepts valid TriMet passes and tickets. There is no charge to riders who travel only within TriMet's Fareless Square. You can buy tickets on streetcars; fare boxes accept coins and $1 and $5 bills, including $1 coins. Debit/credit cards are not accepted.

Streetcar stops are located every three or four blocks downtown. Streetcars run approximately every 13 minutes during most of the day Monday through Saturday and less frequently in the early morning and evenings and on Sundays. A Global Positioning System tracking network that includes reader boards at each of the stops makes it easy to figure out just how long a wait there is before the next car is due. Bicycles and Segways are allowed on the streetcar in the lowfloor section only. For more information, including a downloadable map of the route and how to purchase a streetcar-only annual pass, check the Web site.

TriMet (Buses, MAX, Trolleys)

If the streetcar doesn't get you where you want to go, TriMet can. TriMet (503-238-RIDE [7433]; *www.trimet.org*; offices open Mon–Fri 7:30 A.M.–5:30 P.M.) manages the rest of the Portland area's public transit system, which consists of TriMet buses, Metropolitan Area Express (MAX) light-rail, and the vintage trolleys (see below), which run weekends on part of the MAX lines and on the streetcar line.

Tickets

In Portland there *is* still such a thing as a free ride. Within a 300-block section of downtown called Fareless Square, passengers can ride TriMet buses and light-rail cars for free. Fareless Square includes most of downtown Portland (within the boundaries of the Willamette River, NW Irving Street, and Interstate 405) as well as MAX stations from the Rose Quarter to Lloyd Center and bus stops along NE Multnomah to 13th Avenue.

For travel beyond Fareless Square, adult fares are based on the number of zones you travel through (basic fee: $2/adults, longer rides: $2.30/adults; $0.95 honored citizens [applies to riders ages 65 and older, people on Medicare, or people with mental or physical disabilities], $1.50/children ages 7–17; free/children 6 and under with fare-paying adult; day passes: $4.25/person).

To ride, place exact change or a ticket in the fare box when boarding the bus. MAX tickets can be purchased and validated using the vending machines at each station. (Remember to keep your transfer; it's generally good up to two hours.)

Perhaps the best, and most central, place to purchase tickets is TriMet's ticket office at Pioneer Courthouse Square (SW Sixth Ave and Yamhill), where you can also stop at the visitors' center for tips. You can also purchase TriMet tickets and find schedules downtown in a number of locations, including Portland State Bookstore (1715 SW 5th Ave) and One Main Sundries (101 SW

Main). Throughout the city you can buy tickets at local Fred Meyer, Safeway, and most Albertsons stores. You can usually find different route schedules on racks near the front of the buses.

Buses

Most of TriMet's 93 bus lines loop through the recently revitalized downtown transit mall on SW Fifth and Sixth Avenues. Shelters line the broad brick sidewalks of these byways, and auto traffic is minimized and even eliminated along certain sections of the mall. Television monitors inside most shelters in the heart of downtown show schedules so you can figure out which bus to expect next. If you have a cell phone, you can use Transit Tracker information (503-238-RIDE [7433]) to tell you when the next bus will arrive.

MAX (Light Rail)

There are currently three MAX lines. The **Blue Line** runs east and west from downtown Portland, connecting with Gresham, Beaverton, and Hillsboro. The **Red Line** operates from Beaverton Transit Center through downtown to Portland International Airport, dropping passengers at the airport terminal. And the newest line, the **Yellow Line**, serves North and Northeast Portland between City Center and the Expo Center via Interstate Avenue. Opening in 2009, a new MAX line to Clackamas County—the **Green Line**—will run the length of the Mall, connecting Union Station and Portland State University. Trains typically run every 10 minutes during rush hours and every 15 minutes during the rest of the day.

Portland Aerial Tram

Opened in 2007, the Portland Aerial Tram, linking the South Waterfront and the Oregon Health Sciences University, is the only one in the world that serves as a link with an academic health center and only the second in the nation to provide regular commuter service. The tram cabins rise 500 feet for the three-minute trip over Interstate 5, the Lair Hill neighborhood, and the Southwest Terwilliger Parkway. Take the kids to one of the restaurants on the burgeoning South Waterfront followed by a ride on the tram. The ride is free to children under six and a fun, exciting way to get a bird's-eye view of the city.

More on Getting Around Town

The city of Portland's Office of Transportation (*www.portland transportation.org/getaround*) offers a wealth of information about how to get around town. Especially useful are the bicycle and walking maps. You'll find a link to the maps—along with links to such info as downtown construction projects, the rules for skates and skateboards, and SmartPark locations—at the Web site.

The tram, which departs every five minutes, operates Monday–Friday 5:30 A.M.–9:30 P.M., Saturday 9 A.M.–5 P.M., Sunday 1–5 P.M., May 18–Sept 19 only. The last tram leaves the lower terminal 15 minutes before closing. Adults must purchase a round-trip ticket for $4; TriMet and Portland Streetcar monthly and annual passes are honored, as are C-Tran monthly passes. Tickets can be purchased from the ticket machines at the lower terminal, adjacent to the OHSU Center for Health and Healing at 3303 SW Bond Avenue. The ticket machines accept only credit and debit cards, and quarters. They do not accept paper bills or other coins.

All riders must have a round-trip fare ticket when riding the Tram. The Tram is not a park-and-ride form of transportation. Parking is limited at the South Waterfront. The Portland Streetcar stops at the corner of SW Moody and Gibbs, across the street from the South Waterfront Tram terminal. TriMet riders may ride the bus or MAX downtown and transfer to the Portland Streetcar. Bikes, strollers, and carriages are allowed on the Tram.

Vintage Trolleys

For sheer fun the vintage trolleys still rank as one of the best rides in town. At the turn of the 20th century, electric trolleys offered regular service throughout downtown and into the West Hills. In 1990 four working replicas of the original Council Crest cars were introduced along a light-rail route that links the downtown shopping district with Lloyd Center on the east side.

Always free, the trolleys now run year-round on Saturdays and Sundays along the Portland Streetcar route (see above) between Legacy Good Samaritan Hospital in Northwest Portland and Portland State University. From

March through December the trolleys run on Sundays along the MAX line between Lloyd Center and SW 11th Avenue in downtown Portland. The trolleys run every 30 minutes, stopping at each MAX station along the line. A round trip takes about 40 minutes.

Family Memberships

If your family is the kind that likes to visit and revisit a local attraction—such as a museum or the zoo—purchasing a family membership can make a lot of sense. The benefits usually include more than just admission for your own brood. Newsletters, gift shop discounts, and guest passes often are part of a membership package. Most museums offer a variety of family memberships. A sampling of some of the area's museums is below, along with the cost of a basic family membership. Call individual facilities or check their Web sites for information about memberships that are beyond the basic.

- **Audubon Society of Portland**, 5151 NW Cornell Rd; 503-292-6855; *www.audubonportland.org*; $45.

- **Oregon Historical Society Museum**, 1200 SW Park Ave; 503-306-5198; *www.ohs.org*; $75.

- **Oregon Museum of Science and Industry (OMSI)**, 1945 SE Water Ave; 503-797-4000; *www.omsi.edu*; $90.

- **Oregon Zoo**, 4001 SW Canyon Rd; 503-226-1561; *www.oregonzoo.org*; $69.

- **Pearson Air Museum**, 1115 E. Fifth St, Vancouver, WA; 360-694-7026; *www.pearsonairmuseum.org*; $75.

- **Portland Art Museum**, 1219 SW Park Ave; 503-226-2811; *www.pam.org*; $85.
- **Portland Children's Museum**, 4015 SW Canyon Rd; 503-223-6500; *www.portlandcm.org*; $80.
- **World Forestry Center Discovery Museum**, 4033 SW Canyon Rd; 503-228-1367; *www.worldforestry.org*; $45.

....

Portland Attractions Pass

Designed for visitors, the Portland Attractions Pass ($35/adults, $29/children; prices subject to change) allows you to visit 10 of the city's prime attractions for a fraction of the combined regular price. Best for out-of-town visitors, the pass is available at the Visitor Information Center at Pioneer Courthouse Square (701 SW Sixth Ave; 503-275-8355) and some area hotels and is valid for a seven-day period. (It's not valid with any other discount offer, group rate, or advance ticket sales.) Sites included in the pass:

- End of the Oregon Trail Interpretive Center
- The Japanese Garden
- Oregon Historical Society
- Oregon Museum of Science and Industry (OMSI)
- Oregon Zoo
- Pittock Mansion
- Portland Art Museum
- Portland Children's Museum
- Classical Chinese Garden
- World Forestry Center Discovery Museum

Your week may be hectic, but if you managed to hit all of the attractions included in the pass within the week it's valid, you'd save $23.50 in admissions for a child and $49.75 for an adult!

Information Resources

Portland is home to two free monthly parent-oriented publications, both of which carry calendars of events and articles of interest. Both may be found at public libraries, in some kid-friendly restaurants, and in many area doctors' offices:

- **Metro Parent**, P.O. Box 13660, Portland 97213-0660; 503-460-2774; *www.metro-parent.com.*

- **Portland Family Magazine**, 12725 SW Millikan Way, Ste. 300, Beaverton, OR 97005; 503-906-7952; *www.portlandfamily.com.*

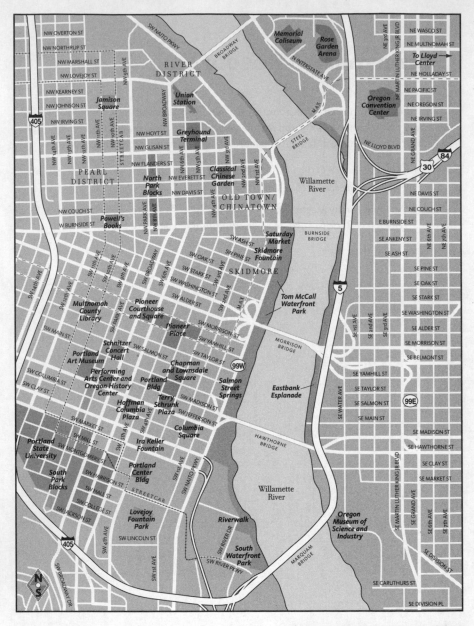

Downtown
Portland

Chapter 1

Exploring Downtown

The best way to see downtown Portland is on foot. Make your visit a treasure hunt, slowing down so that you can appreciate the art in the everyday—from the sidewalk underfoot to the murals on the buildings. Admire the statues, play in the fountains, take a self-guided tour—it's all part of what makes Portland unique.

Landmarks and Public Art

An inscription on the city's oldest artwork, Old Town's Skidmore Fountain, erected in 1888 and newly refurbished, reads: "Good citizens are the riches of a city." In Portland "good citizens" have turned the city into riches.

In 2005 the city of Portland and Multnomah County marked the 25th anniversary of their respective Percent for Art ordinances, which originally required that not less than 1 percent of major publicly funded capital construction budgets be earmarked for public art. (That amount has since been raised to 1.33 percent to cover maintenance and administration.) More than 1,000 artists have been involved with Percent for Art since its inception. From a mammoth hammered-copper statue to computerized water fountains to trompe l'oeil ("fool-the-eye") murals—there's something interesting and curious around nearly every corner downtown.

Benson Bubblers

Parents of thirsty children, rejoice! Almost as recognizable as the rose, the Benson Bubblers that punctuate the downtown streetscape have come to symbolize Portland's free-flowing hospitality. In response to his workers' claims that they frequented the saloons in town because there was no fresh drinking water, in 1912, teetotaling lumber baron Simon Benson donated $10,000 to outfit the city with 20 bronze, four-bowl drinking fountains. A. E. Doyle, architect of the Multnomah County Library, Meier & Frank, and U.S. National Bank buildings, designed the fountains.

There are now some 50 Benson Bubblers in Portland (plus another 75 single-bowl variations located around town). During the drought of 1992 the city installed push buttons for use during periods of water shortage. And in 2005 the Portland Water Bureau began retrofitting the "bubblers" with small devices to reduce the amount of water each fountain uses.

Chinatown

Portland's Chinatown traces its roots back to the 1890s. And with the Classical Chinese Garden, created by Chinese artisans practicing centuries-old craftsmanship, there's an especially good reason to explore this area of the city. Though Burnside tends to be rather shabby near the great Chinatown Gate (NW Fourth Ave and Burnside) and not particularly hospitable to families, it's still fun to get a close-up view of the gate. Dedicated in 1986 to commemorate Portland's Chinese citizens, the authentic design features two fearsome bronze lions, five-tiered roofs, and 64 dragons.

South Park Blocks

From Portland State University at the south (Jackson St) to Salmon Street at the north, the 12 grassy, shaded Park Blocks that form downtown's cultural core are punctuated by sculptures and benches.

Look for statues of Abraham Lincoln and Theodore Roosevelt and for *In the Shadow of the Elm* (Clay St), a granite pavement sculpture constructed in 1984. One of Benson's original bubblers stands at SW Park and Salmon. Can you spot *Salmon on Salmon*? (Hint: It's at the corner of SW Salmon St and Ninth Ave.) To the north, the Studio Building (SW Ninth Ave and Taylor) features a frieze with the busts of famous composers.

Commissioned by the Oregon Historical Society in 1989, Richard Haas' *Oregon History Murals* use a trompe l'oeil technique. Adorning the Sovereign Hotel, the west (SW Park and Madison) and south (SW Broadway and Jefferson) murals depict historical personalities, panoramas, and architectural details.

Just for fun, check out the *Folly Bollards*, a whimsical piece of public art that lines Main Street between Broadway and Park Avenue, between the Arlene Schnitzer Hall and the Newmark Theatre. Bollards are those usually utilitarian posts that separate pedestrian and motor traffic. But these are unique: Each sports a sculpture of a "wise fool" character from the mythology of a different culture.

North Park Blocks

The North Park Blocks (from SW Ankeny to NW Glisan) include some of the city's original park property, given to the city in 1869. Through the years the area's popularity has waxed and waned. With many Portlanders now calling the burgeoning Pearl District home and with the district's reputation for fine dining and shopping, this area can be quite busy (especially during such events as Art in the Pearl, an arts festival that takes place each Labor Day weekend).

For kids, the park's main attraction is the playground. But it's also fun to check out the fountain called *Portland Dog Bowl*, which was designed by the famous Weimaraner dog photographer, William Wegman. And you can't miss the 12-foot bronze sculpture titled *Da Tung* ("Universal Peace"). A replica of a Chinese antique dating from the late Shang Dynasty (1200–1100 BC), this sculpture features a large elephant adorned by figures from ancient Chinese mythology, and on its back it carries a baby elephant, symbolizing safety and prosperity for offspring.

Pioneer Courthouse Square

Affectionately referred to as the city's "living room," Pioneer Courthouse Square (SW Broadway and Yamhill; 503-223-1613; *www.pioneercourthouse square.org*) is a great example of forward-thinking civic planning. Once a parking lot, this grand public space is busy, busy, busy with reportedly more than 26,000 people passing by it each day. It also draws visitors for some 300 planned cultural events (concerts and festivals) as well as for impromptu gatherings. (Find out what's happening at the square by checking the calendar on the Web site.)

You might see brown-bagging executives sprawling on its steps at noon, teens congregating to play Hacky Sack, children climbing up and down the steps under the watchful eye of parents, and commuters lining up for the ride home. (Be aware that the crowd will undoubtedly include a few panhandlers, too.)

To fund the square's construction in 1984, more than 63,000 personalized bricks were sold. Read the names under your feet. Can you find "Wm. Shakespeare," "Sherlock Holmes," "Frodo Baggins," and "Bruce Springsteen"?

Check out the square's echo chamber by standing on the round marble stone in the center of the small amphitheater to the north. Then let the kids discover and explore the square's whimsical artwork: *Allow Me*, a life-size bronze gentleman with an umbrella; *Mile Post*, with distances to nine sister cities and other geographical destinations; and terra-cotta columns that pay homage to the city's architectural roots.

If you're in the square at lunchtime, don't miss the *Weather Machine* in the northwest corner. Each day at noon a musical fanfare kicks off a two-minute sequence that involves the appearance of weather symbols: a stylized sun for clear, sunny skies; a blue heron for drizzly, wet days; and a dragon for stormy weather. Look, too, for the wrought iron gate and fence, which once graced the Portland Hotel. Built in 1890 on this spot, the elegant hotel played host to eight U.S. presidents and Portland's high society until 1951. The whole family can also enjoy the square's outdoor summer movie series, Flicks on the Bricks. Check the Web site for scheduled films. See chapter 5, Outside Fun & Learning, for more open-air movie offerings.

Pioneer Courthouse

Located just east of the square, Pioneer Courthouse (SW Sixth Ave and Yamhill; 503-326-5830; Mon–Fri 8 A.M.–5 P.M.) is the oldest U.S. courthouse on the West Coast. Opened in 1875, it's still in use today by the U.S. Court of Appeals. To protect it against earthquakes, the building underwent a major renovation, which was completed in 2005; now it's open to the public. Be aware that you'll have to go through the courthouse security system to enter the building, which means that adults must have photo ID. Once inside, take the elevator to the third floor and then continue up the stairs to the glass-enclosed cupola for a view of the city and the mountains beyond. The aged, rippled glass and the historic photographs up here put it all in perspective.

Flanking the courthouse on both SW Yamhill and SW Morrison is a series of concrete pools decorated with 25 native animals and birds cast in bronze—seals, bears, ducks, otters. Kids love perching on a deer, petting the beaver, and pretending to feed the ducks.

Plaza Blocks

The Plaza Blocks (SW Third Ave from Madison to Salmon), comprising Chapman and Lownsdale Squares, are separated by Main Street, which curves around a massive bull elk statue given to the city in 1900 by a former mayor. Elk from the West Hills are said to have grazed here before the parks were dedicated in 1852. The squares, which attracted orators and milling crowds of citizens, were designed as gathering places in the 1920s, one for women and children (Chapman) and one for men (Lownsdale). Nearby at Terry Schrunk Plaza (SW Third

Ave and Jefferson), look for another echo chamber as well as a small replica of the Liberty Bell and shrapnel from the Oklahoma City bombing.

Tom McCall Waterfront Park

Portland has been called unsophisticated, provincial, sleepy, and even backward. For instance, there was a time, in 1974, when the governor razed a freeway to build . . . a park! Now named for that governor, this much-loved park stretches for 22 blocks along the west bank of the Willamette River, a testament to progressive visions of civic development.

The Olmsted brothers, Boston's landscaping gurus, first conceived a riverside greenway for Portland in 1904. Today Waterfront Park is a focal point for fair-weather recreation and festivities. It's fun to bike or skate by the harbor (see "Biking" in chapter 5, Outside Fun & Learning). To the north, near the Steel Bridge, check out *Friendship Circle*. Erected in 1990, *Friendship Circle* commemorates Portland's four-decade association with sister city Sapporo, Japan. A collaboration between sculptor Lee Kelly and composer Michael Stirling, the stainless-steel sculpture resonates with sounds that are reminiscent of the flutes and drums of Japan.

Then walk to the area just south of the Burnside Bridge to visit the *Story Garden*, a maze of image and word pathways etched in granite paving stones. *Story Garden* was commissioned in 1993 in response to citizens' requests for a children's playground in Waterfront Park. Move from slab to slab as you would on a game board and create a story, play King of the Hill on the massive granite throne, or share your responses to such tough questions as "What is your sadness?" or "Why is there evil?"

Mill Ends Park

In Portland it sometimes seems there's a park on every corner. But it's easy to miss Mill Ends Park (in the median at SW Naito Ave and Taylor, near Waterfront Park). That's because this one is the world's smallest. Once upon a time, it was just a pothole below the office window of *Oregon Journal* columnist Dick Fagan. Then he planted it with flowers. Visit it so you can say you did, but use caution at this busy intersection.

See Green for Help

If you ever lose your way downtown, just look for a green-and-black-jacketed Sidewalk Ambassador. These friendly folks stroll the streets in the heart of the city (Tues–Sat 10 A.M.–6 P.M., Sun 11 A.M.–6 P.M.) ready to dispense everything from Band-Aids to such information as how to catch a MAX and where to find the nearest restroom. Their mobile information kiosk is stocked with maps, dining guides, and brochures. And with their hand-held Personal Digital Assistants (PDAs), they can access directions, maps, and information about any of the 5,000 businesses in the downtown area.

Fountains Galore

One sure way to get your kids interested in doing a bit of walking downtown, especially on a hot summer day, is to focus the hike on the city's fountains. Have them wear their swimsuits under their clothes, tuck a towel in a backpack, and hit one—or all!—of the following cool spots.

For more information about Portland's fountains, visit the Portland Water Bureau's Web site (*www.portlandonline.com/water*) and search "fountains." There you'll find a printable guide to the best of the city's watery delights.

Essential Forces Fountain
The Rose Garden, 1 Center Ct

This impressive computerized fountain features 500 water jets that emit geyser-force blasts of water.

....

Holladay West Park
NE 11th and Holladay

This tree-filled park sports an interactive water feature where kids delight in the often-changing arc of various water jets.

....

Ira Keller Fountain
SW Third Ave and Market (opposite Keller Auditorium)

Named after an advocate of urban renewal, this park's naturalistic brooks, terraces, and cascading waterfalls are suggestive of the Northwest landscape.

....

Jamison Square
NW 11th between NW Johnson and NW Kearney

This park includes a fountain that simulates a shallow tidal pool.

....

Lovejoy Fountain
SW Third Ave and Hall

This fountain cascades over the lip of an upper pool and splashes down over an irregular series of stairsteps, then out again into a placid lower basin.

....

O'Bryant Square Fountain
SW Park and Stark

O'Bryant Square's fountain is a bronze rose, fittingly titled *Fountain to a Rose*.

....

Salmon Street Springs
SW Naito Pkwy and Salmon

Here the 185 water jets are programmed by computer to keep frolickers on their toes.

Saturday Market

Under Burnside Bridge between SW Naito Pkwy and First Ave
503-222-6072
www.portlandsaturdaymarket.com
Hours: Mar–Dec Sat 10 A.M.–5 P.M., Sun 11 A.M.–4:30 P.M.

If you're out on a weekend, a stop at Portland's Saturday Market can be fun for the whole family. Now more than 30 years old, Saturday Market provides visitors with a sensory adventure. Here you'll find some 300 crafts and food vendors who cluster beneath the west end of the Burnside Bridge to sell their handmade wares and homemade treats. Depending on their age, kids with a little spending money in their pockets gravitate toward the balloon artists, the handcrafted wooden toys, the tie-dyed T-shirts, the scented candles, or the racks of shiny earrings. The challenge is to keep tabs on everyone. If you go fairly early, there's less of a crowd.

After wandering the craft booths, visiting with the artists as you go, you can refuel with a trip to the food area, where the savory options range from fresh cinnamon-sugared elephant ears to peanut-sauce-covered pad thai. Instead of eating on the run, find a bench or chair near the Main Stage to listen to the musicians. Young children love dancing to the live music. Or you can wander over to the Skidmore Fountain area to join the crowd surrounding such acts as a family of tap-dancing kids or a magician at work. (Scheduled entertainment is posted on the market's Web site.)

On the first Sunday of each month, look for the kids' activities booth (generally 11 A.M.–3 P.M.) located next to the market's Main Stage. Here the Portland Old Town Arts and Cultural Foundation sponsors activities that might have your youngster learning to juggle, creating a Chinese block print, or painting a pumpkin to take home.

Skidmore Fountain
SW First Ave and Ankeny

This fountain is the centerpiece of Portland's Saturday Market (see the sidebar later in this chapter).

Tours

Portland's shorter city blocks lend themselves to walkers—and to shorter legs—but even the best hikers can grow weary and need a rest. A downtown walking tour can be especially ambitious, and even more fun, if you incorporate some public transportation into your adventure. Virtually all of the highlights of downtown described in this chapter can be reached—albeit sometimes with a walk of several short blocks—from the MAX, streetcar, or one of the city's many public buses (see "Getting Around" in Portland at a Glance, the book's introduction).

Guided Tours

Where were you in 3rd grade? In Portland that's the year schoolchildren study civics, learn about cities, and explore their hometown. Classrooms sign up en masse with local tour operators to wander the streets and pick up tidbits about the history and architecture of the sights many of us take for granted.

You don't have to be nine years old to get something out of a guided walking tour, though. Families are welcome on these tours, but advance reservations are required. Tour guides are generally amenable to designing a tour to fit your special interests and requirements. Most guides cover lots of territory in upward of two hours of fast walking and talking. If your children are younger than five, consider their attention spans and stamina before booking a tour.

Peter's Walking Tours
503-704-7900 or walkportland@msn.com
www.walkportland.com

Season: Year-round, most weekends and by arrangement (check online schedule or contact Pete by phone or e-mail)

Tickets: $10/adults, $5/children ages 8–19, free/children 7 and under (with paying adult); group rates available

A former elementary- and middle-school teacher, Peter Chausse knows how to captivate children. He stuffs his pockets with magnets, paper, and crayons before a tour, then passes out the materials when the time comes to test the properties of the cast-iron Franz Building (SW First Ave and Yamhill) and make rubbings of the intriguing phrases in *Streetwise* (SW Third Ave and Yamhill). His entertaining downtown walks—running 2 ½ hours at a minimum—highlight art, architecture, urban parks, fountains, and local history. Interested especially in bridges, downtown architecture, parks, or fountains? Just ask, and Chausse will tailor a tour to suit you. Call at least a day ahead to reserve.

....

Portland Bridge Walk

Portland Parks and Recreation (PPR): 503-823-5132 or 501-823-2525
www.portlandparks.org

Season: Spring–fall

Tickets: PPR district residents: $15/adults, $10/children 14 and under; nonresidents: $19.50/adults, $13/children 14 and under

Sharon Wood Wortman literally wrote the book on Portland bridges. The author of *The Portland Bridge Book*, she leads this downtown waterfront tour to the largest mechanical structures in Oregon. You'll visit the tower and pit of the Morrison Bridge and meet a bridge operator. You'll also visit a National Park Service bridge exhibit, learn how to cope with gephyrophobia (fear of bridges), take a short ride on MAX light-rail, walk across a $2.5 million cantilevered sidewalk, and hear the latest poems of bridge walkers. Her Portland Bridge Walk, offered monthly in season for Portland Parks and Recreation since 1991, is made possible, she notes, by the city's compressed layout: Portland has eight notable bridges in close proximity to one another.

Children are welcome on the 3 ½-hour outings, and Wood Wortman, who has lots of experience hosting school groups, can fashion a tour to meet the needs of her guests. Participants view and discuss the eight bridges, walk across two, learn how the city works, and play games to simulate a bridge's balancing act. Reservations are suggested.

Portland Underground Tours

Cascade Geographic Society: 503-622-4798

http://shanghaitunnels.info/

Hours: Year-round, most Thurs–Sat evenings

Tickets: $13/adults, $8/children 12 and under; reservations required

With these tours you actually go underground beneath the city's streets to get a unique glimpse of Portland's past. Offered by volunteers from the Cascade Geographic Society, these educational tours focus on the shanghai trade in Portland and on the West Coast, which survived from 1850 to 1941. During its heyday in Portland at least 1,500 people each year were shanghaied, kidnapped, and sold to sea captains who forced them to work for no pay.

Currently, three main tours are offered: the "Shanghai Tunnels Heritage Tour," the "Shanghai Tunnels Ghost Tour," and the "Shanghai Tunnel Ethnic History Tour." Tours include between 15 and 25 people, last approximately 1 ½ hours, and begin at Hobo's Restaurant (120 NW Third Ave). Note: Due to the subject matter, as well as the fact that it can be hot and stuffy underground, these tours are best for older kids. Consult the tour leader beforehand if you're doubtful about your own child's staying power.

Cascade Geographic Society also conducts tours of the Oregon Trail and other historical sites and trails, as well as tours of old-growth forests and other natural areas. Contact the society for more information.

Urban Tour Group

503-227-5780

www.urbantourgroup.org

Season: Year-round

Tickets: $25/group of 1–5 people, $5/each additional person

A nonprofit volunteer organization with 125 trained guides and more than 35 years' experience leading downtown walking tours (free for school groups), the Urban Tour Group also offers customized guided tours to the public. Call two weeks ahead to schedule a tour. Weekdays are preferable to weekends, when accessibility to many buildings is limited. (For before-you-go fun, check out the virtual walking tour posted at the group's Web site.)

Do-It-Yourself Tours

Are you a do-it-yourself kind of tourist? The Portland Oregon Visitors Association (*www.travelportland.com*) offers a great series of Portland Cultural Tours brochures, which detail self-guided tours around Portland that focus on various cultures, including African American, Chinese, Hispanic, and Japanese. In addition, the *Guide to World Cultures of Portland* lets you know, for example, where you can find a Polish meat market, purchase African crafts, or celebrate the Greek Festival. You'll find these brochures at the visitors center located in Pioneer Courthouse Square, or you can download one from the Web site.

Another valuable resource is the *Public Art Walking Tour* map and brochure, a colorful guide to nearly 100 public art pieces in downtown Portland and the near east side of the city. Available at Portland-area visitors centers, the guide can also be found by visiting the Web site below, or you can ask to have one mailed to you by calling the Regional Arts and Culture Council (503-823-5111; *www.racc.org/walkingtour*, click on "public art").

Chapter 2

Exploring the Natural World

Whether getting an up-close look at a bear's face at the zoo, spotting a giant salamander in the wild, or discovering the wonders of the forest thanks to a fabulously imaginative museum exhibit, introducing our kids to the wonders of our natural world is one of the greatest pleasures of parenting. Portland and environs offer great opportunities for such experiences for all ages at all times of the year.

Animals Up Close

Hart's Reptile World
503-759-3513
www.hartsreptileworld.com

Hart's Reptile World is a menagerie of over 100 snakes, iguanas, geckos, lizards, turtles, tortoises, alligators, and crocodiles. Lovingly cared for by curator Mary Hart, these wonders of nature may not be pretty, but most children (and adults) find them utterly fascinating.

Reptile World used to be open to the public but unfortunately, you can no longer visit and admire the creatures that live there. However, Hart, a renowned reptile handler, will bring reptiles to classrooms, group get-togethers, and birthday parties, for a marvelous lesson and a chance to get a close look and even pet these creatures.

Oregon Coast Aquarium
2820 SE Ferry Slip Rd, Newport
541-867-3474
www.aquarium.org

Hours: Labor Day–Memorial Day daily 10 A.M.–5 P.M., closed Christmas; Memorial Day–Labor Day daily 9 A.M.–6 P.M.

Admission: $14.25/adults, $8.75/children ages 3–12, $12.25/seniors (65+), free/children under 3

Annual family membership: $80

This exceptional aquarium is only 130 miles away, but the road to the Oregon Coast is not a fast one, so plan on a travel time of three hours to reach Newport: It's best to visit as part of an overnight trip to the coast. All ages will love the sea otters and sea lions. For a fun preview take a tour of the aquarium on the Web page and check out the live shark cameras! The aquarium is open year-round, but in summer months expect crowds and long lines.

....

Oregon Zoo
4001 SW Canyon Rd
503-226-1561
www.oregonzoo.org

Hours: Apr 15–Sept 15 daily 9 A.M.–6 P.M. (open at 8 a.m. from Memorial Day through Labor Day); Sept 16–Apr 14 daily 9 A.M.–4 P.M. (grounds open 1 hour after gates close). Open every day except December 25. Check the Web site for the annual Zoolights special evening hours.

Admission: $9.75/adults, $8.25/seniors (65+), $6.75/children ages 3–11, free/children 2 and under; discounted admission second Tues every month: $2/person (children under 3 free); Family Passes available; $2/car for parking; additional fees for train rides, thrill rides, Winged Wonders exhibit, ZooKeys. Show your Max or TriMet ticket for a $1 admission discount.

Annual family membership: $69

Founded in 1887 at the rear of a downtown pharmacy, the Oregon Zoo is the state's leading paid attraction, drawing more than one million visitors each year. On the zoo's 64 rambling acres, you'll find 12 major exhibits that represent various geographic areas of the world. The Oregon Zoo boasts more than 1,000 specimens representing 200 species of birds, mammals, reptiles, amphibians, and invertebrates. One of the things that makes the zoo special and plays a major role in its ongoing popularity is the fact that it is ever-changing. Among the zoo's newer exhibits are a walk-through butterfly aviary called Winged Wonders. Beginning, generally, in late May and running through Labor Day, this exhibit houses butterflies from 40 different species native to North and Central America.

Other exhibits at the zoo include:

- **Red Ape Reserve:** Visitors will have opportunities to observe orangutans and white-cheeked gibbons, indoors and outdoors, exhibiting natural behaviors as they climb and swing over visitors' heads and come nose-to-nose with them at glass viewing windows.

- **Howard Vollum Aviary:** Relax in the warm tropical aviary. Enjoy exotic birds in flight and up close.

- **African Rainforest:** Bats and a variety of tropical birds and waterfowl live among lush vegetation. Tropical thunder, lightning, and a torrential downpour keep the humidity just right for endangered slender-snouted crocodiles, lungfish, and frogs in the swamp area of the exhibit.

- **African Savanna:** Visit the dry, open plains of East Africa, where giraffes, zebras, hippos, and rhinos live along riverbanks and water holes. Be sure to check out the naked mole rats.

- **Fragile Forests, Amazon Flooded Forest, and South American Forest:** Dense rainforest canopy is home to toucans and Saki monkeys; turtles and caimans live in the floodwaters below. This exhibit places visitors within inches of a green anaconda. As they leave the flooded forest, visitors enter the tropical and subtropical forests of southern Brazil, Paraguay, and Argentina, home to shy and illusive ocelots. The exhibit's rock ledges provide a perching place for the cats to hang out.

- **Asian Elephants:** Meet Packy, Portland's star elephant, and his pals.

- **Bears:** Travel beneath the ice floes to see polar bears basking on the shore or taking a dip in the cool waters. See sun bears lounging in trees.

- **Cats of the Amur Region:** Tigers and leopards native to the Russian Far East inhabit this area of the zoo.

- **Great Northwest Exhibit**

- **Cascade Crest:** This replica of an alpine area in the Cascade Mountains features mountain goats and a simulated snow cave.

- **Cascade Canyon Trail**

- **Black Bear Ridge:** Black bears and bobcats await you in this exhibit.

- **Eagle Canyon:** Eagle Canyon walks you through the habitat of the endangered bald eagles and Coho salmon while stressing the importance of forest streams and rivers.

- **Cascade Stream and Pond:** Peer into the beaver den and watch river otters frolic in a cool mountain stream.

- **Cougar Crossing:** Come face-to-face with cougars.

- **Trillium Creek Family Farm:** Feel the wool on a Shetland lamb or brush a pygora goat. This exhibit is run entirely by teen volunteers.

- **Elk Meadow:** This predator/prey exhibit features Roosevelt elk and gray wolves separated by a fence. Watch them interact in close proximity as they would in the wild. Learn about them and their important links.

- **Steller Cove:** Travel through underwater kelp forests and come nose-to-nose with sea otters and sea lions. Use the research station to learn more about the underwater habitat.

- **Insect Zoo:** This seasonal exhibit offers an up-close look at the world of bugs.

- **Island Pigs of Asia:** Meet rare visayan Warty pigs and Babirusa pigs.

- **Lilah Callen Holden Elephant Museum:** Learn about Portland's Asian elephant breeding program and the role elephants play throughout the world.

- **Lorikeet Landing:** Some of the world's most beautiful birds live in this walk-through, open-air aviary. Visitors may purchase small paper cups of "nectar" (actually fortified fruit juice) at the entrance to the aviary. The lorikeets fly down and drink from the cups, making this exhibit highly interactive. Please note that on busy days, the lorikeets may run through their daily allotment of juice before the exhibit closes, therefore the feeding opportunity is not guaranteed.

- **Penguins:** Endangered Humboldt penguins can be seen both above and below the water in this exhibit, which replicates their native habitat. The penguins share their exhibit with a flock of Inca terns.

- **Primates:** Look high to see monkeys and mandrills swinging and resting.

- **Tree Kangaroos:** Meet tree kangaroos native to New Guinea. Watch them balance on tree branches with their thick tails.

- **Warren J. Iliff Sculpture Garden:** The sculpture garden is a way for children to experience animals in a different way: They can see replicas of animals that might be a little less frightening than the real thing.

It's next to impossible to see everything in one day. So our best advice is to wear good walking shoes, study the zoo map (downloadable from the Web site or available at the zoo entrance), and establish your child's priorities. And, of course, it pays to be flexible.

If you have a young child, take along a stroller or rent one ($6) near the zoo entrance. Wheelchairs and electric scooters are available for rental. And though food can be purchased at the zoo from food carts, the AfriCafe (which overlooks an aviary), or the Cascade Grill, you're also free to pack in your own cooler. Many families plan their visit around a relaxed picnic on the grassy lawn by the amphitheater.

When you tire of walking, you might want to hop a ride on the Washington Park and Zoo Railway (whose runs are dependent on weather and crowd conditions). From late March to Memorial Day the train offers a 12-minute trip ($3/person, ages 3 and up) that circles the zoo grounds. Then, from Memorial Day through mid-September, the train runs a daily 35-minute round-trip ride ($5/person, ages 3 and up) that chugs through the hills of Washington Park to the International Test Rose Garden and back. The train schedule is based on the number of train riders, not a fixed timetable, but it typically departs at least once per hour.

You might also want to enrich your zoo experience by purchasing a ZooKey ($2.50; available in Cascade Outfitters Gift Shop) to "unlock" the secrets of various animals at 16 stations around the zoo. For extra fun check out the Kid's Zone on the zoo's Web site. There you'll find amazing animal facts, a behind-the-scenes tour, and fun activities such as tips for drawing animals.

Note: Since 1979 the zoo has hosted a popular summer concert series, which in the recent past has featured such talent as Chris Isaak, Emmylou Harris, the Indigo Girls, the Gipsy Kings, Susan Tedeschi, and Portland's own Pink Martini. (For the current concert schedule, check *www.oregonzoo.org/concerts*.)

Wildlife Viewing

Zoos offer fabulous, up-close views of animals and a chance to see endangered species, but spotting a creature in its natural habitat gives a unique thrill of discovery. Your visit to one of the scenic wildlife areas described below can be turned into a treasure hunt: Give the kids a list (or, better still, a collection of photos) of the plants, birds, and animals they might spot in the area they will be exploring.

Audubon Society of Portland Wildlife Sanctuary
5151 NW Cornell Rd, Portland
503-292-6855
www.audubonportland.org

Hours: Nature Center: Mon–Sat 10 A.M.–6 P.M., Sun 10 A.M.–5 P.M.; trails: year-round dawn–dusk. Wildlife Care Center: daily 9 A.M.–5 P.M.

Admission: Free

Nestled against Forest Park's southwestern flank, the Wildlife Sanctuary provides a tranquil escape from city life. Home to the giant Pacific salamander (it barks like a dog and grows to be a foot long) and bats (look for wooden bat houses nailed high up in trees), in addition to a variety of bird species, the 150-acre park consists of lush native forest and a maze of more than 4 miles of trails. The trails weave and loop over bridges and boardwalks, past a pond, below a rough-hewn picnic hideout, alongside Balch Creek, and up and down steep hillsides. Two longer loops begin south of Cornell (be alert when crossing this busy road).

The Wildlife Care Center, where volunteers tend to injured birds and other forest creatures, is located at the trailhead. Peek in the windows to see them gently handle baby birds and drip nutrients into their beaks using syringes. Permanent residents, whose cages face the outdoor courtyard, include a red-tailed hawk, a northern spotted owl, and a peregrine falcon.

The Nature Center gives an up-close look at the display of birds, nests, and eggs and at the backyard birds and squirrels that come to feast at a large platform feeder. (The Nature Center is wheelchair accessible, but the trails are not.)

The Audubon Society of Portland hosts a regular selection of outstanding nature programs for families and children. Day-camp sessions (pick and choose classes of interest) are offered during winter, spring, and summer vacations. Field trips and workshops are scheduled throughout the year. Call for a program guide or check the Web site, which is frequently updated.

Audubon also offers the Junior Audubon program for the children of members, beginning in 3rd grade. This club includes monthly activities, participation in the annual bird-a-thon, and an overnight trip. Especially good for families with young children is a group called Fledglings, which meets during the week on various days to explore nature together. Call the society for details. In addition, watch for the guest speakers who make presentations at Nature Night (Sept–June second Tues each month, 7 P.M.). Call ahead to assess suitability for children.

Camassia Natural Area
Walnut St, West Linn
http://nature.org

The Nature Conservancy chose to preserve this 26-acre rocky plateau above the Clackamas and Willamette Rivers because of its extraordinary floral diversity, including rare plants and uncommon wetland and grassland communities. Camassia Natural Area is named for common camas—historically a highly valued food source of Pacific Northwest Native Americans—which blooms profusely in April and early May.

More than 300 plant species are found on the preserve, including some rare Willamette Valley species. The shallow soils of this rocky plateau support wet meadows, Oregon white oak and madrone woodlands, vernal and permanent ponds, and even a stand of quaking aspen. The preserve provides habitat for many well-known bird species, including the wood duck, California quail, hairy woodpecker, western bluebird, and golden-crowned kinglet. In spring and summer, green mosses and purple camas pose a stunning contrast to the dark gray basalt bedrock.

Make sure kids stay on the paths and wear long pants to avoid the poison oak. No restrooms are available.

Jackson Bottom Wetlands Preserve
Hwy 219 south of Hillsboro
503-681-6206
www.jacksonbottom.or

Hours: Daily dawn—dusk; Wetlands Education Center: daily 10 A.M.–4 P.M.

Admission: $2/ages 10–99

Located within the city limits of Hillsboro, the 710 acres of Jackson Bottom Wetlands Preserve provide a tranquil sanctuary for both people and animals. The quiet, open waters, rolling meadow, and upland ash and fir woods are home to thousands of ducks and geese, deer, otters, beavers, herons, and eagles.

Songbirds and small mammals, as well as salamanders and rare wetland plants, are also dependent on the marshes of the preserve.

The Wetlands Education Center features hands-on exhibits where kids can learn more about the area's flora and fauna, either before or after exploring the preserve. At the north end of Jackson Bottom a covered viewing shelter is both wheelchair and stroller accessible. There, one of the major attractions had been a nesting pair of bald eagles, whose nest is now on display in the Education Center. The south end of the preserve features 3 miles of hiking trails. Wandering along the Tualatin River and past ponds and marshy areas, these trails are level and therefore easy for kids to navigate. But beware: They are not necessarily stroller friendly; backpack carriers are best for transporting the littlest members of the family. No dogs or bicycles are allowed.

Interpretive signs throughout the preserve, designed by Hillsboro schoolkids, make for easy self-guided tours. Every Wednesday at noon, from September through June, a preserve volunteer shows up at the north end's viewing site for a free "Lunch with the Birds" program. The preserve also hosts occasional family-friendly events, such as bird walks in the morning or night hikes suitable for the entire family. Call or check the Web site for details.

....

Oaks Bottom Wildlife Refuge
SE Seventh and SE Sellwood Blvd, Portland
503-823-PLAY (7529)
www.portlandonline.com/parks/

Hours: Daily 5 A.M.–midnight. North parking lot closed at 10 P.M.

Admission: Free

Covering 140 acres, Oaks Bottom Wildlife Refuge started out as simply a wetland on the east bank of the Willamette River. Now its hiking trails are favored by bird-watchers aplenty. Some 100 species have been identified here, with eagles, hawks, pintails, quail, coots, woodpeckers, kestrels, and mallards all known to make appearances. But the bird that draws many people to Oaks Bottom is the great blue heron, the official bird of the city of Portland. Because it's near one of the rookeries on Ross Island, the refuge is a favorite place for many of these impressive birds.

The Springwater Corridor on the Willamette trail, flanking the refuge's western edge, is a popular biking spot for Portland cyclists of all ages. If you stop on the paved trail to look at birds, just beware of the racers speeding by. No bikes are allowed on the unpaved nature trail in the refuge. For restrooms, go to nearby Sellwood Park.

....

Ridgefield National Wildlife Refuge
Headquarters: 28908 NW Main Ave, WA
360-887-3883
www.ridgefieldrefuges.fws.gov

Hours: May 1–Sept 30 daily dawn–dusk

Admission: Free

It's a bit of a drive to reach the Ridgefield National Wildlife Refuge, located in the town of Ridgefield, Washington, about 20 miles north of Portland, but the whole family will agree it's worth it to see the wide variety of birds and animals in their natural habitat. Covering more than 5,000 acres of marshes, grasses, and wetlands, the refuge is home in fall and spring to migrating sandhill cranes, swans, shorebirds, and songbirds. Year-round residents include red-tailed hawks and great blue herons. Black-tailed deer, coyotes, raccoons, skunks, beavers, river otters, and brush rabbits make an occasional appearance.

The 1.2-mile compacted gravel walking trail is wheelchair and stroller accessible. A 4.2-mile auto tour loop is also open to foot traffic. The newest addition to the area is the Cathlapotle Cedar Plank House, built as an outdoor classroom for learning about the rich natural and cultural history of the area. Ridgefield was the site of Cathlapotle, one of the largest Chinookan villages that Lewis and Clark encountered on their journey west. A map of the area and portable toilets are located at the River "S" Unit visitors contact station of the refuge.

Sauvie Island
Hwy 30, 10 miles northwest of Portland
Oregon Department of Fish and Wildlife area headquarters: 18330 NW Sauvie
Island Rd
503-621-3488 (ODFW headquarters)

Hours: Year-round, many wildlife areas closed during hunting season, Oct–Apr;
call for details

Fees: Parking: $3.50/day, $11/year

Did you know that Sauvie Island is the largest freshwater island in the U.S.? Luckily for us, Oregon Parks and Wildlife has set aside 12,00 acres of the island as the Sauvie Island Wildlife area. This has ensured public access to lakes, beaches, wildlife, and plants that make the island a unique and natural experience.

When visiting Sauvie Island, pick up your parking pass at the general store on the east end of the Sauvie Island Bridge, and head to one of several areas to see songbirds, bald eagles, wading birds, and a resident flock of sandhill cranes. Best places to see a variety of kid-pleasing species include Coon Point, the Oak Island Nature Trail, and the Eastside Wildlife Viewing Platform off Reeder Road.

Stop by the Oregon Department of Fish and Wildlife area headquarters for a map of the area and information about what birds you're likely to see in what season. Metro (the Portland area's regional government) and the Audubon Society of Portland sponsor numerous trips to Sauvie Island at all times of the year, some geared especially toward children and/or beginning bird-watchers.

See chapter 4, Agricultural Adventures, for flower, fruit, and pumpkin picking sites and seasons.

Smith and Bybee Lakes Wildlife Area
On Marine Dr 2.5 miles west of I-5, exit 307, Portland
503-797-1850
www.metro-region.org/parks/smithbybeepage.html

Hours: Daily dawn–dusk

Admission: Free

A collection of facilities completed in 2005, including a covered shelter, interpretive displays, and restrooms, has brought new attention to Smith and Bybee Lakes, one of Portland's best-kept secrets. Tucked away in an industrial area of Portland, the 2,000-acre wildlife area is the largest protected wetland within an American city. Here, just minutes away from downtown, quiet visitors may spot beavers, river otters, nutria, black-tailed deer, ospreys, bald eagles, and western painted turtles.

A 0.5-mile segment of the old Marine Drive has been newly paved for hikers and bikers and is completely accessible by Americans with Disability Act standards. Budding birders can check things out from two different wildlife-viewing platforms. For the best bird viewing, go during winter or spring, when the area has the most water—and therefore the most birds.

If you have access to a canoe or other nonmotorized boat, you might have the upper hand when it comes to seeing wildlife. The canoe launch (0.25 mile east of the larger parking lot) provides convenient access to Smith Lake and even includes 10 parking spaces reserved for paddlers.

Visitors will also encounter pieces of environmental art that are functional as well as beautiful. The sculpted wooden poles, carved boulders, and other pieces invite adults and kids alike to discover the natural and cultural history of the area.

During summer a naturalist offers free weekly programs at the wildlife area for school-age children accompanied by a parent. Program themes vary, with birds, bugs, mammals, and turtles each targeted in turn. Check the Web site for times and days.

....

Tualatin River National Wildlife Refuge

19255 SW Pacific Hwy, Sherwood
503-625-5944
www.fws.gov/tualatinriver

Hours: Daily dawn – dusk

Admission: Free; pets not allowed

Just a few short miles from the center of Oregon's largest city, the honking of geese replaces the honking of car horns. This special place is a refuge, a haven for wildlife and people. Born of a community's dream, and made possible by their support, a wildlife refuge now thrives in the backyard of a growing metropolis.

Located on the outskirts of Portland, Tualatin River National Wildlife Refuge is one of only a handful of urban wildlife refuges in the country. Situated within the floodplain of the Tualatin River, the refuge comprises less than 1 percent of the 712-square-mile watershed. Yet, due to its richness and diversity of habitats, it supports some of the most abundant and varied wildlife in the watershed.

The refuge is now home to nearly 200 species of birds, over 50 species of mammals, 25 species of reptiles and amphibians, and a wide variety of insects, fish, and plants. The refuge has also become a place where people can experience and learn about wildlife and the places they call home.

Be sure to check out the information kiosks before heading out on the trails. Trails are for walking only. To minimize disturbance to wildlife, no bicycling, jogging, or running is permitted.

Pets are not allowed on the refuge. They disturb wildlife and will scare animals away even before you get a chance to see them.

....

Whitaker Ponds Natural Area
7040 NE 47th Ave, Portland
www.portlandonline.com/parks/

Whitaker Ponds Natural Area is another hidden gem, this one located in a gritty section of Northeast Portland. Part of the site was once a junkyard full of scrap metal, old cars, and 2,000 tires. After public acquisition of the land, the junk was removed, and the site has since been restored with thousands of native plants. A black cottonwood forest stretches eastward from NE 47th between the two ponds and the Whitaker Slough. The trail around the western pond provides a scenic walk for kids of all ages. Look for great blue herons, ospreys, brown-headed cowbirds, willow flycatchers, and perhaps even a great horned owl. Bring a snack to eat in the gazebo, and you might see deer come out to graze. Portable toilets are available near the parking area.

Museums That Teach Natural Science

Oregon Museum of Science and Industry (OMSI)
1945 SE Water Ave, Portland
503-797-OMSI (6674)
www.omsi.edu

Hours: Mid-June–Labor Day daily 9:30 A.M.–7 P.M.; Labor Day–mid-June Tues–Sun 9:30 A.M.–5:30 P.M.; closed Thanksgiving and Christmas

Admission: $11/adults, $9/seniors 63 and up and children ages 3–13; additional fees for other attractions—Omnimax: $8.50/adults, $6.50/children and seniors; planetarium: $5.50/person; submarine: $5.50/person; laser matinee: $5.50/person; laser evening: $7.50/person; motion simulator: $4/person; combo ticket (includes one museum admission, Omnimax, and choice of submarine, planetarium, or laser matinee): $21/adults, $17/children and seniors (each ticket redeemable up to 60 days past purchase date); special "2 for 1 Thursdays"—after 2 P.M. buy one ticket to any attraction and get one free (offer not applicable to combo tickets or motion simulator and not valid during peak periods, including summer, winter break, and spring break)

Annual family membership: $90

Parking: $2

The Oregon Museum of Science and Industry's stated goal is to "put the '*wow!*' in science for the kid in each of us." And it succeeds on a grand scale. A world-class tourist attraction and educational resource, OMSI resides in a gleaming steel-and-glass structure on the east bank of the Willamette River. The museum's five exhibit halls and eight science labs offer hundreds of interactive exhibits and hands-on demonstrations, covering a space of more than 200,000 square feet with make-you-think fun.

Here the signs read: "Please touch!" And kids—and adults alike—don't hesitate to dive in and take advantage of the opportunity. One of the museum's most popular spots for kids is Turbine Hall, to the right of the museum entrance, where there are a multitude of hands-on exhibits and labs to explore. You can learn about space by launching a water rocket or climbing into a replica of the Gemini space capsule; program a robot or build an aqueduct to bring water to a model town; design your own flying machine; build a contraption of hoses to send balls bouncing all around; or discover the hair-raising effects of static electricity with the Van de Graff Generator.

Upstairs, the museum's second floor harbors both the Earth Science and Life Science halls, along with a variety of labs, including the Paleo Lab and Life Lab. Among other things, you can step into the middle of a 5.5-magnitude earthquake; touch a twisting vortex of air that simulates the wind dynamics of a tornado; meet Bubba, a 13-foot python; and compare your foot size to that of a dinosaur's.

Also on the second floor are the Science Playground and Discovery Lab, geared especially for kids from birth to age six and their families. Sandland is populated by budding paleontologists who sift and dig in the "fossil pit" to unearth dinosaurs. The "Illumitune" draws toddlers eager to experiment with making music, and the Waterworks area—with its buckets for pouring and boats to float—is always awash with avid hydrologists. In the Discovery Lab youngsters learn about basic chemical reactions by mixing colors, painting, and playing with Flubber.

Along with its permanent exhibits, OMSI is also popular for the temporary exhibits it brings in, such as "Magic: The Science of Illusion," which let kids explore the art and science behind entertainment magic like mind reading and levitation and "Dinosaurs, China's Ancient Giants," a touring exhibition including more than 20 original fossils, complete with interactive displays. Be sure to check out the Omnimax Theater, where films including *Mystery of the Nile*, *Dinosaurs Alive*, *Grand Canyon Adventure*, and *Lewis and Clark: Great Journey West* play. (The Omnimax has also started showing such well-known films as *Harry Potter and the Prisoner of Azkaban* and *Charlie and the Chocolate Factory*.) Also well liked are shows (including laser shows) at the Kendall Planetarium and tours of the USS *Blueback*, a naval submarine in service for 31 years that is now permanently docked in the river.

Somewhere in the midst of all the fun, remember to take time for refueling. You can bring in your own snacks or purchase some in the vending area near the Omnimax Theater or at the museum's cafe, which overlooks the river.

There's no doubt about it: There's a lot to see at OMSI. Because of that, many families opt for a membership and make the museum part of their regular schedule. If you're averse to crowds, be aware that the museum is busiest on holiday weekends—especially during cold, rainy weather. Be sure to check the OMSI Web site for special events, including traveling science shows and live satellite viewings of a total eclipse of the moon.

....

Rice Northwest Museum of Rocks and Minerals
26385 NW Groveland Dr, Hillsboro
503-647-2418
www.ricenwmuseum.org

Hours: Wed–Sun 1 P.M.–5 P.M.

Admission: $7/adults, $5/students, free/children under 5

Bring your rock hounds to one of the finest collections of rocks and minerals in the Pacific Northwest. See petrified wood, fossils, gemstone crystals, thunder eggs, a large agate collection, and more. Group tours daily by appointment.

....

World Forestry Center Discovery Museum
4033 SW Canyon Rd, Portland
503-228-1367
www.worldforestry.org

Hours: Daily 10 A.M.–5 P.M., except Thanksgiving, Christmas Eve, and Christmas Day

Admission: $7/adults, $6/seniors 62 and up, $5/children ages 5–18, free/children under 5; group rates available

Annual family membership: $45

Founded in 1964, the World Forestry Center has completed a $7.5 million exhibit and building renovation and opened the doors of its Discovery Museum. Located in Washington Park, near the Oregon Zoo and the Portland Children's Museum (see map on page 180), the Discovery Museum's goal is to change the way we look at trees.

A great way to begin a visit here is to step into the small theater just to the right of the entrance to view a short film about what makes a forest. After glimpses of forests around the world—boreal, tropical, subtropical, and temperate—and learning that no two forests are alike, you're ready to dive in and explore.

On the first floor the Dynamic Forest exhibit lets you consider trees from every angle. By manipulating a video camera, you can search a tall conifer for a pine marten, a brown creeper, a nest of red-tailed hawk chicks, and more. Then, by climbing through a hollow log, you discover the animals and insects that call it home. And finally, you can "go underground" to discover and play with (stuffed) animals that live there: skunks, weasels, coyotes, and more.

Other exhibits teach visitors about diversity, forest management challenges, and the benefits of forests and trees. You can learn how to plant trees, go for a white-water raft ride without getting wet, test your skill at hitting a target in a smoke jumper's parachute, and try your hand using a simulator at maneuvering a huge timber harvester.

On the second floor you continue exploring via videos that have you ride the Trans-Siberian railway, take a jeep through Kruger National Park in South Africa, and step into a canopy crane for a visit to a tropical forest.

No food is allowed inside the museum, but you can bring your own snacks and eat them outside while checking out "Peggy," a refurbished 1909 locomotive used to haul an estimated billion board feet of logs during her career with a logging company. Check out the Web site for special exhibits and events.

....

Natural Geologic Wonders

To explore the natural wonders of the world, you have to pack up the kids and go. Bring along a picnic and maybe even read a book or check out a Web site in advance for some background so you can answer the inevitable questions. This kind of "in-the-field" exploration is perfect for young scientists—plenty of chance to run and shout and discover natural treasures for themselves.

John Day Fossil Beds National Monument

Visitors center: 420 W. Main, John Day
541-987-2333
www.nps.gov/joda/home.htm

Season: Visitors centers, seasonal; trails and beds, year-round. Check Web site for seasonal hours.

Admission: Free (donations welcome)

Located about 230 miles (about a five-hour drive) east of Portland, this national monument necessitates an overnight trip, but it is well worth it. Within the volcanic deposits of the scenic John Day River basin is a well-preserved fossil record of plants and animals, spanning more than 40 million of the 65 million years of the Cenozoic Era (the "Age of Mammals and Flowering Plants"). More than 160 kinds of mammals were discovered in this world-renowned site, whose three units—Clarno, Painted Hills, and Sheep Rock—are scattered around the John Day area in north-central Oregon.

Regularly scheduled ranger-conducted programs are offered year-round, as well as fossil museum talks, trail hikes, and off-site presentations, all featuring the geologic and paleontologic story. The schedule of activities changes during each of the four seasons. There is also an extensive field trip program, and children can learn online about the Junior Ranger program.

Mount St. Helens National Volcanic Monument

U.S. Forest Service Mount St. Helens National Volcanic Monument, WA
360-247-3900 (headquarters), 360-274-2100 (visitors centers)
www.fs.fed.us./gpnf/mshnvm/

You can't live in or visit the Northwest without seeing the lateral blast zone of the 1980 eruption of Mount St. Helens. See "Mount St. Helens" in chapter 10, Out-of-Town Excursions, for details.

Sky Above

Although a fascination with the night sky is something adults and children share, we often forget that we can explore the world of comets, moons, and planets together as a fun family outing.

Haggart Astronomical Observatory
John Inskeep Environmental Learning Center: 19600 S. Molalla Ave, Oregon City
503-657-6958 ext. 5665
http://depts.clackamas.edu/haggart/

Hours: Hours are dependent upon the weather and volunteer staffing. Call the observatory on the day of your visit to confirm.

Admission: $3/person donation suggested

The Portland area's only public observatory, Haggart Astronomical Observatory, houses both a 24-inch reflecting telescope and a 13-inch telescope in a 45-foot tower. Each Saturday evening, volunteers staff the observatory, dedicated to helping all comers view stars, planets, and deep-space objects. The tower accommodates just eight visitors at a time, and you might have to wait a bit for your turn at the lens if a night is particularly clear—especially during summer when it's warm and more stargazers are likely to turn out. While you wait, though, you can tinker with various star-related activities, learning to identify constellations or playing with a solar system model. You can also take a turn at the 10-inch telescope, when it's available, set up in the parking lot where a volunteer offers stargazing tips there as well.

Planetarium Sky Theater

Mount Hood Community College: 26000 SE Stark St, Gresham
503-491-7297
www.mhcc.edu/pages/

Hours: Public shows: Jan–Aug second Mon every month, 7 P.M. and 8 P.M.; for current show information, visit Web site

Admission: $1/person

With a 30-foot hemispherical dome, comfortable seating for 70, special effects, and an enhanced audio system, the Mount Hood Community College planetarium puts on a star-studded show. Planetarium director Douglas McCarty, an astronomy instructor for more than 25 years, tailors the monthly public show to his audience. Children are always welcome (McCarty encourages questions), and the programs use the current night sky as a springboard to discuss recent discoveries in astronomy and space science. Visitors are seated on a first-come, first-served basis, so arrive early to be sure of a seat.

Culture for Kids

Most kids naturally love art, music, and drama. So while the word "culture" may sound a bit daunting, attending a museum or a cultural event shouldn't be. The key is to consider both what is age-appropriate and what is fun. In Portland there's plenty to do that scores high in both those categories. And don't worry: Your adventures don't have to be costly. This chapter offers a listing of free or almost-free arts opportunities for families. Check out the Web sites and get out and about and enjoy exploring the rich world of the arts with your child!

Chapter 3

Art Museums

Museum of Contemporary Craft
724 NW Davis St, Portland
503-223-2654
www.museumofcontemporarycraft.org

Hours: Tues–Sun 11 A.M.–6 P.M., Sun 1 P.M.–5 P.M., Thurs 11 A.M.–8 P.M.

Admission: Free

In 1937 a group of women who believed in the importance of creativity and the power of the handmade created the Oregon Ceramic Studio on a hill overlooking Portland. This museum showcases some of the best in Northwest crafts from nationally recognized craftspeople as well as emerging artists.

Portland Art Museum
1219 SW Park Ave, Portland
503-226-2811, 503-276-4225 (education department)
www.pam.org

Hours: Tues, Wed, Sat 10 A.M.–5 P.M., Thurs–Fri 10 A.M.–8 P.M., Sun noon–5 P.M.; closed Mondays and major holidays

Admission: $10/adults, $9/seniors 55 and up and students 18 and up, free/ children 17 and under (children under 14 must be accompanied by an adult); prices vary for special exhibitions

Annual family membership: $85

The Portland Art Museum is known especially for its holdings of French paintings, English silver, and the arts of the native peoples of North America; for its graphic arts collection; and for a center devoted to the artists of the Pacific Northwest. When it comes to families, the museum is also known for its efforts to provide family programming, which includes Museum Family Sundays, held several times a year in conjunction with different exhibitions (see "Arts and Crafts" in chapter 6, Inside Fun & Learning).

....

Oregon Historical Society

1200 SW Park Ave, Portland
503-306-5198
http://www.ohs.org/

Hours: Tues–Sat 10 A.M. - 5 P.M.,Sun Noon–5 P.M. , closed Mon

Admission: $10/adults, $8/students (over 18) and seniors (over 60), $5/children (6–18), free/children 5 and under. Free to the public on the 3rd Sat of every month.

Easily identified by its huge trompe l'oeil *Oregon History Murals*—covering one entire side of the building—the Oregon Historical Society has been the keeper of the state's historical treasure trove since 1898. The Society houses over 85,000 fascinating artifacts, including ancient objects from the earliest settlements and objects that illustrate exploration in the Oregon Country, the growth of business and industry, the development of artwork and crafts, maritime history, and many other topics. There is certainly something to incite the imagination of every member of your family.

Dance

Jefferson Dancers

Jefferson High School Performing Arts Department: 5210 N. Kerby Ave, Portland
503-916-5180
www.jeffdancers.pps.k12.or.us

Season: Year-round

Tickets: Varying prices, depending on performance.

Established in 1974, the Jefferson Performing and Visual Arts Magnet Program was devised to improve inner-city school enrollment along with student motivation and self-esteem. Drawing from a multi-ethnic student body, the program offers training in dance, theater, music, television, and visual arts.

One of the program's unbridled success stories is the Jefferson Dancers. An ensemble composed of the department's most advanced dance students, the Jefferson Dancers have been known to tour throughout the Northwest, in western Canada, and in France. They also attend the National High School Dance Festival in Miami. And, of course, they offer a series of performances at Jefferson High School's auditorium in the spring that are open to the public. Unlike most professional companies, this dance troupe maintains an ambitious repertoire of works in all dance styles—tap, ballet, jazz, modern, ethnic, and musical-theater numbers. The resulting potpourri productions are all the more exciting to children in the audience.

Oregon Ballet Theatre

818 SE Sixth, Portland
503-2-BALLET (222-5538), 503-227-0977
www.obt.org

Season: Oct–June

Tickets: $15–$127/person; season subscriptions available. No children under 3 allowed at some performances.

Established in 1989, Oregon Ballet Theatre (OBT) is the metro Portland area's flagship ballet company, offering an annual season of five productions performed at the Keller Auditorium (SW Third and Clay) and the Newmark Theatre (1111 SW Broadway).

Pacific Festival Ballet

4620 SW Beaverton–Hillsdale Hwy, Portland
503-977-1753
www.pacificfestivalballet.org

Season: *The Nutcracker:* late Nov–early Dec

Tickets: *The Nutcracker:* $20/adults, $17/children (18 and under) and seniors; group discounts available

Founded by professional ballet dancer John Gardner in 1980, this community-based nonprofit organization performs *The Nutcracker* each year to growing and enthusiastic audiences.

....

Going to the Movies

With first VCRs and now DVDs in just about every household, going to the movies is not quite the treat that it was at one time. It's simpler, less expensive, and more convenient to rent a movie, take it home, and settle in on the couch together to watch it. But when you do want to try something different or there's something that you've just got to see on the big screen, check out the following. See also "Movies Under the Sky" in chapter 5, Outside Fun & Learning.

....

McMenamins
503-249-7474
www.mcmenamins.com

The McMenamins chain of eateries operates a number of theaters (listed below) that show movies in cinemas adjacent to full-service pubs. Order from the restaurant and eat while watching the movie. Children are allowed at matinees only, or at an early showing when accompanied by an adult. Call in advance to make sure the current film is suitably rated for your family.

Bagdad Theater & Pub
3702 SE Hawthorne Blvd, Portland

Showtimes: Sat–Sun 2 P.M.

Tickets: $3/adults, $1/children 11 and under

Edgefield Power Station Theater
2126 SW Halsey, Troutdale

Showtimes: Daily 6 P.M.

Tickets: $3/person

Kennedy School Theater
5736 NE 33rd, Portland

Showtimes: Daily 5:30 P.M.; Mommy Matinees (babies and toddlers welcome): Mon–Fri 1 P.M., Sat–Sun noon and 2:30 P.M.

Tickets: $3/adults, $1/children 11 and under

Mission Theater
1624 NW Glisan, Portland

Showtimes: Daily 5:30 P.M., Sat–Sun 2:30 P.M.

Tickets: $3/adults, $1/children 11 and under

St. Johns Theater & Pub
8203 N. Ivanhoe, Portland

Showtimes: Daily 6 P.M., Sat–Sun 1:30 P.M. (times may vary)

Tickets: $3/person

Music

Chamber Music Northwest
522 SW Fifth Ave, Ste 920, Portland
503-294-6400 (tickets), 503-223-3202 (administration)
www.cmnw.org

Season: Year-round; family concerts Apr and July

Tickets: Family concerts: $5/person; other concerts: $19–$43/person; Friday concerts are free to students 7–18 when accompanied by a paying adult.

For more than 35 years Chamber Music Northwest has been building a national reputation on the strength of its programming and informal, intimate settings. Children younger than age seven are not admitted to evening performances; check the Web site for special performances for younger children.

Columbia Symphony Orchestra
P.O. Box 6559, Portland 97228
503-234-4077
www.columbiasymphony.org

Season: Oct–May

Tickets: $30/adults, $25/seniors, $10/students 13 and over, $5/students 12 and under, $65/family pass; season subscriptions available

Founded in 1983 at Lewis & Clark College, the Columbia Symphony Orchestra is a semiprofessional metropolitan group. The orchestra takes pride in performing works that are considered undiscovered classics and offers audiences the chance to hear and meet some of the finest classical musicians in the Portland area.

Metropolitan Youth Symphony

4800 SW Macadam, Ste 105, Portland
503-239-4566
www.metroyouthsymphony.org

Season: Dec–June

Tickets: $3–$32/person; season subscriptions available

The Metropolitan Youth Symphony (MYS) draws more than 600 student musicians (elementary-school age through college) from throughout northwest Oregon and even southern Washington to perform in its more than eight orchestras and bands. Under the direction of Lajos Balogh since 1974, the MYS holds rehearsals every Saturday during the school year. Students' skills vary from beginning to advanced, and emphasis is placed on enjoyment through learning and satisfaction through accomplishment. The annual performance schedule features three major concerts in December, March, and June, as well as several free concerts at local schools. Auditions are held each summer and in January to welcome new students. If your child is interested, call early or check the MYS Web site to find out more.

Oregon Symphony

923 SW Washington, Portland
503-228-1353 (ticket office), 503-228-4294 (administration)
www.orsymphony.org

Season: Aug–June

Tickets: $7–$100/person; season subscriptions available

The Oregon Symphony is committed to reaching diverse audiences with a full season of varied music, including newly commissioned works, works dropped from active repertoires, and works of contemporary composers and U.S. composers.

The popular Kids Concerts series is consistently rated among the city's highest-caliber musical events. These fast-paced performances are kept to about an hour in length and are designed to introduce children ages four and up to the instruments and sounds of the orchestra. Each of the three Sunday-matinee concerts is performed twice, and seating is reserved.

....

Portland Opera
211 SE Caruthers St, Portland
503-241-1802 (tickets), 503-241-1407 (administration)
www.portlandopera.org

Season: Sept–May

Tickets: $35–$127/person; dress-rehearsal discount: $10/students, $12/educators or chaperones; $10 "rush tickets" for students, active military, and seniors (62+); season subscriptions available

The Portland Opera has cultivated an "anything but stuffy" style, which has resulted in consistently sold-out productions at the Keller Auditorium (SW Third Ave and Clay).

In an effort to nurture a new generation of opera fans, the Portland Opera makes final dress rehearsals available to the region's students. The demand for these discounted tickets is high. Learn more about how to apply for these tickets online at the Portland Opera Web site.

The opera also increases its accessibility by selling any unsold tickets on each performance night to students, active military personnel, and senior citizens at the Keller Auditorium box office one hour prior to curtain (just $10; identification required; one ticket per qualifying person) for any available seat.

Portland Youth Philharmonic

421 SW Sixth Ave, Ste 1350, Portland
503-223-5939
www.portlandyouthphil.org

Season: Nov–May

Tickets: $11–$37/person

The nation's oldest youth orchestra, the Portland Youth Philharmonic (PYP) was founded in 1924 and continues its long-standing commitment to excellence in musical education. Students ages 7 to 22 audition for seats in the PYP, the Conservatory Orchestra, the Young String Ensemble, and the Portland Youth Wind Ensemble.

The Philharmonic and Conservatory Orchestras perform four concerts for over 10,000 schoolchildren in grades 3 through 8 at the Arlene Schnitzer Concert Hall each year. These concerts introduce children to classical music in a concert hall setting in a less formal way than the evening concerts. They include segments such as "Meet the Instruments" and "Be a Conductor."

If your own child is a budding musician, you should know that auditions take place every May or June (and sometimes in August). Applications are available in April. Strings players must be at least seven years old; winds, brass, or percussion players must have played their instrument for at least one year.

Singing Christmas Tree

7360 SW Hunziker St, Ste 102, Portland
503-557-8733 (tickets), 503-244-1344 (administration)
www.singingchristmastree.org

Season: Thanksgiving–early Dec

Tickets: $12–$75/person

Launched with a single performance at Benson High School in 1962, the Singing Christmas Tree is a Portland tradition and one of the city's most popular holiday extravaganzas. From its perch atop a 26-foot-tall, 34-foot-wide lighted and flocked Christmas "tree," a 325-member volunteer choir—including 45 children—performs with a 60-piece orchestra. Staged at Keller Auditorium (SW Third Ave and Clay) beginning the day after Thanksgiving, the pageant's musical lineup blends Santa and popular commercial Christmas music with the Christ child and more traditional carols. Be aware: Shows run about two hours—a length that may test the interest span of toddlers. Check the Web site for guest performances.

Summer Concert Series

A picnic at an outdoor summer concert has got to be as American as baseball, hot dogs, and apple pie. And if we're lucky, the sun shines just long enough in Portland for families to get their fill of all of the above.

In reality, the Rose City seems to have more than its fair share of concert series in the summer. Nearly every municipality with a patch of green lawn hosts one. Not that we're complaining. Events such as these have "family" written all over them. Yours won't be the only kids digging for ants and stepping on neighboring blankets.

Many of the concerts are free, but some are not. Call for details. The following listings are merely a sampling.

Beaverton Community Band Concerts
Beaverton City Library, front lawn: 12375 SW Fifth St, Beaverton
503-228-2288
www.beavertonoregon.gov

Hours: July–Aug, dates and times vary

Concerts on the Commons
Tualatin Commons: 8325 SW Nyberg St, Tualatin
503-691-3062
www.ci.tualatin.or.us

Hours: July–Aug, Fri 6:30 P.M.

Forest Music Series
Tryon Creek State Park: 11321 SW Terwilliger Blvd, Portland
503-636-4398
www.tryonfriends.org

Hours: July–Aug, Sun 2 P.M.–3 P.M.

Lunchbox Concerts
Oregon Square Courtyard: NE Holladay between Seventh and Ninth, Portland
503-233-5696

Hours: June–Aug, Wed noon–1 P.M.

Noon Tunes Concert Series
Pioneer Courthouse Square: SW Broadway between Yamhill and Morrison, Portland
503-223-1613
www.pioneercourthousesquare.org

Hours: July–Aug, Tues and Thurs noon–1 P.M.

Oregon Symphony in the Neighborhoods
Selected Portland parks
503-228-4294
www.orsymphony.org

Hours: Aug–Sept, dates and times vary

Wells Fargo Summer Concert Series
Oregon Zoo Amphitheater: 4001 SW Canyon Rd, Portland
503-226-1561
www.oregonzoo.org

Hours: June–Aug, days vary 7 P.M. These are ticketed events. Check the Web site for ticket prices.

Theater

Broadway Rose Theatre Company
P.O. Box 231004, Tigard 97281
503-620-5262
www.bwayrose.com

Season: Summer and holiday shows

Tickets: $30/premier seats, $25/adults and seniors, $20/youth ages 6–25, $6/children's show

The Portland metro area's only professional summer-stock theater troupe, the Broadway Rose Theatre Company, got its start in 1991 when a group of four experienced actors, directors, and designers began mounting professional—and affordable—productions at Tigard High School's 600-seat Deb Fennell Auditorium (9000 SW Durham Rd, Tigard). Its ambitious eight-week season consists of three main-stage shows and two children's musicals. The theater also runs summer camps for budding actors.

Do Jump! Movement Theater
Echo Theatre: 1515 SE 37th Ave, Portland
503-231-1232
www.dojump.org

Season: Oct–June

Tickets: $25–$35/person

Under the direction of Robin Lane, a performance artist of the best kind, Do Jump! Movement Theater, founded in 1977, has outlasted all comparably sized local arts organizations. Yet what it does continues to defy description. "Cirque du Soleil meets Oregon Ballet Theatre" may have to suffice. With a repertoire that consists of 20 full-length shows, the seven-member troupe fills a nine-month season with elements of dance, acrobatics, physical comedy, aerial movement, and live original music. Watch for performances by the Zig Zags—a youth performance group—in early spring and early summer. Do Jump! also offers classes; check their Web site for more information.

....

Imago Theatre

17 SE Eighth Ave, Portland
503-231-9581 (tickets), 503-231-3959 (administration)
www.imagotheatre.com

Season: Aug–May

Tickets: $14–$24/person

Recognized as one of the nation's most innovative masked ensembles, Imago continues to grow and evolve. Having established its reputation with the family favorite *Frogz*, the company has since staged complex, even dark, adult dramas that center on classic themes from literature by, for example, Chekhov and Sartre. It premiered another popular family show in 2003 called *Biglittlethings*, which the *New York Times* has called "a mad-cap review that leaves everyone feeling giggly." But *Frogz*—in which amphibians with a sense of humor intermingle with ethereal globes and an overfed baby—remains a favorite, and though it tours internationally now, it also plays to an appreciative home crowd once a year.

Krayon Kids Musical Theatre

P.O. Box 59, Oregon City 97045
503-656-6099
www.krayonkids.org

Season: Fall, Fri and Sat evenings, Sat and Sun matinees

Tickets: $10/adults, $8/seniors and students (ages 13–18), $5/children 12 and under

The Krayon Kids Musical Theatre company is a nonprofit community theater that offers children the chance to display their varied talents in original musical productions. And what talents they have!

Founded in 1993 by Dianne Kohlmeier and Vicki Mills O'Donnell, the repertory company includes more than 60 children ages 6 to 16, who perform an original musical theater production each fall at the Barclay Community Theater (817 12th St, Oregon City). The motto of the organization is "kids performing for kids." Auditions are held each spring to identify children with acting, vocal, instrumental, dance, comedic, and gymnastic talent.

Ladybug Theater

8210 SE 13th Ave, Portland
503-232-2346

Season: Call for up-to-date schedule

Ladybug Theater performs fairy tales with a twist for children and adults alike. Its productions, with actors from 11 to 70 years old, include improvisation and audience participation. Productions on Wednesday and Thursday mornings at 10:30 A.M. are geared for preschool children. Family shows on some weekends vary from casual to original musicals.

Lakewood Theatre Company

Lakewood Center for the Arts: 368 S. State St, Lake Oswego
503-635-3901 (tickets), 503-635-6338 (administration)
www.lakewood-center.org

Season: Children's: fall–spring

Tickets: $6–$28/person

Lakewood Theatre Company (LTC) is the oldest continually operated, not-for-profit theater company in the Portland metropolitan area. Each year it provides more than 700 theater artists the opportunity to learn and display their craft, and it attracts more than 40,000 people to its shows annually. While the primary emphasis is on adult theater, the Lakewood Theatre Company is also dedicated to theater-arts education. In hosting an array of drama workshops for children as well as three children's theater productions each year, the LTC continues to serve the metro area with engaging arts experiences.

Each season's trio of kids' shows, mostly adaptations of fairy tales, feature young actors, many of whom are students in Lakewood classes. In partnership with 10 Portland-area high schools, the LTC also sponsors a holiday breakfast-theater event for children in December. The LTC offers classes for children (in grades K–12) in spring, fall, and winter, as well as a popular summer drama camp. Check the theater's main-stage season too for a variety of shows, including various musicals that will appeal to the whole family.

Miracle Theatre Group

425 SE Sixth Ave, Portland
503-236-7253
www.milagro.org

Season: Sept–June

Tickets: $14–$22

The Miracle Theatre Group oversees three professional companies: Miracle Mainstage, Teatro Milagro, and Bellas Artes. It also produces and presents a diverse variety of cultural programs in El Centro Milagro, which houses the organization's theatrical and administrative operations and a community resource, Portland's first Hispanic Arts and Cultural Center. All performances are held at the Miracle Theatre, 525 SE Stark Street, Portland.

Missoula Children's Theatre

200 N. Adams St, Missoula, MT 59802-4718
406-728-1911
www.mctinc.org

Season: Year-round

Tickets: Prices vary

Each year, this Montana-based band of traveling actors and directors criss-crosses the globe overseeing full-length productions that star legions of singing schoolchildren. Hired by a local school, recreation department, church, or scout troop to put on a show, one of MCT's 35 or so creative duos comes to town and, all within the course of a week, auditions and casts 50 to 60 students; conducts rehearsals of lines, staging, songs, and dances; and then oversees two performances.

Take a look at the company's Web site for a frequently updated listing of upcoming tour locations, and you'll see that the MCT makes many stops in Portland and outlying communities throughout the year. (Interested in bringing the MCT to town yourself? The cost of a weeklong program is $2,400 to $2,600.)

Northwest Children's Theater and School

1819 NW Everett St, Portland
503-222-4480 (tickets), 503-222-2190 (administration)
www.nwcts.org

Season: Year-round

Tickets: $14–$18/person; season subscriptions available

One of the largest children's theater companies on the West Coast, this non-profit organization operates out of the Northwest Neighborhood Cultural Center. Each season the NWCT offers five family-oriented, thought-provoking shows that feature adult actors and designers working beside talented young actors. The theater has a reputation for showcasing top-quality classic plays and original adaptations of children's literature.

In choosing the season, NWCT looks for scripts with literary merit, relevance to local school curriculum, and appeal to audiences of diverse ages, genders, and ethnicities. The theater creates guides to enhance the educational impact of the plays, and provides "Talk-Backs" and workshops for school audiences. In addition to a main stage season, they offer two TeenStage productions especially geared to older teen audiences.

The NWCT also offers what it calls "family date nights," held the second Friday of every show. Families are invited to come for a catered dinner just prior to the play. Also, on "grandparent days," a grandparent attending either the 2 P.M. or 7 P.M. show with a child is given a $2 discount on the cost of his or her ticket (child's ticket is not discounted). After the show, grandparents and their guests are invited to attend a special reception.

In addition to its many performances, the NWCT also runs a year-round theater school for children ages 3 to 18, with skills classes and play-lab classes, as well as an internship program, summer employment, and volunteer opportunities for teens.

Costumes anyone? You can rent great costumes—from 15 productions such as *Alice in Wonderland*, *The Hobbit*, and *Little Women*—through the NWCT rental shop. And just for fun, keep an eye out for word on the school's annual fundraising event, a costume rummage sale that takes place in late October each year.

....

Oregon Children's Theatre
600 SW 10th Ave, Ste 313, Portland
503-228-9571
www.octc.org

Season: Late Nov–early May

Tickets: $13–$24/person; season subscriptions available

A nonprofit professional theater company and a resident of the Portland Center for the Performing Arts, the OCT presents four productions per year for children ages 4 to 18. It also plays to more than 80,000 children, parents, and educators throughout Oregon and Washington each year. The selected scripts tend to be based on favorite children's books, such as its recent productions of *Ramona Quimby* and *Charlotte's Web*, so audiences benefit by not only experiencing live theater but also being exposed to great literature.

Play After Play

...nklin St, Bay K, Portland

...205

www.brooklynbay.org

Season: Year-round, starting in Oct, then every other month (with one special show in Jan)

Tickets: $6/person, free/children 12 mos. and under, $20/family of 4 or more (for selected shows); reservations strongly recommended

Part of the Brooklyn Bay Performance Space, Play After Play was launched by Melanya Helene and Marc Otto. The shows feature professional actors in a unique theater experience that includes a high-quality, musical, and action-packed performance (about 20 minutes long) followed by the chance for kids to interact with the performers. Each month brings a new production that's based on folk and fairy tales from around the world.

Portland Revels

P.O. Box 12108, Portland 97212

503-224-7411

www.portlandrevels.org

Season: Year-round

Tickets: $7–$35/person

The Portland affiliate of the national Revels organization provides unique opportunities for communal celebration, usually centered on the changing of the seasons. Revels' events, which blend traditional music, dance, drama, comedy, and ritual, will appeal to just about everyone in the family, although they're not recommended for children under four.

    The Portland Revels are best known for their Christmas production, which is held in early December at the Scottish Rite Theater (1512 SW Morrison). Each production is different, though most are historical in character with songs, dances, comedy, and the playing of instruments characteristic of whatever period is depicted.

Performances always feature a large volunteer chorus of children and adults drawn from the community along with a number of highly talented professional actors, musicians, artists, directors, and "bearers of tradition" from many cultures. And you should know before you go that audience participation is a hallmark of Revels productions, so be prepared to sing along on some songs and to join the cast in a rousing, audience-wide dance.

....

Shakespeare-in-the-Parks Program

P.O. Box 8671, Portland 97202
503-467-6573
www.portlandactors.com

Season: Summer

Tickets: Free

Since the summer of 1970, a band of volunteer actors, writers, and artists called the Portland Actors Ensemble has been performing a minstrel-like summer Shakespeare series in metro-area parks. Sometimes traditionally Elizabethan, other times set in the golden age of Hollywood, the Wild West, or sometime in the near future, these free plays are largely faithful to the Bard's text. Each season brings a new title—*As You Like It*, *Love's Labour's Lost*, *A Midsummer Night's Dream*, *Two Gentlemen of Verona*, and *Julius Caesar* have all made the rounds in recent years.

Plays are performed on consecutive weekend afternoons before being repeated the following week in a different neighborhood park, library, or college campus. Because the stage is designed to conform to its natural surroundings with minimal props and sets, each new location adds an unexpected twist to the proceedings. Audiences are encouraged to picnic on the grounds while watching the show. Sometimes hundreds of people turn out, so arrive early for a "front-row" patch of ground. The actors have now added a second show, performed Friday and Saturday evenings at a downtown park. For a schedule of performance locations and times, check the ensemble's Web site. Final shows coincide with Labor Day weekend.

Tears of Joy Puppet Theatre

P.O. Box 1029, Vancouver, WA 98666
503-248-0557, 360-695-3050
www.tojt.com

Season: Nov–Apr

Tickets: $13–$16/person; season subscriptions available

Tears of Joy develops inspirational productions that entertain and enlighten audiences about distant peoples and far-off lands. The puppets, custom-built for each show, are otherworldly—big as sequoias or small as shrews. Visit with the puppeteers after the show to touch their creations and learn how they're manipulated. No doubt you'll be surprised at how versatile the performers are; most take on multiple parts. Almost better than the puppets is the innovative use of simple materials and indigenous music to evoke a mood.

Typically the company presents six productions each year at Portland Center for the Performing Arts' Winningstad Theatre (111 SW Broadway) and in Vancouver, Washington, at the Royal Durst Theater (32nd and Main). The theater offers puppet classes for children each June in Portland.

Theatre in the Grove

2028 Pacific Ave, Forest Grove
503-359-5349
www.theatreinthegrove.org

Season: Sept–June

Tickets: $12/person; $10/students and seniors

An amateur community theater troupe formed in 1970 to produce musicals, Theatre in the Grove continues to thrive in a remodeled Forest Grove movie theater. Its season consists of a half-dozen or so shows, chosen to appeal to a wide range of ages. Invariably, each season's lineup includes a fair number of musicals. Casts for these productions are often family affairs—with parents and children on stage side by side.

Theatre in the Grove also offers a Young Actors' Summer Theatre that allows children in grades 1 through 12 to discover and hone their acting talents by creating original improvisational plays. At the end of each two-week session the kids open the doors of the theater and perform for the public for free.

Storytelling

Everybody loves a good story, and Portland is home to many accomplished writers, poets, and storytellers. Many bookstores in the metropolitan area, including various large chain stores (think Barnes & Noble and Borders) as well as the smaller local favorites such as A Children's Place (4807 NE Fremont; 503-284-8294), offer story times on a regular basis.

PoetSpeak
Kurt Kristensen (organizer), 503-625-2340
www.poetspeak.com

Hours: Fall, spring Sun afternoons

Tickets: $5/person, free/children 9 and under

You can celebrate the oral tradition with PoetSpeak, a forum for Northwest poets of all ages since 1995. These readings are a wonderful way to expose children to the oral tradition of songwriting and poetry. Performances are held at Sherwood Community Friends Church (950 S. Sherwood Blvd in Sherwood).

Portland Storytellers' Guild
www.portlandstorytelling.org

Hours: Cavatica Center: generally Sept–May every fourth Sat 2 P.M., check Web site to verify; Kennedy School: Sept–May every third Sat 7–9 P.M.

Tickets: Cavatica Center: donations accepted; Kennedy School: $4/adults, $3/children, $10/family donation suggested

You can hear some of the city's best storytellers through regular shows offered by the reinvigorated Portland Storytellers' Guild at the Charlotte A. Cavatica Center (NE Sixth and Prescott)—named, by the way, for the title character of *Charlotte's Web*. Performances are recommended for children ages three and over and their families; the story times feature tales that might highlight the antics of fairies and gnomes or perhaps the adventures of heroes from far-off lands.

The Portland Storytellers' Guild also offers shows at the Kennedy School's Community Room (5736 NE 33rd Ave). These shows are recommended for ages eight and up, and each one has a theme. Recently these have included "Exponentially Exaggerated and Exquisitely Embroidered Half-Truths and Downright Lies," "Earth, Air, Fire, Water, and the Stories They Tell," and "Stories Your Heart Remembers."

....

Tapestry of Tales Family Storytelling Festival
www.multcolib.org

Season: Nov

Tickets: Prices vary; check Web site for details

Watch for this annual storytelling festival sponsored by the Multnomah County Library Foundation. This event happens each November—National Storytelling Month—in Portland, and during the celebration nationally renowned storytellers as well as regional tellers perform at many different libraries. You'll find a complete schedule of events on the Multnomah County Library Web site.

Public Libraries

Libraries around town offer free scheduled story times throughout the year. Babies, toddlers, and preschoolers are typically treated to separate sessions. For older kids there are book groups at most library branches. Many of these groups are geared for parents and kids to participate together, and they generate lively discussions. Check out Multnomah County Library's story times Web site (*www.multcolib.org/events/storytime.html*).

Multnomah County branches also host an impressive array of crafts sessions, pajama parties, puppet shows, and other special events year-round. Find out what's going on at the library's events finder (*http://events.multcolib.org/*). They pull out the stops during summer vacation to inspire young readers to keep up their skills. And speaking of summer, don't miss signing up for the

popular summer reading program—available at any of the area's libraries—
which rewards kids for the time they spend reading, usually by letting them
select a trinket or gift certificate from various treasure boxes.

Drop by your local library to pick up an events flyer, or call the appropriate
department below for information about branches in your neighborhood.

- **Library Information Network of Clackamas County**, 503-723-4888; *www.
lincc.lib.or.us*

- **Multnomah County Library Administration**, 503-988-5402; *www.multcolib.
org*

- **Washington County Cooperative Library**, 503-846-3222; *www.wilinet.wccls.lib.
or.us*

Chapter 4

Agricultural Adventures

It's all too easy in our urban and suburban worlds for a child to grow up without knowing that the real source of food and plants is land and farms. In Portland, though, you don't have to go far to help your kids make the connection. Here's all the help you'll need to discover a fabulous farmers market, pick out a place to pluck a pumpkin in the fall, or learn how you can secure your own little piece of land to tend. And your family will surely be better off for your agricultural adventures.

Berry Picking

Just about the time summer vacation begins, ripe strawberries, raspberries, and blueberries are ready for picking, and for many Portland families, berry picking is a favorite summer ritual. All ages can participate—from babes in backpacks to teens; the more years of berry picking experience in your group, the more berries you'll bring home.

Boxes are supplied at U-pick farms. Bring sunscreen and hats, plus food and drinks. A staff member will assign you and your kids a row where you can pick to your heart's content. When you've finished picking, someone weighs your berries and you pay by the pound. Reservations are not necessary, but do call ahead to make sure ripe berries are available. Try to go early in the day, when the selection is best and before the day heats up. It's hard work, but the rewards are immediate. Just don't forget that what comes home with you will quickly have to be eaten, frozen, or turned into jam and pies, because berries are highly perishable.

For farms in addition to what's listed below, look for the Tri-County Fresh Produce Guide (*www.tricountyfarm.org*), which lists both U-pick and ready-picked farms, at area libraries or in *The Oregonian* FOODday section. This free publication includes maps, a crop calendar, and a list of farms in Multnomah, Clackamas, and Washington counties.

- **Albeke Farms**, 16107 S. Wilson Rd, Oregon City; 503-632-3989; blueberries, boysenberries, marionberries, raspberries, strawberries.

- **Bonny Slope Blueberries**, 3565 NW South Rd, Portland; 503-645-1252; blueberries.

- **Columbia Farms**, 21024 NW Gillihan Rd, Sauvie Island; 503-621-3909; blackberries, blueberries, boysenberries, marionberries, raspberries, strawberries.

- **Duyck's Peachy-Pig Farm**, 34840 SW Johnson School Rd, Cornelius; 503-357-3570; blackberries, blueberries, marionberries, raspberries, strawberries.

- **Glovers Century Farm**, 29177 SE Hwy 224, Eagle Creek; 503-637-3820; blueberries.

- **Hartnell Farms**, 8481 SE Jannsen Rd, Clackamas; 503-657-5498; raspberries.

- **Hoffman Farms**, 22307 SW Munger Ln, Sherwood; 503-572-6063; blueberries, strawberries.

- **Hoffman Farms Store**, 18407 SW Scholls Ferry Rd, Beaverton; 503-628-0772; blueberries.

- **Kelso Blueberries**, 28951 SE Church Rd, Boring; 503-663-6830; blueberries.

- **Klock Farm**, 931 NE Salzman Rd, Corbett; 503-695-5882; blueberries.

- **Kruger's Farm Market**, 17100 NW Sauvie Island Rd, Portland; 503-621-3489; blueberries, boysenberries, marionberries, raspberries, strawberries.

- **LifeRoses.com**, 32235 SE Pipeline Rd, Gresham; 503-757-0670; organic blueberries.

- **Morning Shade Farm**, 8345 S. Barnards Rd, Canby; 503-651-2622; blackberries, blueberries, boysenberries, elderberries, marionberries, raspberries.

- **Pumpkin Patch Produce Market**, 16511 NW Gillihan Rd, Sauvie Island; 503-621-3874; marionberries, raspberries, strawberries.

- **Sara's Blueberries**, 5301 SE Patterson St, Hillsboro; 503-649-6000; blueberries.

- **Sauvie Island Blueberry Farm**, 15140 NW Burlington Ct, Portland; 503-621-3332; blueberries.

- **Sauvie Island Farms**, 19818 NW Sauvie Island Rd, Sauvie Island; 503-621-3988; blueberries, cherries, marionberries, raspberries, strawberries.

- **Smith Berry Barn**, 24500 SW Scholls Ferry Rd, Hillsboro; 503-628-2172; blackberries, boysenberries, loganberries, marionberries, raspberries.

- **Sweet Home Blues**, 27818 SW Graham's Ferry Rd, Sherwood; 503-682-1962; organic blueberries.

- **Thompson Farms**, 24727 SE Bohna Park Rd, Demascus; 503-667-9138; blueberries, boysenberries, marionberries, raspberries, strawberries.

- **West Union Gardens**, 7775 NW Cornelius Pass Rd, Hillsboro; 503-645-1592; blackberries, black raspberries, boysenberries, gooseberries, loganberries, marionberries, raspberries, strawberries.

Bulb Farms

In spring these four Willamette Valley bulb farms put on quite a show. Arrayed in neat rows, acres of flowers—a symphony of nature's purest colors—take their bows in unison. Children are welcome to explore the display fields, which are planted with hundreds of varieties so customers can select favorites to order, but farmers ask that the kids take care to stay in between rows to avoid damaging the flowers. There's no charge to visit these farms—unless you wind up going home with fresh flowers and bulbs.

Cooley's Gardens Inc.
11553 Silverton Rd NE, Silverton
503-873-5463
www.cooleysgardens.com

Hours: Early–mid-June daily 8 A.M.–7 P.M.

Ten acres of iris display gardens and seedlings, a weekend food booth, and an indoor cut-flower show are offered.

Schreiner's Iris Gardens
3625 Quinaby Rd, Salem
503-393-3232, 800-525-2367
www.schreinersgardens.com

Hours: May 9–June 8, daylight hours

There's a one-acre iris display garden as well as picnic tables. A gift shop is open, too, during bloom season.

Swan Island Dahlias
995 NW 22nd Ave, Canby
503-266-7711, 800-410-6540
www.dahlias.com

Hours: Aug–Sept daily 8 A.M.–8 P.M.

The largest dahlia grower in the nation, this farm features more than 40 acres of the flowers for public viewing. Fresh-cut flowers are available in season as well. Visit the farm for the Indoor Dahlia Show in late August—early September, and view more than 250 arrangements with 30 varieties of the colorful bulbs and blossoms.

Wooden Shoe Bulb Company
33814 S. Meridian Rd, Woodburn
503-634-2243, 800-711-2006
www.woodenshoe.com

Hours: Mar 20–Apr 20 daily 9 A.M.–6 P.M.

In addition to the 50-acre daffodil display garden and 30-acre tulip display garden, there's entertainment, demonstrations, picnic tables, and a weekend food booth.

Christmas Tree Farms

Bundle up the family and visit one of the area's Christmas tree farms for a special outing during the winter holidays. Many farms offer hot cider, coffee, and holiday goodies, as well as such special attractions as tractor rides and visits with Santa. Admission to farms, as well as most of the attractions, is free. Each year the Pacific Northwest Christmas Tree Association (503-364-2492; *http://nwtrees.com*) publishes a guide with its member Christmas tree farms, including addresses, phone numbers, and hours of operation for each farm, as well as special amenities. The Web site also includes great tips for picking a tree, setting it up, and keeping it fresh. Call or go to the Web site to find out where to get this free guide. We list just a few of the local tree farms below.

Before leaving on your outing, it's a good idea to check with the farm you hope to visit, to make sure trees are still available. In some years stock may be low at a particular tree farm, causing it to close early—or, in some cases, never open that year. Be sure to bring along boots, towels, a change of shoes, some blankets to warm the kids up in the car, as well as other wet-weather gear. This is a damp time of year.

Tip

As romantic as they sound, family outings to find a Christmas tree have the potential to turn into a tortured experience in failed group decision-making. Whether you search for your tree at a Christmas tree lot in the city or venture out to a tree farm, remember that this is not a ride into the snowy woods in a one-horse open sleigh. Discuss in advance how the group will choose a tree (a lesson in compromise) and caution the kids (and adults) that the perfect tree will not be found. It's also a good idea to measure the height and width of the room the tree will stand in before you leave the house—and then bring a tape measure along with you. Trees always look much smaller in the great outdoors than they do when you bring them into your house.

Beck's U-Cut and Sheep Farm

16700 S. Gerber Rd, Oregon City
503-631-7947

Free hot chocolate and candy canes round out the U-cut experience at this Oregon City farm. Check out the gift shop for ornaments and decorations.

Historic Kirchem Farm

19723 S. Bakers Ferry Rd, Oregon City
503-631-8817
www.historickirchemfarm.com

This beautiful old farm borders the Clackamas River. Come on the weekend to enjoy a hayride, followed by hot chocolate in front of a warm fire.

Lee Farms

21975 SW 65th, Tualatin
503-638-1869
www.leefarmsoregon.com

Get your mistletoe and holly, wreaths and swags, in addition to your tree at Lee Farms. Kids will enjoy the farm animal displays and the petting animals.

Loch Lolly Christmas Forest
28366 NW Dorland Rd, North Plains
503-647-2619
www.lochlollychristmasforest.com

Loch Lolly offers 28 acres of trees from which to choose. After you find that almost-perfect tree, visit the ducks and geese in the large pond, then scoot inside for hot chocolate (coffee is available for the grown-ups). Kids can visit with Santa on the weekend and browse in the gift shop.

Oxbow Rim Tree Farm
34623 SE Holman, Gresham
503-663-6815

Oxbow Rim's large selection of trees, including noble fir, Douglas fir, grand fir, Fraser fir, and Scotch pine, and their equally large selection of food, from hot dogs to elephant ears and candy canes, make this a popular spot. A gift shop and woodstoves for warming up are available as well.

Parry's Tree Farm
45627 NW David Hill Rd, Forest Grove
503-348-9601
www.parrysfarm.us

From the cinnamon-scented pinecones to the custom-made ornaments in the gift shop, Parry's has an old-time feel to it. Sip hot spiced cider or hot chocolate in the covered warming shed. Many related products—mistletoe, wreaths, greens, and holly—are also available for sale.

U-Cut

Another option for those who like to get a really fresh tree is to get a permit from the U.S. Forest Service. This can be a wonderful adventure for your family. But be forewarned: The areas designated by the Forest Service can be quite remote, requiring that you drive on primitive roads. You may be directed to an area at a fairly high elevation, making it more likely that there will be snow on the road. Be sure to carry chains in your car, a snow shovel in the trunk, extra warm clothing for everyone (including a change of shoes), and a few snacks.

The Forest Service issues permits for $5, allowing the permit holder to cut a tree (up to 12 feet tall) in a specific area. Call the local ranger station for areas and permit information: Mount Hood National Forest at Dufur (541-467-2291), Estacada (503-630-6861), Hood River (541-352-6002), Zigzag (503-622-3191), or Willamette National Forest at Detroit Lake (503-854-3366).

....

Community-Supported Agriculture

Community-supported agriculture (CSA) has really taken off in the Portland area. A CSA farming operation is a combined effort between a farm and a community of supporters, usually called harvest shareholders or members. Each season the harvest shareholders provide the money needed for the farm to operate by purchasing a share of the season's projected harvest. By making this commitment, harvest shareholders share with the farmer in the risks and rewards of growing the food they will eat. In turn, the farm distributes to the shareholders the entire production of the farm: a wide variety of seasonally harvested fresh produce, usually on a weekly basis, throughout the growing season(s).

Some CSAs deliver directly to the shareholder's door, some have centralized drop-off locations such as the Portland Farmers Market, and others ask that you come out to the farm to pick up your share. Many farms also allow, and even encourage, members to visit the farm to help with planting, tending, and harvesting the produce. You'll be amazed at the vegetables kids will try if they've had a hand in growing and picking them!

In addition to fruits and vegetables, many farms offer other freshly raised goods, ranging from eggs and chickens to flowers and honey. Some operate only in the warmer months; others offer winter shares as well, often at lower prices. To find a complete list of local CSA farms and to choose one that is right for you and your family, visit *www.greenpeople.org/listing/Pacsac_portland_area_20479.cfm*.

Braeside Farm

P.O. Box 1141, Estacada
503-630-5861
michaelm@aracnet.com

Braeside grows vegetables, herbs, salad mix, chicken, rabbit, lamb, beef, pork, honey, berries, and eggs. Both home delivery and farm pickup are offered.

Dancing Roots Farm

29820 E. Woodland Rd, Troutdale
503-695-3445
dancingroots@hevanet.com

This farm grows vegetables, herbs, flowers, and fruit. Also available at an extra charge are eggs and beef. Delivery to Northeast and Southwest Portland are offered, along with farm pickup.

47th Avenue Farm

6632 SE 47th Ave, Portland
503-777-4213
The47thAveFarm@aol.com

Here, vegetables, herbs, and flowers are grown. Pickup is required: Tuesday at the farm, Thursday in Lake Oswego at Luscher Farm (see "Gardening Programs" later in this chapter).

Hidden Oasis Farm

5410 NE 229th Ct, Vancouver, WA
360-256-6896
tmaxwell@mail2.cu-portland.edu

Hidden Oasis grows vegetables, herbs, free-range chicken eggs, shiitake mushrooms, Asian pears, blackberries, and plums. Delivery to Vancouver locations and farm pickup are offered.

La Finquita del Buho

7960 NW Dick Rd, Hillsboro
503-647-2595
lynjuve@earthlink.net

This farm grows vegetables, herbs, and fruit. Also available at an extra charge are free-range eggs and goat cheese. Pick up your share at the farm.

Natural Harvest Farm

P.O. Box 1106, Canby
503-263-8392
info@osalt.org

This farm grows vegetables, fruits, herbs, and grapes. Also available at an extra charge are lettuce mixes and free-range chicken and duck eggs. Your share is delivered to your door.

Pumpkin Ridge Gardens

31067 Pumpkin Ridge Dr, North Plains
503-647-5023
pumpkinridgegdns@aol.com

Pumpkin Ridge grows vegetables and herbs. Also available at an extra charge are eggs, flowers, and fruit. Shares are delivered to your door (limited to Multnomah County west of E. 82nd Ave and Washington County north of Lake Oswego).

Sauvie Island Organics LLC

20233 NW Sauvie Island Rd, Portland
503-621-6921
www.sauvieislandorganics.com

This farm grows vegetables and herbs. Also available at an extra charge are salad mix, flowers, and eggs. Delivery to Southeast, Northeast, and Northwest Portland or pickup at the farm are offered.

Square Peg Farm
6370 NW Evers Rd, Forest Grove
503-357-1214
squarepegfarm@yahoo.com

Square Peg grows vegetables, herbs, and fruit. Also available at an extra charge are eggs and flowers. Pick up your share in Southeast and Northeast Portland and Lake Oswego.

Farm Visits

When you hanker for a drive out to the country and a full day of amusement for the family, consider a visit to a local farm. However, don't come expecting Old McDonald and his cows and horses. Many of these "farms" have changed with the times, so you're not likely to hear a *moo* or an *oink*—or, for that matter, spot a farm animal—anywhere on the premises.

Alpenrose Dairy
6149 SW Shattuck Rd, Portland
503-244-1133
www.alpenrose.com

Hours: Year-round, hours vary by event

Admission: Free

In the 19th century the rolling hillsides of Southwest Portland were dotted with dairy farms, which were largely operated by Swiss immigrants. One pioneering dairyman, Florian Cadonau, owned a small farm at SW 35th Avenue and Vermont and began delivering milk in 3-gallon cans by horse-drawn wagon in 1891. More than a century later, Cadonau's ancestors are still in the dairy business. Though it no longer milks cows, the Alpenrose operation purchases milk from local Tillamook and Willamette Valley farms for its lines of milk, ice cream, cottage cheese, and sour cream. Local families may not associate Alpenrose with milk,

however, because the farm has evolved to include a unique array ~~~~~ ~~~~~~~~~~~~~~
ment facilities and an annual series of family holiday events.

Built by Florian's son and grandson, Dairyville is a replica of a Western
frontier town. Its dozen false-front shops—among them a doll museum, old-
fashioned ice-cream parlor, harness shop, and music store—are filled with
period antiques. The grand old opera house, with seats for 600, harbors the
majestic pipe organ that once played in the Portland Civic Auditorium. Elsewhere, an impressive collection of antique music boxes, nickelodeons, and Vic-
trolas is on public display.

No less impressive are the Alpenrose sports facilities: a baseball stadium,
velodrome, and miniature racetrack. Initially built to provide athletic diversion
for Cadonau children and cousins, it wasn't long before these facilities were
made available to the larger community (see "Nonprofessional Leagues" in
chapter 8, Spectator Sports).

....

Flower Farmer
2512 N. Holly, Canby
503-266-3581
www.flowerfarmer.com, www.phoenixandholly.com

Hours: Train: summer Sat—Sun, holidays 11 A.M.—6 P.M. or by appointment; Oct
Mon—Sat 10 A.M.—9 P.M., Sun 10 A.M.—6 P.M.

Tickets: $3.75/adults, $3.25/children ages 2–12

The Flower Farmer's main attraction isn't its many acres of either colorful
U-cut flowers or its farm animals. Kids come in droves to ride the Phoenix and
Holly Railroad, a half-size, narrow-gauge train with a 30-horsepower diesel
locomotive named Sparky and a bright red caboose named Fred. All aboard for
a half-mile loop through the fields, with a pit stop to see the chickens, turkeys,
ducks, and miniature donkey. The train's hours vary, so it's best to call ahead to
be sure you're on schedule. For Halloween pick pumpkins and check out the
spooky railroad tunnel, hay maze, and straw mountain. Christmas features a
special lighting display.

Sauvie Island

This island in the Columbia River, off Highway 30, 10 miles northwest of Portland, is an agricultural oasis. A haven for bicyclists, bird-watchers, and sunbathers (there are four beaches along its northeastern shoreline), Sauvie Island also boasts some of the metro area's finest produce. Come in spring for fresh berries; in summer for peaches; in fall for pears, apples, and pumpkins; or just about anytime to pick and choose from the bountiful farm-stand displays of fruits, vegetables, and homemade specialty goods. There's a $3.50/day parking fee. See "Berry Picking" at the beginning of this chapter for information about farms on Sauvie Island.

Magness Memorial Tree Farm
31195 SW Ladd Hill Rd, Sherwood
503-228-1367
www.worldforestry.org

Hours: Memorial Day–Labor Day, daily 9 A.M.–5 P.M.

Admission: Free

Donated to the World Forestry Center in 1977, this 70-acre forest on Parrett Mountain has been developed and maintained to demonstrate different methods of woodland management—from selective harvesting to clear-cutting. View examples of the various techniques from one of the farm's two hiking trails (the third, a paved trail, is wheelchair accessible), then scale the 60-foot fire tower for a panoramic view of the Cascades. Year-round on Sundays at 2 P.M., a naturalist leads a free guided hike. Facilities include a picnic shelter; rustic log cabins for outdoor schools, overnight camping, and retreats; and a visitors center with restrooms.

Old McDonald's Farm, Inc.
Corbett
503-695-3316
www.oldmcdonaldsfarm.org

Season: Year-round

Admission: Varies, depending on program

Hands-on, structured, educational experiences are at the heart of Old McDonald's Farm, a nonprofit, charitable organization that uses livestock, agriculture, and natural resources as educational tools. As the executive director explains, here the point is "not necessarily to teach children and youth to be farmers but, rather, to use the farm to teach kids to be kind, caring, compassionate, capable, 'can-do' people." Summer programs, day visits, Saturday workshops, after-school programs, and more are offered. The newest offering is the Farmer for a Day program, featuring a family overnight—great for birthday parties.

Children can learn such skills as how to feed and care for all types of livestock, how to ride a horse, how to compost, and how to weed and cultivate a garden. The farm encourages drop-in visits.

Farmers Markets

Find the idea of a trip to the country more than you can manage? During the local growing season, chances are good there's a farmers market not far from your neighborhood, and there you will find not only fresh produce but much of the sights and smells of a trip to a real farm—with much less travel time. For a complete list of markets in Oregon, go to *www.oregonfarmersmarkets.org*.

Alberta Farmers Market
NE 15th Ave and Alberta St, Portland
Hours: End of May–mid-Nov Sat 10 A.M.–2 P.M.

Beaverton Farmers Market
Across from Beaverton City Library, on SW Hall Blvd, between Third and Fifth, Beaverton
www.beavertonfarmersmarket.com
Hours: May–Oct Sat 8 A.M.–1:30 P.M., Wed 3 P.M.–6 P.M.

Canby Farmers Market
NW First Ave, between Holly and Grant, Canby
503-263-5151
www.mthoodterritory.com/farmersmarkets.jsp
Hours: May–late fall Sat 9 A.M.–1 P.M.

Cedar Mill–Sunset Farmers Market
NW Cornell Rd, 1 block west of Murray Blvd, Beaverton
503-913-7733
Hours: End of May–Sept Sat 8 A.M.–1 P.M.

Clackamas Sunnyside Grange Farmers & Artists Market
13100 SE Sunnyside Rd at 132nd Ave, Portland
503-407-3403
www.windancefarmsandart.com
Hours: Apr–Oct Sun 11:30 A.M.–3:30 P.M.

Eastbank Farmers Market
SE 20th Ave and Salmon St, Portland
971-506-8569
www.ebfm.org
Hours: June–Sept Thurs 3:30 P.M.–7:30 P.M.

Estacada Farmers Market
SE Third Ave and S. Broadway St, Estacada
503-630-6058
www.estacadafarmersmarket.4t.com
Hours: May–late fall Sat 9 A.M.–3 P.M.

Fairview Farmers and Artist Market
Fairview City Hall: 1300 NE Village St, Fairview
503-407-3403
www.windancefarmsandart.com
Hours: Apr–Oct Thurs 4 P.M.–8 P.M.

Gresham Farmers Market
Third St between Miller and Main, Gresham
503-341-4153
www.greshamfarmersmarket.com
Hours: Mother's Day weekend–Oct Sat 8:30 A.M.–2 P.M.

Hillsboro
Courthouse Square: Second and E. Main, Hillsboro
503-844-6685
www.hillsboromarkets.org
Hours: May–Oct Sat 8 A.M.–1 P.M., Tues 5 P.M.–8:30 P.M.

Hillsboro–Orenco Station Farmers Market
NW Cornell Rd and Orenco Station Pkwy, Hillsboro
503-844-6685
www.hillsboromarkets.org
Hours: May–Oct Sun 10 A.M.–2 P.M.

Hillsdale Farmers Market

Wilson High–Rieke Elementary parking lot (behind Hillsdale Shopping Center), Portland

503-475-6555

www.hillsdalefarmersmarket.com

Hours: Mid-May–Oct Sun 10 A.M.–2 P.M.

Hollywood Farmers Market

NE Hancock St between 44th and 45th, Portland

503-709-7403

Hours: Mid-May–Oct Sat 8 A.M.–1 P.M.

Interstate Farmers Market

N. Fremont St, directly south of Overlook Park off N. Interstate Ave, Portland

971-344-0115

Hours: May–Sept Wed 3 P.M.–7 P.M.

Lake Oswego Farmers Market

Millennium Park: First and Evergreen, Lake Oswego

www.ci.oswego.or.us/farmersmarket

Hours: Mid-May–Oct Sat 8 A.M.–1 P.M.

Lents International Farmers Market

SE 92nd and Foster Rd, Portland

503-621-7655

www.zenger.eroi.com/lents-internation-farmers-market.com.

Hours: Mid-June–mid-Oct Sun 9 A.M. – 2 P.M.

Lloyd Farmers Market

NE Holladay St. between Seventh and Ninth, Portland

503-730-8367

Hours: June–Sept Tues 10 A.M.–2 P.M.

Milwaukie Farmers Market

SE Main, between Harrison and Jackson, Milwaukie

503-407-0956

www.mthoodterritory.com/farmersmarkets.jsp

Hours: May–late fall Sun 9:30 A.M.–2 P.M.

Montavilla Farmers Market

7600 block of SE Stark St, Portland

Hours: June–early Oct Sun 10 A.M.–2 P.M.

Moreland Farmers Market

SE Bybee and 14th St, Portland

503-341-9350

www.morelandfarmersmarket.org

Hours: Mid-May–Sept Wed 3:30 P.M.–7:30 P.M.

OHSU Farmers Market

OHSU Auditorium Courtyard (near the fountain)

SW Sam Jackson Park Rd, Portland

503-494-8792

www.ohsu.edu/farmersmarket

Hours: Mid-May–mid-Oct Tues 11:30 A.M.–3:30 P.M.

Oregon City Farmers Market

2051 Kaen Rd at Beavercreek Rd, Oregon City

503-734-0192

www.oregoncityfarmersmarket.com

Hours: Mid-May–Oct Sat 9 A.M.–2 P.M.

Parkrose Farmers Market

NE 122nd St and Shaver St, Portland

503-890-7152

www.parkrosefarmersmarket.org

Hours: May–Oct Sat 8 A.M.–2 P.M.

People's Farmers Market

3029 SE 21st Ave, Portland
503-236-5388
www.peoples.coop
Hours: Year-round Wed 2 P.M.–7 P.M.

Portland Farmers Market

South Park Blocks near Portland State University, between SW Montgomery and Harrison, Portland
www.portlandfarmersmarket.org
Hours: Apr–mid-Dec Sat 8:30 A.M.–2 P.M., Wed 10 A.M.–2 P.M. at SW Salmon and Main; Thurs 4 P.M.–8 P.M. at Ecotrust Building parking lot, NW 10th Ave between Irving and Johnson

Scappoose Farmers Market

Columbia Ave and First St, Scappoose
503-543-3469
www.scappoosefarmersmarket.com
Hours: May–mid-Oct Sat 9 A.M.–2 P.M.

Sherwood Farmers Market

Old Town Veterans Park: corner of First and Main, Sherwood
503-682-1604
Hours: Mid-May–Oct 1 Sat 9 A.M.–1 P.M.

Tigard Farmers Market

Hall Blvd and Oleson Rd, Tigard
www.tigardfarmersmarket.com
Hours: May–Oct Sun 9 A.M.–2 P.M.

Vancouver Farmers Market

W. Eighth St near Esther Short Park, Vancouver, WA
360-737-8298
www.vancouverfarmersmarket.com
Hours: Apr–Oct Sat 9 A.M.–3 P.M.; Apr–Sept Sun 10 A.M.–3 P.M.

West Linn Farmers Market
Willamette Falls Dr between 12th and 14th, West Linn
www.mthoodterritory.com/farmersmarkets.jsp
Hours: May–Oct Tue 4 P.M.–8:30 P.M.

Gardening Programs

Picking a berry is one thing—growing the berry bush is another. Nothing matches the awe of slowly pulling a vivid orange carrot from the deep brown soil. You don't need three acres in the backyard to let your children experience the joy of growing one's own food. Check out the opportunities below.

Community Garden Program
6437 SE Division St, Portland
503-823-1612
www.portlandonline.com/parks

If you're interested in doing a little farming of your own but don't have the space, consider adopting a Community Garden plot. This program, run by Portland Parks and Recreation since 1979, leases garden plots for a nominal fee to city dwellers. Most plots are 20 feet by 20 feet, providing families with enough room to grow raspberries, corn, carrots, and plenty of zucchini. There are 29 Community Gardens scattered throughout the city, so you and your kids are sure to find one close to home, maybe even within walking or biking distance.

The Community Garden program also offers children's gardening classes, many of them free. Some sites are also wheelchair accessible, with raised beds designed to make gardening easier for those with physical disabilities. Check the Web site for information about classes, exact location of garden sites, and how to sign up for a plot of your own.

Growing Gardens

2003 NE 42nd Ave, Ste 3, Portland
503-284-8420
www.growing-gardens.org

This nonprofit organization offers after-school programs, summer garden camps, and a Learn and Grow program to teach children and adults how to grow their own food. Learn how to start seeds, make worm bins, and preserve produce and more in Growing Gardens' frequent, inexpensive workshops. Their Web site also has links to other great sites with information on gardening with kids.

Luscher Farm

125 Rosemont Rd, West Linn
503-675-2546
www.ci.oswego.or.us/parksrec/Luscher

Built around the turn of the 20th century, the Luscher Farm is the most intact historic farm in Clackamas County. It includes a farmhouse in the Queen Anne style, a gambrel-roof barn, a chicken coop, a garage bunkhouse, and several smaller outbuildings on a 47.71-acre site. The farm's primary historical use was for dairy farming and cattle breeding.

Now owned and operated by the city of Lake Oswego, Luscher Farm offers workshops in farming, gardening, crafts, and environmental education, as well as children's summer camps. The grounds include community gardens, organic garden plots, a composting site, and a farm museum. Partnerships with other organizations, such as Oregon Tilth and area scout troops, provide endless opportunities for kids to get their hands dirty.

Zenger Urban Agricultural Park
11741 SE Foster Rd, Portland
503-282-4245
www.zengerfarm.org

Located near Portland's Lents neighborhood, Zenger Urban Agricultural Park includes 6 acres of farmland bordered by a 10-acre wetland. It is a classroom, an ecosystem, a community anchor, and a farming operation. Its mission is to promote sustainable food systems, environmental stewardship, and local economic development through a working urban farm.

Zenger's Grow Wise Youth Education program gives kids firsthand farmwork experience and illustrates the relationship between farming and environmental stewardship. The program shows kids that good food comes from healthy ground and that healthy ground can be anywhere, as long as people take care of it. Contact the farm to find out more about their programs and to schedule a visit.

Pumpkin Patches and Mazes

Squirrels collect nuts. Birds fly south. Another rite of autumn: People go to the pumpkin patch. At last count, more than a dozen Portland metro-area farms were featuring these colorful squashes in time for Halloween. Some make a monthlong party of it, with hayrides, spooky trails, funny dioramas, and festive goodies. Corn mazes are a popular twist, often open at the end of August or early September. Sometimes these are located at a farm in conjunction with pumpkin patches, and sometimes they are created at a different location. Call ahead to confirm dates and hours, then pray for a break in the clouds. Find even more pumpkin patches at *www.pickyourown.org*. Most pumpkin patches charge no admission fee, but hayrides and mazes often cost a few dollars.

Duyck's Peachy-Pig Farm

3480 SW Johnson School Rd, Cornelius

503-357-3570

This farm, which offers a variety of U-pick items and ready-picked produce throughout the seasons, is especially great for school groups and day-care centers. Groups can arrange complete tours of this working farm, which usually include holding baby chicks, bunnies, pigs, and kittens. And don't forget to choose a pumpkin from the field before you leave!

Fantasy Trail at Wenzel Farm

19754 S. Ridge Rd, Oregon City

503-631-2047

At Halloween the lighted, wooded Fantasy Trail at Wenzel Farm may be full of spooky sights and sounds, but it's never too scary. All ages will enjoy the trail as well as the 40-foot castle, which is haunted at Halloween but turns into a winter wonderland at Christmastime. Return in December to experience the magical scene.

Fir Point Farms

14601 Arndt Rd, Aurora

503-678-2455

The annual Pumpkin Fest packs this 75-acre spread every weekend in October, when special activities include a deep, dark hay maze (carry a flashlight just in case), a corn maze, a hay slide, pony rides and hayrides, a half-mile haunted trail, and refreshments.

You can also pick your own flowers and vegetables here, examine the apiary and greenhouse, and gape at the goats that romp on ramps amid the treetops. Your youngest will enjoy seeing the chickens, turkeys, and rabbits, too.

Flower Farmer

See "Farm Visits" earlier in this chapter.

Lakeview Farms

34059 NW Mountaindale Rd, North Plains
503-647-2336

Lakeview Farms' 15-acre spread has lovely views out over rolling agricultural land, but most visitors are too intent on finding the perfect pumpkin to notice. This is the place to come if you prefer literally "picking" pumpkins (bring a pocketknife or garden shears). The vines are tall and prickly, so you may opt instead to peruse the supply of prepicked pumpkins in the mown meadow.

The Lakeview theme is transportation. Take the four-car miniature train to the pumpkin patch through a haunted tunnel. Return across the lake by barge, but beware of a pair of Loch Ness monsters. The grounds—green grass punctuated by a grove of tall evergreens—also feature farm animals, a gift shop, a snack shack (weekends only), a hay maze, and educational displays about farming. There are no restrooms, just portable toilets.

Plumper Pumpkin Patch

11435 NW Old Cornelius Pass Rd, Portland
503-645-9561
www.plumperpumpkins.com

In addition to a quarter-acre corn maze, two hay mazes, and pumpkins galore, Plumper Pumpkin Patch is the only farm in the area to offer a pumpkin-flinging trebuchet, a sort of medieval catapult that sends pumpkins flying across the picturesque fields, just for fun (weekends in October only). Kids will also enjoy the farm animals, produce, U-cut flowers, and pony rides (also weekends only).

The Pumpkin Patch
16511 NW Gillihan Rd, Sauvie Island
503-621-3874
www.thepumpkinpatch.com

Check out the bunnies, birds, bees, and other animals in the Pumpkin Patch's 100-year-old red barn, which opens each year in mid-July. The farm's annual Harvest Festival on Labor Day weekend is a popular event. The farm is also busy during October, when you can catch a free hayride out to the U-pick pumpkin fields to select your own jack-o'-lantern-to-be from an assortment that comes in all shapes and sizes. Older children especially will enjoy the challenge of figuring out the farm's amazing Maize, carved out of a cornfield where the stalks are 9 feet tall. There are a number of pumpkin patches on Sauvie Island; head out and explore!

Rasmussen Fruit and Flower Farm
3020 Thomsen Rd, Hood River
541-386-4622, 800-548-2243
www.rasmussenfarms.com

This 20-acre farm with U-pick sunflowers and pumpkins hosts several distinct harvest festivals. In July there's a celebration of cherries. In September there's the Pear Party, with free samples, pear cider, pear pie, and live music. The Apple Express follows, with free samples, apple cider, apple pie, and *aebelskivers*—tiny Danish apple pancakes. And in October there's Pumpkin Funland, a holiday tradition. During the pumpkin festival, the greenhouse is decorated for fall with as many as 50 scenes with storybook characters as well as farm and zoo animals created from vegetables, squashes, and gourds. Other activities include a mildly scary Halloween Hut and a corn maze.

State and County Fairs

Q: What sounds like a farm and smells like a farm, but isn't a farm? A: The Oregon State Fair (see listing below for details). Held each summer, this is the best place to get your fill of farm animals. You'll see barns full of cows, horses, goats, sheep, pigs, rabbits, and fowl and exhibit halls full of farming displays. As the kids mature, they may grow less interested in livestock and more interested in carnival rides, but all generations agree that the Oregon Dairy Women's ice cream earns a blue ribbon.

The state fair is the granddaddy, but local county fairs are fun, too, and can be more intimate. When arranging your visit, call ahead to ask about special admission and carnival-ride discounts. Prices below are subject to change.

....

Clackamas County Fair and Rodeo
Clackamas County Fairgrounds, Canby
503-266-1136
www.clackamascountyfairandevents.com

Season: Mid-Aug

Admission: $7/adults, $4/seniors ages 65–74, $3/children ages 8–15, free/ seniors 75 and over and children 7 and under

....

Clark County Fair
Clark County Fairgrounds: 17402 NE Delfel Rd, Ridgefield, WA
360-397-6180
www.clarkcofair.com

Season: Early Aug

Admission: $8/adults, $6/seniors, $4/children ages 7–12, free/children 6 and under

....

Multnomah County Fair
Oaks Park, 7100 SE Oaks Park Way, Portland
503-761-7577

Season: Late July

Admission: $3/adults, $1/children ages 5–13, free/children 4 and under

Oregon State Fair

Oregon State Fairgrounds, 2330 17th St, Salem
503-947-FAIR (3247)
www.fair.state.or.us

Season: Late Aug–early Sept

Admission: $10/adults, $6/seniors, $5/children ages 6–12, free/children 6 and under

Washington County Fair and Rodeo

Washington County Fair Complex, Hillsboro
503-648-1416
www.faircomplex.com

Season: Late July

Admission: Free; parking $5/vehicle

Chapter 5

Outside Fun & Learning

Myth has it that rain is our constant companion in Portland. The truth is, it doesn't *always* rain. But there's no doubt that when there's a break in the clouds, everyone wants to take a break outdoors. And what an outdoors! The Portland metro area is one of the nation's most scenic. So when the weather is fine, get outside and get moving. Go for a paddle on a lake, head to the hills for some sledding or skiing, or enjoy an outdoor amusement park. It's all here, just waiting for you.

Amusement and Action Parks

When it is out-of-the-ordinary entertainment you seek and you have a variety of ages in your group, consider an outing to one of the places below. While your budget probably can't afford this kind of treat often, these places make a great way to mark an important occasion—end of the school year, end of summer, graduation, and birthdays, to name a few. See also Enchanted Forest under "Salem" and Mount Hood SkiBowl Action Park under "Mount Hood" in chapter 10, Out-of-Town Excursions.

Family Fun Center

29111 SW Town Center Loop W., Wilsonville
503-685-5000
www.fun-center.com

Hours: Year-round, rain or shine; hours vary by season

Tickets: Around $5.50/person per activity; bargain packages available

Located 20 miles south of Portland, the Family Fun Center provides 6 acres of good times for preschoolers, adults, and all ages in between. This clean, well-run place has many options for all kinds of weather, and outdoors facilities are well lit at night. Dress appropriately for the season, but if you're caught off guard in a rainstorm, the center sells ponchos ($1).

Prices are reasonable, but with so many tempting choices, the cost can add up. If you plan to allow each person more than three activities, buy a bargain package. Also, to give yourself a good time, consider declaring your dollar limit per child in advance (which also provides a good math lesson!).

Outdoors there's miniature golf, bumper boats, go-karts, and a batting range, plus, for serious thrill-seekers, the Sling Shot and a 28-foot climbing tower. Miniature-golf fans can choose from one of two 18-hole courses: a castle theme with cave and waterfall or a Western town with totem poles and sawmill. Three sizes of putters accommodate all ages. Go-karts race on a 1,000-foot course with dips and hairpin turns. Go-kart drivers must be at least 58 inches tall; passengers must be at least three years old and ride with someone 18 or older. Everybody's likely to get soaked when bumper boats travel down a cascading waterfall into the bumper pond, so plan accordingly. Boat drivers must be at least 44 inches tall; passengers must be at least three years old and ride with someone 18 or older. Squirters are available spring through fall. The eight batting cages offer a range of pitching speeds, with bats and hats provided.

If it is too rainy, hot, or cold, go indoors, where you'll find a climbing wall, a laser tag arena, more than 80 video and arcade games, and the Flight Cyber Coaster, a simulator pod that allows two riders to dictate whether the unit flips, turns, rotates, or spins. Kids less than 5 feet tall will like Playland and the Frog Hopper (bouncing fun).

When hunger strikes, Bullwinkle Restaurant serves standard kid fare with an animated performance on stage.

....

Malibu Grand Prix

9405 SW Cascade Ave, Beaverton
503-641-8122
www.maliburaceway.com

Hours: Mon–Sat 11 A.M.–11 P.M., Sun 11 A.M.–9 P.M.

Tickets: $3.25/lap; discounts for multi-lap packages

A popular birthday-party destination, Malibu Grand Prix showcases two racetracks and two different car models. The larger half-mile road course accommodates the Virage (a three-quarter-scale, gas-powered formula Indy car) and the F-50 Sprint racer. Equipped with brake and gas pedals (the transmissions are automatic), the cars can reach speeds of up to 30 miles an hour in races against the clock. The small oval racetrack is an easier course for younger kids to try out the F-50 Sprint racers. On this track drivers race each other.

All drivers wear helmets and are strapped in using a four-point harness. On-track supervisors monitor the activity at all times. Not all children are tall enough to get behind the wheel at Malibu Grand Prix. Drivers must be at least 4 feet 6 inches tall and eight years old to drive the Sprint cars. To drive the Virage, you must have a current driver's license or be at least 14 years old and complete the Car Control Clinic.

There's also a high-powered two-seat race car that uses the larger track. Drivers for this car must be at least 18 years old and have a current driver's license; the passenger must be at least 3 feet 6 inches. When it rains, only the Sprint racers are available.

....

Oaks Amusement Park
East end of Sellwood Bridge, Portland
503-233-5777
www.oakspark.com

Season: Open the week of Spring Break, then weekends only until school's out in June; summer Tues–Sun; Sept weekends only (check Web site for hours); roller rink open year-round

Tickets: $11.50/5-hour limited bracelet (excludes roller coaster, bumper cars, Scream 'N Eagle, Looping Thunder, and The Disco); $14.25/5-hour deluxe bracelet; roller skating included with limited and deluxe bracelets; go-karts, miniature golf, and carnival games priced separately; individual ride tickets available

In 2005 Oaks Amusement Park celebrated its 100th birthday, making it one of the nation's oldest continuously operating amusement parks, and as such it has entertained generations of Oregonians at its rambling facilities on the banks of the Willamette River. Home to one of the West Coast's largest roller rinks (see "Skating" in chapter 6, Inside Fun & Learning), in addition to a full complement of rides, this place may lack high-tech razzamatazz, but it serves up generous portions of old-fashioned charm.

Spread over 44 acres, the amusement park is operated as a nonprofit community resource, and it teems with children. Corporate picnics fill the park on summer weekends, so try to go on weekdays to avoid a big crowd. Bring lunch from home, or feast on snack foods from the concession stands. Dozens of picnic tables overlook the river, and shelters that are booked by groups on weekends are vacant on weekdays and evenings.

The park is continually reevaluating its mix of rides. The miniature train, bumper cars, and Ferris wheel remain favorites, but some of the park's more recent additions, such as Scream 'N Eagle, the Tea Cups, and the Frog Hopper, are gaining a following. Kiddieland features a historic wooden carousel, Skyfighters, Jump Cycles, and Toon Cars.

Biking

There will be skinned knees and elbows and close calls Mom need not hear about. Learning to ride a two-wheeler is one of the major accomplishments of childhood and the first true taste of freedom. Because kids often have more stamina biking than hiking (it helps that you get farther faster!), bike rides are often a better option for a family outing. And Portland is a great city for family cycling. The following are some of the recommended bike trails for family outings.

Blue Lake Regional Park
Off Sandy Blvd and NE 223rd Ave, Fairview
503-797-1850, 503-665-4995 (shuttle)
www.oregonmetro.gov/index.cfm/go/by.web/ie=149

Hours: 8 A.M.—sunset

Admission: $4/car, $7/bus; pets not allowed

Operated by Metro Regional Parks and Greenspaces, Blue Lake Regional Park is 185 acres of recreational opportunity for the Portland region. The big draw is the 64-acre natural lake fed by underground springs. Bring bikes to tour the interior or to explore the scenic 40-Mile Loop, which runs adjacent to the park. Picnic tables and shelters abound, as do restroom facilities. Bring a lunch or purchase hot dogs or other snack foods at the concession stand. In the summer of 2005, the park added a shuttle bus from the Gresham Transit Center to the park on summer weekends and holidays. Call for availability.

Biking Resources

Maps: City of Portland (503-823-CYCL; *www.portlandonline.com/transportation*) provides family-friendly bicycle maps for Southeast, North, Northeast, and outer Southeast Portland. You may also request a Waterfront Bike Loop map for the 12-mile loop along the Eastbank, Esplanade, Springwater, and Greenway trails.

Bikes on Buses: All TriMet buses and MAX trains are equipped with bicycle racks.

Community Cycling Center: The Community Cycling Center is a nonprofit organization that uses the bicycle as a tool for teaching positive life skills to youth. Children learn bicycle safety and maintenance and earn their own bicycles, locks, and helmets. The center provides year-round programs for low-income youth and adults and a professional retail bike shop that is open to the public and sells refurbished bicycles.

Champoeg State Heritage Area
Champoeg Rd, St. Paul
503-678-1251
www.oregonstateparks.org/park_113.php

Hours: Dawn–dusk

Admission: $3/vehicle

At the 615-acre Champoeg (pronounced "sham-POO-ee") State Park, the Willamette is slow and wide, the trees dangle lichens and ferns, and the frogs offer a serenade. Bring bikes for a ride along the 4-mile paved trail (it's wheelchair accessible). You can also rent bikes from the park's Butteville General Store (503-678-1605).

Eastbank Esplanade

Between Hawthorne Bridge and Steel Bridge, Portland
503-823-PLAY (7529)

Open since 2001, the 1.5-mile-long Eastbank Esplanade is tucked between Interstate 5 and the Willamette River. With its fabulous views of downtown, the esplanade has become popular with walkers, bicyclists, and skaters. Along the walk, 13 markers provide information about the river and the area's rich history. For those who tire along the way or who just want to savor the views, there are seating walls, benches, and overlooks that invite visitors to stop and relax. Kids especially enjoy being right down at river level as they ride or walk the 1,200-foot-long floating walkway, the longest such walkway in the United States.

On weekends, especially during Saturday Market season (see sidebar in chapter 1, Exploring Downtown), it's fun to bike the esplanade, then cross over the river on the Burnside Bridge, park your bike, and visit the market, and then continue along the river through Waterfront Park.

You can enter the Eastbank Esplanade from several places. If you're on public transportation, take your bikes on the MAX or bus to the Rose Quarter. Walk southwest from the MAX platform until you see the entrance to the esplanade on your right (just past Wheeler Street).

If you're driving, park under the Hawthorne Bridge via SE Main or Madison Street to the large fee parking area. Ride south on the esplanade (1.5 miles from the Rose Quarter) past the Oregon Museum of Science and Industry, where it turns into the Springwater Corridor (see below).

Forest Park

North of W. Burnside St to NW Newberry Rd, west of NW St. Helens Rd (Hwy 30) to SW Skyline Rd
503-823-PLAY (7529)

Hours: Daily dawn–dusk

The largest natural area in any U.S. city, this more than 5,000-acre park is crisscrossed by some 50 miles of trails. Navigating the expansive tangle of trees with children takes some forethought, though, because few of the paths make loops and some are too challenging for young riders. One obvious place to start is the end of NW Thurman Street (continue west from NW 25th Avenue, across a small bridge to the dead end). Especially popular with cyclists, Leif Erickson Drive begins here. A public throughway that was closed in the 1950s, this broad, relatively flat trail is still paved in spots and continues for about 7 miles.

Henry Hagg Lake

Off Hwy 47 near Gaston, south of Forest Grove (about 30 miles southwest of Portland)

503-359-5732

Hours: March 1–late Oct, daily sunrise–sunset

Admission: $5/vehicle, $6 with boat; seasonal pass: $30/vehicle, $35 with boat

Owned by the U.S. Bureau of Reclamation and maintained and operated by Washington County, Hagg Lake is a recreational paradise with boating, swimming (no lifeguard but a quiet zone for nonmotorized boats and swimmers), and a 15-mile biking trail along the forested shores of the lake. In addition, a 10.5-mile bike trail in Scoggins Valley Park adjoins the trail at Hagg Lake.

Tip

Sometimes a picnic is best as a spontaneous event, but if you want to plan ahead to be sure you'll have just the right picnic site, you can make a reservation with Portland Parks and Recreation. You can even reserve a ball field next to your picnic, if one is available. Fees vary by site. For more information, go to *www.portlandonline.com/parks* and look under Picnic Sites.

Sauvie Island

Hwy 30, 10 miles northwest of Portland

503-621-3488 (Oregon Department of Fish and Wildlife area office)

www.sauvieisland.org

Hours: Year-round, many wildlife areas closed during hunting season, Oct–Apr; call for details

Fees: Parking: $3.50/day, $11/year

The flat 12-mile bike ride here, a scenic loop through farmland and nature preserves, is well suited to inexperienced riders. To reach the trail, take Highway 30 north to the Sauvie Island Bridge. Turn right, cross the bridge, loop left, and park in the gravel parking lot. Ride left out of the parking lot and under the bridge on Gillihan Road. After approximately 6 miles you'll reach a stop sign at Reeder Road, where you take a left turn. Stay on Reeder Road until you come to a stop sign on Sauvie Island Road (approximately 10 miles). Turn left and ride along the Multnomah Channel for 2 more miles until you reach the parking area.

••

Springwater Corridor
503-823-2223 (trail map available)
www.portlandonline.com/parks/

Springwater Corridor was originally an interurban electric railway corridor that carried passengers between Portland and Estacada from 1903 to 1943. Today the paved, 10-foot-wide, 16.5-mile path is the Portland area's premier multi-use regional trail and is very popular for bicycles, strollers, and wheelchairs. Not surprisingly, it can get quite congested, so on weekends with good weather it is not the best place for a new cyclist who has trouble not wobbling all over the trail.

Starting near the OMSI, the Oregon Museum of Science and Industry (1945 SE Water Ave), the trail travels along the Willamette River and Oaks Bottom to the Sellwood Bridge. The rest of the trail parallels Johnson Creek east to the Clackamas County line in Boring, past wetlands, farmlands, nature parks, and residential and industrial neighborhoods. Trailheads with parking, restrooms, and picnic tables are found near SE Johnson Creek Boulevard at 45th Avenue and in Gresham at SE Hogan Road.

Bike Rentals

There are several bicycle shops in Portland renting bikes for kids. The following are excellently located.

....

Fat Tire Farm
2714 NW Thurman, Portland
503-222-3276
http://fattirefarm.com

Hours: Mon–Fri 11 A.M.–7 P.M., Sat 10 A.M.–5 P.M., Sun 10 A.M.–5 P.M.

Fees: Prices vary depending on the type of bike. Bicycle or trailer for bike: $5/hour, $30/day; tandem: $10/hour, $60/day

This shop has an ideal location a few blocks from Forest Park's Leif Erickson Drive, a very popular place for cycling in Portland. Trail maps for Forest Park are available here.

....

Waterfront Bicycle and Skate
315 SW Montgomery St, Ste 360, Portland
503-227-1719

Hours: 7 days a week 10 A.M.–7 P.M.

Fees: $9/hour (price goes down as hours increase), $35/daily

This is conveniently located in RiverPlace near Waterfront Park in downtown Portland (see "Tom McCall Waterfront Park" in chapter 1, Exploring Downtown).

Boating

Poised at the confluence of two rivers not far from the Pacific, Portland made its mark early as a significant seaport. Though the River City now relies less on the shipping industry for economic vitality than it once did, the Columbia and Willamette Rivers continue to be a focal point of tourism and recreation, which suits kids just fine.

Take a sightseeing cruise on a sunny afternoon and marvel at a new perspective. Children may have little patience for scenery, but they'll enjoy tossing crumbs to the seagulls, counting bridges, waving to passing watercraft, and watching the captain navigate.

Choose a smaller vessel for a more vivid and intimate boating experience, but be wary of taking younger kids on a dinner cruise. If "perfect for romantic celebrations" is in the promotional literature, best steer clear with the little tykes.

Belle of the Falls
503-286-7673

Season: May–Sept

Tickets: $15/adults, $7/children ages 3–11, free/children 2 and under; $38/Family Pass (2 adults and 4 children)

Belle of the Falls, a stern-wheel paddle wheeler and sister ship to the *Sternwater Rose*, began making trips to Willamette Falls in May 2005. The *Belle* operates in the Oregon City area during the summer months, giving passengers rides from Oregon City to the Willamette Falls.

Canby Ferry

Mountain Rd, Stafford–Holly St, Canby

503-650-3030

Hours: Daily 6:45 A.M.–9:15 P.M.

Tickets: $2/car

The Canby Ferry, built right here in Portland by Diversified Marine, Inc., and in operation almost continuously since 1914, has a loyal following. The ferry is a small, simple platform that holds nine vehicles and stays on course by means of an underwater cable. Most kids are thrilled by the short sailing across the Willamette, from Mountain Road in Stafford to Holly Street in Canby. In nice weather families out for a drive in the country often combine a train ride at Flower Farmer (see "Farm Visits" in chapter 4, Agricultural Adventures) with the short trip on the Canby Ferry. There may be a wait during poor weather or busy summer days, so bring some books or games just in case.

Cascade Sternwheelers

1200 NW Naito Pkwy, Ste 110, Portland

503-223-3928, 800-643-1354

Season: Year-round, except Jan

Tickets: Prices vary by cruise

An authentic replica of stern-wheelers from a previous century, the *Columbia Gorge* resembles local stern-wheelers of the 1890s and, with triple decks, can accommodate 599 passengers. Learn about the Lewis and Clark expedition on a cruise aboard the *Columbia Gorge*. You board from Marine Park at Cascade Locks (45 minutes east of Portland), in the heart of the Columbia River Gorge National Scenic Area.

Portland Spirit
842 SW First Ave, Portland
503-224-3900, 800-224-3901
www.portlandspirit.com

Season: Year-round

Tickets: Prices vary by cruise

Scenery takes a backseat to food aboard the three-story, 350-passenger yacht *Portland Spirit*. Operating from a dock at Naito Parkway (formerly Front Avenue) and SW Salmon, the vessel focuses on dinner and brunch cruises, including historical narrative on some trips. The two-hour champagne-brunch cruise and the historical cruise to Willamette Falls are best suited for families. If it is just a boat cruise you want without the food, you can forgo the meal and enjoy the sights. There's also a popular Cinnamon Bear Christmas Cruise, especially for kids. The Web site is chock-full of pricing and other important information about the cruises.

Sternwheeler Rose
6211 N. Ensign St, Portland
503-286-7673
www.sternwheelerrose.com

Season: Year-round

Tickets: Prices vary by cruise

This jaunty little red-and-white stern-wheeler offers a regular schedule of public cruises south to Lake Oswego from its dock at OMSI, the Oregon Museum of Science and Industry. Families might prefer the hourlong harbor tours that run during summer months rather than the more formal brunch and dinner cruises.

Willamette Jetboat Excursions
1945 SE Water Ave (behind OMSI), Portland
503-231-1532
www.willamettejet.com

Hours: Late Apr–mid-Oct; hours vary by season

Tickets: $33/adults, $21/children ages 4–11, free/children 3 and under

Since 1997, this company has been showing visitors 37 miles of sights in the Portland metropolitan area on its two-hour trips. Giant cargo and military ships, elegant riverfront homes, majestic Willamette Falls, and bald eagles are all part of the scenery on one of these thrilling jet-boat trips.

Boat Rentals

Alder Creek Kayak & Canoe
250 NE Tomahawk Island Dr, Portland (Jantzen Beach); 503-285-0464
49 SE Clay, Portland; 503-285-1819
www.aldercreek.com

Hours: Winter daily 10 A.M.–6 P.M.; summer Sun–Thurs 9 A.M. 6 P.M., Fri–Sat 9 A.M.–7 P.M.

Fees: Canoes, kayaks: $30/half-day, $50/day; double kayak: $40/half-day, $70/day

At the Jantzen Beach location you put rental boats in at a harbor on the Columbia River. At the SE Clay location you paddle on the Willamette. Paddlers must have previous experience, and your itinerary must be approved. Alder Creek also offers kayaking classes for youths and adults, all-day family canoe outings in the Ridgefield National Wildlife Refuge, and a summer kayaking camp for kids.

Island Sailing Club
515 NE Tomahawk Island Dr, Portland
800-303-2470
www.islandsailingclub.com

If you hanker to sail the Columbia with your tykes and have the sailing proficiency to do so safely, this sailing club will rent you a 20-foot or 23-foot boat. You aren't allowed to take rentals through the locks, but that might be more excitement than the family needs anyway. With locations in Washington as well as Oregon, the club offers a low-cost alternative to boat ownership.

Fishing

Bait a hook with a wiggly worm, drop it in the water, and you'll have a child's attention, if not a bite from a fish on the line. In Oregon, children under age 14 can fish for warm-water panfish, such as trout and bass, without a license. Youths ages 14 to 17 are required to purchase an annual juvenile angling license, but anglers of all ages can try to nab clams, crayfish, and bullfrogs without shelling out for a license. Licenses and information are available at local sporting goods stores, such as Joe's and Fred Meyer, and at Department of Fish and Wildlife offices (*www.dfw.state.or.us/free_fishing/*). When purchasing a license, ask for a copy of the Oregon Sport Fishing booklet of information and regulations, updated every December.

The best fishing for kids occurs at lakes. Rivers with fast-moving currents are much more dangerous and challenging. Choose lakes that are flushed and cleaned naturally, either by tidal action or by in-flowing rivers. Fish from a raft or canoe only if your child knows how to swim. If you are fishing on a lake bank, your child can catch frogs, hunt for cool rocks, and skip stones should the fishing get slow (as it always does). And remember: *Always* have children wear personal flotation devices (life jackets) when on or near the water. The following lakes and ponds are among the region's finest for fishing with kids.

Free Fishing Weekend

O n one of the first June weekends every year, families in the Portland metro area have many opportunities to try fishing without having to buy any licenses or fancy gear. Adults who fish, or who have fished in the past, can teach kids the sport at one of several Portland-area lakes stocked with legal-sized trout. Parents who have never fished or have no fishing equipment can bring their kids to one of several fishing events where rods, bait, and instruction are provided to children free of charge.

The events are all part of the annual Free Fishing Weekend, when licenses and tags are not required to fish or crab anywhere in Oregon. All regulations related to fishing locations, species, and catch limits must be followed.

Just before the Free Fishing Weekend, the Oregon Department of Fish and Wildlife stocks 11 easily accessible lakes in the Portland metro area with more than 40,000 eight-inch trout. In addition, numerous fishing events happen this weekend around the region. Additional information may be found on the ODFW Web site (*www. dfw.state.or.us/free_fishing/*).

Henry Hagg Lake
Off Hwy 47 near Gaston, south of Forest Grove (about 30 miles southwest of Portland)
503-359-5732

Hours: Late Apr–late Oct daily sunrise–sunset

Admission: $5/vehicle, $6 with boat; seasonal passes: $30/vehicle, $35 with boat

Owned by the U.S. Bureau of Reclamation and maintained and operated by Washington County, Hagg Lake (a reservoir) is stocked with rainbow trout each spring, but smallmouth-bass anglers are lured by the prospects of catching a record-breaker bass. The best thing about Hagg Lake may be something other than the fishing, however. Canoes, kayaks, and paddleboats as well as small boats with electric motors are available for rental. Boat rental is available by the hour or the day, although hours of the rental facility are irregular, so don't count on it. The grassy banks sport picnic areas especially hospitable to young anglers. Swimming is allowed, but no lifeguard is on duty. Disabled persons who want to fish are catered to as well with a short, accessible hiking trail, special picnic sites, and boat ramps.

....

Horning's Hideout

21277 NW Brunswick Canyon Rd, North Plains
503-647-2920
http://horningshideout.com

Hours: Daily 8 A.M.–dusk

Fees: $2/person ages 6 and up, for either fishing or paddleboats

Admire the peacocks as you fish in a pond brimming with trout, barbecue in one of the many covered pavilions, play on the playground, or just wander around and take in the pretty surroundings. Fishing gear can be rented, and bait is always available. Fly fishermen should check in advance on current releasing rules. You'll also find horseshoe pits and paddleboats. Several times during the year, grassroots festivals are hosted in the amphitheater. Call ahead or check the Web site so you don't arrive hoping to fish during a big event! The pond is located adjacent to Highway 26, the highway to the Oregon Coast, about 20 minutes from Portland.

Promontory Park

Hwy 224, 7 miles east of Estacada
503-630-7229

Season: June–Oct

Admission: Free

Located on the 350-plus-acre Portland General Electric North Fork Reservoir, Promontory Park features campsites, picnic facilities, boat rentals, and docks. Like Hagg Lake, the reservoir is divided into two speed zones, with the slower portion most suited to angling. However, kids have an even better reason to come to Promontory Park to fish: Small Fry Lake, a shallow, 1-acre pond developed and stocked for the exclusive use of anglers up to age 14. The daily catch limit for kids is three fish.

Rainbow Trout Farm

52560 E. Sylvan Dr, Sandy (off Hwy 26)
www.rainbowtroutfarm.com

Hours: Mar 1– Oct 15, daily 8 A.M.–dusk

Fees: Vary by size of fish, $0.50–$22.50

Located just 7 miles east of Sandy, Rainbow Trout Farm offers a fun chance to fish and, even better yet, catch something! You can bring your own fishing gear or rent gear and purchase bait at the farm. Fishing instruction is also offered, free of charge. Fish-cleaning facilities are provided, or they will clean your fish for you. You can take your fish home to cook or barbecue it on the premises (you provide side dishes and charcoal briquettes or purchase them at the farm). Broad pathways and restrooms are built to handle wheelchairs.

Roslyn Lake Park

North of Ten Eyck Rd, 3.5 miles north of Sandy
503-464-8515

Season: Late Apr–early Sept

Admission: Free

The forebay of Portland General Electric's Bull Run Hydroelectric Project, Roslyn Lake is stocked annually with rainbow trout. A day-use area has six picnic areas (three with shelters), in addition to a playing field, horseshoe pits, a concession store, and boat rental. The park is particularly well suited to families; no motorboats or alcoholic beverages are permitted. Wheelchair-accessible features include a fishing dock, picnic area, sunbathing area, and restrooms.

Sauvie Island

Oregon Department of Fish and Wildlife area office: 18330 NW Sauvie Island Rd, off Hwy 30 northwest of Portland
503-621-3488 (ODFW area office)

Season: Year-round, certain areas closed Oct–Apr; call for details

Fees: Parking: $3.50/day, $11/year

A popular destination for fruit picking in summer (see sidebar under "Farm Visits" in chapter 4, Agricultural Adventures), Sauvie Island also boasts nice beaches along the Columbia River, as well as lakes and sloughs for fishing. For a map, stop at the Oregon Department of Fish and Wildlife kiosk. Good fishing options include Gilbert River, accessible via two fishing piers: one on the west side at Big Eddy, off Sauvie Island Road, the other on the east side on Gilbert River Boat Ramp Road, off Reeder Road. Expect to catch bullhead and channel catfish, walleye, crappie, and perch. Parking permits are required, available from the Cracker Barrel store on the island near the bridge or anywhere fishing licenses are sold, including Joe's and Fred Meyer stores.

Golf

Miniature golf is a fun family outing, but when you've had enough of windmills, castles, and loop-the-loops, perhaps your clan is ready for the real deal. The following courses are particularly well suited for families.

The Children's Course
19825 River Rd, Gladstone
503-722-1530

Hours: Summer daily 6:30 A.M.–dusk; winter daily 7:30 A.M.–dusk

Fees: $5/youth ages 17 and under, and $10/adult for 9 holes; $8/youth, $15/adult for 18 holes

This course was renamed in July 1996 with the goal of providing youngsters with a low-cost opportunity to learn golf. The layout of the nine-hole, par-3 course is ideal for kids. Junior golfers receive hefty fee discounts and are encouraged to enroll in lessons and weekend clinics. Those who pass a written rules and etiquette test receive greens-fee discounts.

Eagle Landing Golf Course
10220 SE Causey Ave, Happy Valley
503-698-PUTT (7888)
www.eaglelandingsite.com/golf

Hours: Summer Sun–Thurs 7:30 A.M.–9 P.M., Fri and Sat 7:30 A.M. – 10 P.M.; check the Web site or contact the course for winter hours. Weekend tee times required; contact Pro Shop for course closures due to special events

Fees: $11.75/adult, $9.75/ages 6–12, $8.75/ages 5 and under for 36 holes; $7.75/adult, $6.75/ages 6–12, $4.75/ages 5 and under for 18 holes

Your family will enjoy playing this 36-hole scenic-style miniature golf course. The landscape winds around trees, waterfalls, and natural rock formations giving you a peaceful place to enjoy your time. The course was built to accommodate all ages and skill levels.

....

Frontier Golf Course
2965 N. Holly St, Canby
503-266-4435

Hours: Year-round; daily 8 A.M.–7 P.M.

Fees: Mon–Fri $6.50/adult and child, Sat–Sun $7.50/adult and child

This countryside course is a mom-and-pop operation that has been open since 1964. Lovingly maintained, the course offers a mix of short and long holes that make it fun for all ages.

....

Meriwether National Club
5200 SW Rood Bridge Rd, Hillsboro
503-648-4143

Hours: Daily dawn–dusk (weather permitting)

Fees: Prices vary by day and time of play

This club offers three full-length sets of nine holes as well as a short course and an 18-hole, all-grass putting course. The best deal for young players ages 17 and under is Monday through Thursday, when the price for nine holes is $7.

....

The Pub Course
2126 SW Halsey, Troutdale
503-669-8610
www.mcmenamins.com

Hours: Daily dawn–dusk

Fees: $8–$9/person for 9 holes, $13–$14/person for 18 holes

This 18-hole pitch-and-putt course set at McMenamin's Edgefield Brewery is hilly and picturesque. Holes range from 40 to 80 yards, wrapping precariously around the Edgefield estate. All ages and skill levels are welcome, as long as players keep pace.

....

Tualatin Island Greens
20400 SW Cipole Rd, Tualatin
503-691-8400
www.tualatinislandgreens.com

Hours: Apr–Sept daily 8 A.M.–10 P.M., Oct–Mar daily 8 A.M.–9 P.M.

Fees: $6/adults, $4/children ages 17 and under

The putting course here consists of 18 famous golf holes that have been copied and reduced to scale (30–50 yards each), including an island green that's accessible only by footbridge. There's also a covered driving range.

Miniature Golf

Even if the kids argue over who gets the blue ball, who keeps score, or who putts first, miniature golf is one of those outings that really is great for the whole family. In addition to the listings below, see also "Amusement and Action Parks" earlier in this chapter and "Mount Hood" in chapter 10, Out-of-Town Excursions.

....

Glowing Greens Miniature Golf
509 SW Taylor St, Portland
503-222-5554
www.glowinggreens.com

Hours: Sun–Thurs noon–10 P.M.; Fri–Sat noon–midnight

Fees: $9/adult, $8/youths ages 7–12, $6.50/children under 7, seniors, and military; $5/second game and half-round

This is the miniature golf course rainy Portland has waited for: pirate-themed (complete with sound effects), super friendly, and indoors! The 18-hole course is two stories down, under downtown's Hilton Executive Tower. And, just as the name implies, it's glow-in-the-dark fun.

Scappoose Mini Golf

50418 Columbia River Hwy, Scappoose

503- 543-6500

Hours: Late Apr–Oct (weather permitting) Mon–Fri 10 A.M.–11 P.M., Sat–Sun 10 A.M.–11 P.M.

Admission: $4.50/adults, $4/children 12 and under

This 18-hole course set in a natural landscape offers a variety of challenges suitable for ages five and up.

Hiking and Walking

When your kids are young, let them make some of the decisions about how long and how far your group will hike. They are more likely to want to go out the next time if they have positive memories of their time on the trail. If they need to stop every five minutes to examine a wonder of nature, enjoy their keen observation skills and tell yourself that you'll get your real exercise some other time. Dress them in layers and emphasize that they need to stay within your view at all times. Also, remember bribery as a proven parenting method. The promise of a treat at the top of the hill can work wonders.

Forest Park

3339 NW Skyline to St. Helens Rd, Portland

503-823-PLAY (7529)

www.portlandonline.com/parks/

Hours: Daily 5 A.M.–midnight

Admission: Free

"Whose woods these are . . ." In Portland these woods in the West Hills belong to everybody, and we couldn't be luckier. The largest natural area in any U.S. city, 5,000-acre Forest Park is crisscrossed by some 50 miles of trails. Navigating the wilderness with children takes some forethought, though, because few of the paths make loops. Hoyt Arboretum (4000 SW Fairview; 503-865-8733) has free Forest Park trail maps and staff who can offer suggestions for family walks.

One good place to start is the end of NW Thurman Street (continue west from NW 25th Avenue, across a small bridge to the dead end). Leif Erickson Drive, a broad, relatively flat trail, begins here. A public throughway that was closed in the 1950s, this trail is still paved in spots. Although it continues for about 7 miles, you will likely tire before then and turn for home.

Sample another bit of Forest Park from Cumberland Road (ascend Westover from NW 25th Avenue, then continue up Cumberland to the dead end). The dappled Cumberland Trail hugs the hillside along a ravine. Connect with the Wildwood Trail, then the Upper Macleay Trail, and emerge on Macleay Boulevard for a short walk back to the car. Ambitious (and strong) hikers can remain on the Wildwood Trail for a steep climb to the Pittock Mansion (see "Restored Homes" in chapter 6, Inside Fun & Learning).

A great hike for younger kids starts at Macleay Park, at NW 29th and Upshur. Walk on the Lower Macleay Trail along pretty Balch Creek for about 0.75 mile and you'll reach the old Stone House (some kids think of it as a fairy house); the building used to house restrooms, but the roof was torn off by the Columbus Day Storm in 1962 and it was never rebuilt.

Continue uphill on the Wildwood Trail another 0.25 mile and you'll reach the Audubon Society of Portland Wildlife Sanctuary; this 150-acre park consists of lush native forest and more than 4 miles of trails open dawn to dusk year-round. The maze of trails weaves and loops over bridges and boardwalks, past a pond, below a rough-hewn picnic hideout, alongside Balch Creek, and up and down steep hillsides. Two longer loops begin south of Cornell—be alert when crossing this busy road. (See "Wildlife Viewing" in chapter 2, Exploring the Natural World.) See also the map on page 180.

Hoyt Arboretum

4000 SW Fairview Blvd, Portland
503-865-8733
www.hoytarboretum.org

Hours: Visitors center: Mon–Fri 9 A.M.–4 P.M.; Sat 9 A.M.–3 P.M. Closed Sundays and major holidays

Admission: Free

Established in 1928, 175-acre Hoyt Arboretum boasts one of the nation's largest collections of conifers. This city-owned garden of trees is adjacent to Washington Park, and many of its 10 miles of trails link with its neighbor Forest Park.

When you arrive in Hoyt Arboretum for a walk, stop first at the visitors center to get oriented. The restrooms are here, and a large picnic shelter is directly across the street. A trail map is available; seasonal trail maps for spring's wildflower displays and fall's foliage fiesta are free. You can also pick up various maps for trails in Forest Park.

The Vietnam Veterans Memorial Trail and Bristlecone Pine Trail are wheelchair accessible; most other trails are rugged and steep at times. Scenic outlooks over Portland and toward mountain peaks are worth the climb, even when you're toting a child.

Oxbow Regional Park

3010 SE Oxbow Pkwy, Gresham
503-797-1850 (events), 503-663-4708
www.metro-region.org/parks/oxbowpage.html

Hours: Daily 6:30 A.M.–sunset

Admission: $4/car, $7/bus; pets not allowed

Come to Oxbow's 1,000 acres of ancient old-growth forest and an oxbow in the Sandy River, one of the state's most scenic waterways, to hike, bike, or ride horseback on the 15 miles of trails throughout the park. Please leave your pets at home; they're not allowed, in or out of your vehicle, due to conflicts with resident wildlife. Owned and managed by Metro Regional Parks and Greenspaces, Oxbow has been left relatively undeveloped, though there are picnic facilities, a campground, and nature programs. See "Portland and Environs" in chapter 7, Parks & Gardens.

Tualatin Hills Nature Park
15655 SW Millikan Way, Beaverton
503-629-6350
www.thprd.com

Hours: Daily dawn–dusk

The Tualatin Hills Nature Park is a 222-acre wildlife reserve in the heart of Beaverton. Designed for walking and nature study, the park features 5 miles of trails (one of them handicapped accessible), a visitors center, and a covered shelter. The park offers family programs throughout the year. Check the Web site for details about days and times.

Horseback Riding

Horseback riding isn't for everyone. Some people exude the scent of anxiety, which tips off horses to their vulnerability. The very riders who are praying that their horse won't trot are the first whose mounts veer off the trail in a cloud of dust. But for true horse lovers—the kids who collect plastic horses and read horse books—there's no rest until they've had a chance to handle the reins of a real beast.

owing ranches and stables in the Portland area rent horses and
ponies to ride on their property. Dress appropriately in long pants (jeans are best), and shoes or boots with a sturdy heel. Children must be about six or older to ride. Check with individual stables for age regulations. (See also "Mount Hood" in chapter 10, Out-of-Town Excursions.)

....

Beaverton Hill Top Riding Stables
20490 SW Farmington Rd, Beaverton
503-649-5497

Season: Year-round (weather permitting)

Fees: $25/horse

Choose a guided trail ride through Hill Top's scenic, wooded acres. Trotting and cantering are allowed. Pony rides are available for children under age five if parents are willing to lead the pony. Hill Top accepts same-day reservations for individuals and families only; larger groups are asked to provide advance notice.

....

Chehalem Mountain Ranch
23185 SW Jaquith Rd, Newberg
503-314-3176
www.chehalemmountainranch.com

Season: Year-round

Fees: $175/Basic Cowboy Party Package

The Chehalem Mountain Ranch, featuring Norwegian fjord horses and Barbado hair sheep, is conveniently located approximately 10 miles west of the Washington Square Mall in the Scholls area. It specializes in pony parties for kids. The Basic Cowboy Party Package includes 1½ hours of fun for up to 10 wranglers, use of the party room and indoor riding arena, games, and crafts. Chehalem Mountain Ranch also offers summer horse day camps as well as beginner private riding lessons and an after-school riding club.

Once Upon a Horse
Lake Oswego
503-635-7403
www.onceuponahorse.com

Located in the Stafford area, between Wilsonville and Lake Oswego, Once Upon a Horse specializes in lessons and riding experiences for children ages 2 to 11. The emphasis is on a gentle and easy introduction to horsemanship. Group, mom-and-me, and private lessons are offered, as well as summer day camps, birthday parties, pizza play days, and other special events.

Hot-Air Ballooning

Sometimes our kids take us to places we never expected to go. If your child hankers for a view from on high, and you can manage the cost, here's how.

The Portland Rose
18965 SW Olson Ct, Lake Oswego
503-638-1301
http://portlandroseballoons.com

Season: Mar–Oct

Tickets: $159/person

Panoramic views of the Willamette Valley and Lake Oswego are the order of the day when you sign on for a ride in a Portland Rose hot-air balloon. The adventure begins just before sunrise and ends approximately three hours later. Layered clothing, including a warm jacket, comfortable shoes, and long pants are advised. Passengers are invited to participate in the inflation and launching process under the guidance of the pilot and ground crew. A light lunch (with a glass of champagne for the grown-ups!) follows touchdown.

....

Vista Balloon Adventures
701 SE Sherk Pl, Sherwood
503-625-7385
www.vistaballoon.com

Season: Apr–late Oct daily (weather permitting)

Tickets: $189/person, $170/person for group of four or more

Arrive before dawn, when the air is cool and still, to help set up and inflate the balloon. Climb into the basket and find a comfortable spot in which to stand. Glide for an hour, wherever the wind takes you—over the rolling vineyards, orchards, and farmlands of the Willamette Valley. Touch down in an open field and await the ground crew, then head to the launch field for a picnic. In business since 1989, the company recommends this trip for children ages eight and older. (For one thing, they have to be taller than 4 feet to see over the basket!)

....

Movies Under the Sky

When warm weather finally arrives in Oregon, we all want to spend as much time outdoors as possible. In addition to drive-ins and movies in the park, keep an eye out for summer's Dive-In Movies. which you can watch while you swim at one of Portland Parks and Recreation's (*www.portlandonline.com/parks/*) various outdoor swimming pools.

Ninety-Nine West Drive-In

Hwy 99 W., just west of Springbrook Rd, Newberg
503-538-2738
www.99w.com

Hours: Mid-Apr–late Oct, Fri–Sun, showtime at dusk (weather permitting)

Tickets: $7/adults, $4/children ages 6–11, free/children 5 and under; minimum: $11/vehicle

For a fun taste of the past, check out this cool place, one of just 10 or so drive-ins still operating in Oregon. The Ninety-Nine West Drive-In was built by the late J. T. Francis, the grandfather of the theater's current proprietor, and opened in August 1953. It's been in operation ever since. Its popularity has waxed and waned, but now, with a capacity of 275 to 300 cars, the drive-in is quite popular again. In fact, in hopes of getting the best parking spot, drivers have been known to line up outside the theater as early as three hours before a show. Films are usually suitable for families, but it's always best to call and check what's playing before you go. And don't miss a visit to the theater's original snack bar.

Movies al Fresco

Now it's even possible to go to the movies outdoors without a car. All the offerings listed here are free; they begin around dusk, and many have preshow entertainment. Arrive early with a blanket and a folding or beanbag chair for the best seat.

Flicks by the Fountain

Beaverton City Park (across from Beaverton City Library), Beaverton
503-526-3706
www.beavertonoregon.gov

In Beaverton, Flicks by the Fountain draws hundreds who come to enjoy free movies projected on an inflatable screen.

Flicks on the Bricks
Pioneer Courthouse Square (SW Broadway and Yamhill), Portland
www.pioneercourthousesquare.org

Flicks on the Bricks transforms Portland's "living room" into an outdoor movie theater. Films are shown on a gigantic inflatable movie screen.

Summer of Love Outdoor Movies at the Little Red Shed
McMenamin's Edgefield, Troutdale
www.mcmenamins.com

Consider this series a great excuse to visit one of the McMenamin brothers' finest spots. Films range from 1950s-era to the present.

Check *www.aroundthesunblog.com* for more information about these outside movie options:

- **Big Screen on the Green in Portland's parks:** Assorted evenings in July, August, and September
- **Multnomah Outdoor Cinema at Multnomah Arts Center:** Selected Friday evenings in June, July, and August
- **Movies on Ecotrust's back patio:** Tuesday evenings through September 2
- **Movies in the Pearl (Jamison Square):** August 7 and September 4
- **Movies at Millennium Plaza Park in Lake Oswego:** Thursday evenings in July and August
- **Movies in Vancouver parks:** Friday evenings in August
- **Uptown Movie Nights in downtown Vancouver:** Saturday evenings until August 9
- **Movies at Mary S. Young Park in West Linn:** Saturday evenings in June and July
- **Movies at Memorial Park in Wilsonville:** Friday evenings in July and August
- **Movies at Tualatin Commons:** Saturday evenings in July and August
- **Flicks in Columbia Park in Troutdale:** Saturday evenings in August
- **Movies in North Clackamas Parks:** Selected Fridays and Saturdays in July and August; a different park each time
- **Pix on the Plaza in Downtown Hillsboro:** Thursday evenings in August.

Skateboard Parks

Portland has pulled out all the stops to create an environment that is friendly to skateboarders while protecting the safety of nonboarders. For an up-to-date list of the area's skate parks, including tips on the skill levels required for fun skating at the various parks, check out the Web site *www.skateoregon.com*. Here are just a few of the parks to visit.

Chehalem SkatePark
1201 Blaine St, Newberg
503-538-7454

Hours: Daily dawn–dusk (weather permitting)

Admission: Free

This huge skate park, designed and built by Dreamland Skateparks, is hailed by skaters as one of the world's best. Helmets are required. Bikes are not allowed, but there's a BMX track right next to the park.

Davis Park
NE 19th Ave and Glisan, Gresham
503-618-2485

Hours: Daily dawn–dusk (weather permitting)

Admission: Free

Developed and managed by the Gresham Parks Department, which recommends that all users wear safety equipment, this small concrete skate park is ideal for beginners. Situated in a quiet neighborhood and bordering an elementary school, Davis Park features two benches and a low mountain.

Department of Skateboarding
15 NE Hancock St, Portland
503-493-9480
www.departmentofskateboarding.com

Hours: Times vary (check Web site)

Admission: $10/person for 3-hour session

The Department of Skateboarding was created in 2002 by the people who own and operate Cal's Pharmacy (a Portland skate shop). Their goal is to fill the need for an indoor park for the inevitable rainy days in Portland. The park is cleverly street-oriented in design, with obstacles you might find when on any city street (banks, rails, stairs, ledges, gaps, etc.). To skate without parents, kids under age 18 must have a signed waiver from parents.

Snow Sports

Portland's wet weather is legendary. But there is a silver lining to all those winter clouds: the snow. Just enough falls in town to remind us that Mother Nature still has the upper hand. And within a little more than an hour's drive, at Mount Hood, there's enough snow to allow near year-round skiing.

Even before your kids are ready to ski (or you're brave enough to teach them), the Mount Hood area offers ample winter recreation opportunities. For toddlers, it's often enough just to taste a snowflake, make snow angels, and build a snowman. For kids just a little older, sledding and tubing offer lots of fun.

Before You Go

Whatever your snow sport of choice, always check the Oregon Department of Transportation's road condition report (800-977-6368; *www.tripcheck.com*) before driving up into the mountains. Be prepared with traction devices and emergency supplies for the car, including water, blankets, and snacks.

To park in many of the Western states' winter recreation areas from November 15 through April 30, drivers are required to purchase and display in their vehicles valid Sno-Park permits. Available at Department of Motor Vehicle offices, sporting goods stores, some gas stations, and ski resorts (the latter usually tack on a service fee), permits come in three options: one-day ($3),

Cool Deals on Hot Equipment

Outfitting the kids for skiing or snowboarding is a financially daunting task. Many families in the Portland area are dedicated attendees of ski swaps. In fall, high-school ski teams often host weekend sales to raise funds for their endeavors. Sellers bring outgrown skis and related equipment and then donate a portion of their proceeds to the ski team. For news of sales watch your local community paper or call your neighborhood high school to inquire.

The granddaddy of all ski sales takes place at the Expo Center (2060 Marine Dr; first weekend of November). Sponsored by the Oregon Snowsports Industries Association (*www.oregonski.org*), the Subaru Ski Fever and Snowboard Show (503-249-7733; *www.portlandskifever.com*) features representatives from Portland-area ski resorts, dozens of vendors selling new equipment, and lots of used equipment for sale as well.

three-day ($7), and 12-month ($15). For more information, check the state Department of Transportation's Web site *www.oregon.gov/ODOT*.

Dressing children appropriately for winter sports is also essential. Start with a layer of long underwear, a pair of cold-weather socks, a fleece or wool pullover, a warm hat, gloves, and a winter jacket. Pack a change of clothes and shoes for each family member so you can ride home dry and cozy (consider thermoses of hot chocolate and coffee, too). Sunscreen is a necessity, regardless of the time of year; the glare off snow and ice can cause sunburns even on overcast days.

Alpine Skiing and Snowboarding

People who learn to downhill ski as adults will tell you they wish they had learned when they were younger. It goes without saying that a child's body—with its agility and low center of gravity—is better designed for the slopes than an adult's. So if your kids have even the slightest interest in skiing or snowboarding, let them try it.

Mount Hood, the state's highest peak, boasts some excellent slopes, and some runs are groomed for skiing even into the summer. Several local resorts make it especially affordable for parents to introduce their kids to the sport by allowing youngsters under age seven to ski free with a paying adult. And various resorts offer packages that allow you to cut costs—for instance, by buying a pass early in the season.

If alpine skiing is not your idea of a good time, wait a few years until your kids are a little more self-sufficient. Schoolchildren are eligible to participate in special weekend ski-lesson packages that include bus transportation to and from the slopes.

Rentals and Lessons

Depending on your circumstances, it might make sense to lease ski equipment in Portland, not at the mountain. You can save a considerable amount of money doing so. Of course, your vehicle must be equipped to carry a family's worth of gear, and you have to plan ahead to get outfitted at a reasonable cost. But with a little forethought, you can circumvent the resort rental shops' early-morning crowds and save money, too. Several outdoor retail stores in the Portland area, as well as in Sandy, Welches, and Government Camp, lease alpine and Nordic ski equipment, snowboards, and snowshoes.

The resorts listed below also offer ski and snowboarding lessons for kids, from beginning to advanced. There are also the following schools based in Portland:

- **Mogul Busters Snow Sports School**, 11010 SE Mill Ct, Portland; 503-254-0847; *www.mogulbusters.com.*

- **Powder Hounds Ski School**, P.O. Box 68331, Portland 97268; 800-747-7603 (Portland), 360-883-6725 (Vancouver, WA); *www.powderhound.com.*

....

Cooper Spur Ski and Recreation Area
Mount Hood
541-352-7803
www.cooperspur.com

Hours: Winter Fri noon–9 P.M., Sat 9 A.M.–9 P.M.; open Mon–Wed only on holidays

Tickets: $25/adults, $20/children ages 14 and under; night skiing: $15/person; rope tow only: $5/person per day

Popular with families since the 1940s, Cooper Spur still markets itself primarily to families and novice skiers and snowboarders. Because it's small—a T-bar provides access to just 10 runs—it's easy to keep tabs on the kids. And the price is right: Cooper Spur is the most inexpensive resort around. Lessons are offered. For those who want to tube instead of ski, a small fee ($10) includes the tube rental and a rope tow ticket so you can ride both ways on the mountain!

Mount Hood Meadows Ski Resort
Hwy 35, Mount Hood
503-337-2222, 503-227-SNOW (7669; snow conditions)
www.skihood.com

Hours: Mid-Nov–late Apr Mon–Tues 8 A.M.–4 P.M., Wed–Sun 8 A.M. 10 P.M.

Tickets: $54/adults, $32/children ages 7–12, $9/children 6 and under; night skiing: $25/person; discounts for late spring and beginner chair tickets

With 10 chairlifts (including four high-speed quads) and 2,150 acres, Mount Hood Meadows is the largest ski resort on the mountain. Equipment rentals, lessons, and groomed slopes and tracks are available for alpine and Nordic skiers and snowboarders. The resort oversees a variety of youth lesson packages.

Mount Hood SkiBowl
Government Camp
503-272-3206, 503-222-BOWL (2695; snow conditions), 503-254-0874 (ski school)
www.skibowl.com

Hours: Winter Mon–Tues 3:30 P.M.–10 P.M., Wed–Thurs 1 P.M.–10 P.M., Fri 9 A.M.–11 P.M., Sat 8:30 A.M.–11 P.M., Sun 8:30 A.M.–10 P.M.

Tickets: $33–$39/adults, $21/children ages 7–12, free/children 6 and under

Mount Hood SkiBowl, the resort nearest Portland, is one of the last to get snow. But when it does, SkiBowl offers the nation's largest night-skiing area, with skiing on 34 lighted runs beginning daily at 3:30 P.M. Sixty-five day runs with 960 acres, including a 300-acre outback, are served by four chairlifts and five surface tows. A variety of ski and snowboard lessons are offered. While kids are in ski school, parents can be too: Parents whose children are enrolled in a four-session Mogul Busters program are treated to a special concurrent-lesson package at Mount Hood SkiBowl. (For details regarding the summer season's Mount Hood SkiBowl Action Park, see "Mount Hood" in chapter 10, Out-of-Town Excursions.)

....

Summit Ski Area
Government Camp
503-272-0256

Hours: Skiing: Nov–Apr Sat–Sun, holidays 9 A.M.–4 P.M.; tubing: Nov–Apr Mon–Fri 9 A.M.–4 P.M., Sat–Sun 9 A.M.–5 P.M.

Tickets: Skiing: $21/full day, $13/half day; $10 all-day tube rental

Opened in 1927, the Summit Ski Area is the oldest developed ski area in the Pacific Northwest and the first area developed on Mount Hood. It is a good choice for beginners, with its single chairlift that provides access to two runs. Summit may not be the glitziest ski area near Portland, but for families trying to satisfy skiers of varying abilities, it may be the best choice.

Timberline

Hwy 26, Timberline

503-272-3391 (ski area), 503-222-2211 (snow conditions), 503-231-5402 (ski school)

www.timberlinelodge.com

Hours: Year-round (only upper lifts open Sept–Oct) 9 A.M.–4 P.M. (varies according to conditions); night skiing: Sat–Sun, holidays

Tickets: Daytime: $38/adults, $22/children ages 7–12, free/children 6 and under; night skiing: $18/adults, $16/children ages 7–12

Grand, historic Timberline Lodge, built in the 1930s as a Works Progress Administration project, sits near the summit of Mount Hood and watches over the activity of six chairlifts and 32 runs. Timberline hosts the nation's most extensive spring and summer skiing. Ticketmaster sells adult lift tickets for a small savings. Ticketmaster also offers the Bus and Ski Package. This round-trip, chartered bus service to Timberline makes stops on weekends and holidays in season at G.I. Joe's stores in Beaverton, Eastport, and Gresham. The bus is not chaperoned and there is only one price—not discounted for kids.

Nordic Skiing

Whereas many Mount Hood resorts feature groomed trails for cross-country skiing, as well as Nordic rental equipment and ski lessons, their emphasis is on alpine skiers and snowboarders who purchase lift tickets. At Mount Hood Meadows, Nordic skiers are treated to 15 kilometers of groomed tracks ($10/adults, $5/children ages 7–12).

If you'd prefer a more backwoods experience, the Mount Hood region offers a maze of trails for all abilities. To receive a comprehensive list of Nordic ski trails near Government Camp, call the Mount Hood Information Center (503-622-4822) or check the Forest Service Web site (*www.fs.fed.us*).

The trails below are short and relatively flat and easy—good for youngsters just learning to cross-country ski.

- **Clark Creek Trail:** This easy, 2-mile marked trail begins at the Clark Creek Sno-Park on Highway 35.
- **Meadows Creek Tie Trail:** This easy, 1.2-mile trail branches off the Pocket Creek Trail (see below).
- **Pocket Creek Trail:** The first mile of this 4.5-mile trail is relatively flat. It begins on the east side of Highway 35, 3 miles north of Mount Hood Meadows.
- **Snow Bunny Trail:** Slightly more difficult than the Summit Trail, this marked 2-mile road begins at the Snow Bunny Sno-Park.
- **Summit Trail:** This flat, 2-mile marked road begins at the east end of the Mount Hood SkiBowl parking lot.

Sliding and Sledding

Sliding on saucers, inner tubes, sleds, and toboggans may look like child's play, but on a crowded, unsupervised hill it can be more dangerous than skiing. Teach your children the basic rules:

1. Stay on slopes that are within your abilities.

2. There should be only one slider on the hill at a time.

3. Ascend along the sides of the slope, not in the sledding area.

4. Don't build or use jumps.

5. Clear out from the bottom as soon as you stop (most accidents occur there).

The following are designated areas in the Mount Hood region where sledding is currently allowed.

....

Little John Snow Play Hill
Hwy 35, 31 miles south of Hood River
541-352-6002

Fees: Sno-Park pass required

Built by the U.S. Forest Service, Little John Snow Play Hill has two sledding slopes—one easy, the other more difficult. Bring your own discs, saucers, or inner tubes: sleds, toboggans, and snowboards are prohibited. Outhouses and a wooden shelter outfitted with a fireplace grill are open to the public. Haul some firewood from home if you want to use the grill. Little John Snow Play Hill is located on the edge of the snow zone, so it's wise to call ahead to check snow conditions before heading out for the mountains.

....

Snow Bunny Play Area
Government Camp
503-272-0256

Hours: Nov–Apr Sat–Sun, school holidays 10 A.M.–4 P.M.

Fees: $10/tube rental

Monitored by the ski patrol, Snow Bunny Play Area, just 2 miles from Summit Ski Area, features two hills with five lanes each, a small snack bar, and an outhouse. Leave your own sledding equipment at home: All patrons must use Snow Bunny inner tubes. Kids are also allowed to tube on a designated slope at Summit Ski Area (daily 9 A.M.–5 P.M.; $10/tube rental).

....

Swimming—Outdoor Pools

Most years the summer season in Portland is not all that hot or long, but nevertheless there are a surprisingly high number of outdoor swimming pools in the area. Better yet, most are not hidden away in private clubs but easily accessible for everyone to enjoy for a minimal fee. All pools offer classes, family swims, and just about the easiest place imaginable to throw a summer birthday party.

Tip
Have you ever wished that you and your friends could have a swimming pool all to yourselves? Portland Parks and Recreation's pools are available for rental—a great place to hold a birthday party, family reunion, or neighborhood gathering! For more info, call 503-823-5130.

Portland Parks and Recreation Outdoor Pools
503-823-SWIM (7946)
www.portlandonline.com/parks/

Hours: Summer only, hours vary

Fees: $1.75–$3.50

The following pools are open summer only. Several have extra fun features, such as waterslides, hot tubs, and fountains that spray the pool. Water temperature is about 84 degrees. Sellwood and Wilson pools host a very popular "Dive-In" movie night in August, where kids can watch a movie from the pool. For details about each pool, check the Web site.

- **Creston Pool**, SE 44th and Powell Blvd; 503-823-3672
- **Grant Pool**, NE 33rd and US Grant Pl; 503-823-3674
- **Montavilla Pool**, 8219 NE Glisan St; 503-823-4101
- **Peninsula Pool**, 700 N. Rosa Parks Wy; 503-823-3620
- **Pier Pool**, N. Seneca St and St. Johns Ave; 503-823-3678
- **Sellwood Pool**, 7951 SE Seventh Ave; 503-823-3679
- **Wilson Pool**, 1151 SW Vermont St; 503-823-368

Trains and Trolleys

Like the effect of a high-pitched whistle on dogs, the *clickety-clack* of trains and *ding-dong* of trolleys bring forth visceral reactions in children. Take them on a ride. It doesn't have to be a big-deal, all-day affair. Sometimes spontaneous afternoon treats are the most fun. See also Oregon Zoo under "Animals Up Close" in chapter 2, Exploring the Natural World, and Flower Farmer under "Farm Visits" in chapter 4, Agricultural Adventures.

Mount Hood Railroad

110 Railroad Ave, Hood River
800-872-4661
www.mthoodrr.com

Hours: Late Mar or early Apr–Dec daily 10 A.M. and 3 P.M., Nov–Dec daily 10 A.M.

Tickets: $30/adults, $18/children ages 2–12, free/children under 2

You don't need to love trains to love this ride. A four-hour, 44-mile round-trip excursion from Hood River to Parkdale snakes through orchards and along country roads. With its restored railcars from the 1910s and '20s, locomotives from the 1950s, a refurbished depot from 1911, and original track laid in 1906, the entire railroad is designated a National Historic Site. Special events include train-robbery reenactments and seasonal special festivities.

In autumn you'll see the orchard landscape at its peak. The trip to Parkdale takes about 90 minutes, so young children might want to bring along a few travel games. Kids enjoy walking through the train and checking out the open-air car at the rear, plus a snack bar. If you take the morning train, plan to eat lunch during the hour layover in Parkdale, where there are a few cafes, a general store, and picnic tables. Reservations are strongly advised, and you are encouraged to arrive at least a half-hour before departure.

Shady Dell Pacific Railroad

31803 S. Shady Dell, Mollala
503-829-6866
www.pnls.org

Hours: May–Oct Sun 11:30 A.M.–5 P.M.

Fees: Free; donation suggested

Pacific Northwest Live Steamers (PNLS), dedicated groups of miniature-train devotees, created this 4-acre train park located about 23 miles southeast of Portland. The railroad is equipped with eight operating miniature trains (engines are steam, gas, and electric) and just under a mile of rails. Trains depart approximately every 15 minutes, beginning at noon. Climb aboard to travel through woods, over bridges, across a pond, and along a canal (all in 3,800 feet!).Volunteers donate train parts and construction. There is no charge to ride the trains; however, donations are greatly appreciated. Bring your own picnic or buy something to eat at the park's snack bar.

....

Willamette Shore Trolley

Depot: 311 N. State St, Lake Oswego
503-697-7436
www.trainweb.org/oerhs/wst.htm

Season: Jan–Feb Sat–Sun; Mar–May, Oct–Dec Fri–Sun; June–Sept Thurs–Sun

Hours: Lake Oswego: departs on even hours 10 A.M.–4 P.M., also Memorial Day–Labor Day Fri–Sat 6 P.M.; Portland (RiverPlace): departs on odd hours 11 A.M.–5 P.M. (also one-way trip Memorial Day–Labor Day Fri–Sat 7 P.M.)

Tickets: $10/adults, $6/children ages 3–12, free/lap sitters 3 and under

This sightseer's delight boasts two cars—a double-decker from England that was "modernized" in 1921 and a Portland Broadway trolley from 1932—that trace the Willamette River between Lake Oswego and RiverPlace four times daily in summer. The round-trip lasts an hour and 45 minutes. Stop at Willamette Park or at either terminal to give kids a chance to frolic, then return on a later trolley. Watch, too, for special runs, including ones for the Christmas ships and Fourth of July fireworks.

Chapter 6

Inside Fun & Learning

It's bound to happen: It seems like the rain will never stop. Summer vacation has begun to wear thin. Or the post-holiday blues have hit the kids hard. Whatever the reason, there will be those days when you just need a change of scenery. So pack up the kids and get out of the house. There's plenty of action indoors at these local establishments.

Archery

No unusual physical strength is required by this sport: Children as young as five years old are capable of mastering it.

Archers Afield

Tigard Plazas: 11945 SW Pacific Hwy, Ste 121, Tigard
503-639-3553
www.archersafield.com

Hours: Mon–Fri 10 A.M.–8 P.M., Sat 9 A.M.–5 P.M., Sun noon–5 P.M.

Fees: Prices vary; bow rental available

Archers Afield, a carpeted indoor archery range and store, features 30 shooting lanes and 60 targets. Serious archers come here for lessons and practice. Curious beginners are welcome but are encouraged to take a lesson before renting equipment. One of the most popular ways of learning, for beginners of all ages, is the Big Kids Little Kids League offered Tuesday and Wednesday evenings. During these six-week sessions a coach and equipment are provided. In addition, classes are offered in the community several times a year, including special sessions for homeschoolers. Archers Afield stocks rental equipment for kids, and rental fees may be applied toward equipment purchases at the store. Patrons are allowed to bring snacks from home to enjoy at the tables provided.

Arts and Crafts

A child does not have to love art to be enthusiastic about creating a ceramic masterpiece. An outing to one of these pottery studios is a fine idea a few weeks in advance of Mother's Day, Father's Day, or any other time your child wants to give a gift.

Amazin' Glazin'!

8128 SE 13th Ave, Portland
503-233-2566

Hours: Tues–Fri 11 A.M.–7 P.M., Sat 10 A.M.–6 P.M., Sun noon–5 P.M.

Fees: Vary

This paint-your-own-pottery studio offers a variety of ceramic pieces to paint.
Art classes are also available, as is a private party room for rental.

Mimosa Studios—Paint Your Own Pots

1718 NE Alberta Ave. Portland
503-288-0770
www.mimosa-studios.com

Hours: Tues–Sat 11 A.M.–6 P.M., Sun noon–5 P.M.

Fees: Vary

This small, friendly studio is in the Alberta arts district of Portland. Family Art
Night is on Wednesday evenings.

Multnomah Arts Center

7688 SW Capitol Hwy, Portland
503-823-ARTS (2787)
www.multnomahartscenter.org

Hours: Mon–Fri 9 A.M.–9:30 P.M., Sat 9 A.M.–12:30 P.M.

Fees: Vary

The Multnomah Arts Center, located in the former Multnomah School, offers a wide range of services to the Portland community, including outstanding arts education for children and adults.

Paint Pots with Laura

6360 SW Capitol Hwy, Portland
503-244-5976

Hours: Mon–Fri 11 A.M.–8 P.M., Sat–Sun 10 A.M.–6 P.M.

Prices: Vary

A visit to a paint-your-own studio is the perfect, and affordable, way to both provide an afternoon of entertainment for your kids and enable them to create an attractive gift for an upcoming holiday or birthday. Fired pieces can be picked up four days after your visit, and are held for 60 days.

Portland Art Museum
1219 SW Park Ave, Portland
503-226-2811, 503-276-4225 (education department)
www.pam.org

Hours: Tues, Wed, Sat 10 A.M.–5 P.M., Thurs–Fri 10 A.M.–8 P.M., Sun noon–5 P.M.;
closed select holidays

Admission: $10/adults, $9/seniors 55 and up and students 18 and up, $6/children ages 5–18, free/children 4 and under

The Portland Art Museum frequently offers family arts and crafts projects in conjunction with current exhibits. Museum Family Sundays (usually free with admission), held several times a year in conjunction with different exhibitions, are designed to augment the theme of a current installation through interactive activities, performances, and demonstrations that help make the exhibits more tangible and accessible to children. Here you might find children learning calligraphy, creating a sculpture from pipe cleaners and coat hangers, or making a mosaic using squares of colored construction paper. During the museum's once-a-month Family Drop In events (free with admission), kids of all ages visit the classroom for an art-making activity. Call the museum's education department or visit the Web site for upcoming events and classes.

Bowling

Once upon a time, bowling meant a night out for Mom and Dad. Now bumper bowling, along with so-called extreme, cosmic, or glow-in-the-dark bowling, has given new life to the sport. Bumpers are pads, or in some cases inflatable rails, that deflect the ball away from the gutters and turn what was once a physically technical pastime into a forgiving one. In bumper bowling, even the weakest, meekest novice throws strikes.

The following alleys offer bumper bowling at various times. They also offer birthday-party packages for kids, and some even sponsor bumper-bowling leagues on Saturday mornings for children ages three and up. Call ahead for hours of operation and to ensure lane availability. Call, too, to get the scoop on when cosmic bowling (especially popular with the older kids) takes place.

Rental-shoe sizes vary, but if your child's feet are too small for available rentals, he or she is usually welcome to bowl in sneakers or socks. Prices for rental shoes vary (usually they cost about $1.75); some places offer free shoe rentals for kids on weekdays. Cost of a game is typically around $3.50 for adults, with about a $1 discount for kids.

- **AMF Cascade Lanes**, 2700 NE 82nd Ave, Portland; 503-255-2635.
- **AMF Rockwood Lanes**, 18500 SE Stark St, Portland; 503-665-2123.
- **Gladstone Lanes**, 20100 McLoughlin Blvd, Gladstone; 503-656-4266.
- **Hollywood Bowl**, 4030 NE Halsey St, Portland; 503-288-9237.
- **Interstate Lanes**, 6049 N. Interstate Ave, Portland; 503-285-9881.
- **Kellogg Bowl**, 10306 SE Main St, Milwaukie; 503-659-1757.
- **Milwaukie Bowl**, 3056 SE Harrison St, Milwaukie; 503-654-7719.
- **Sunset Lanes**, 12770 SW Walker Rd, Beaverton; 503-646-1116.
- **Tigard Bowl**, 11660 SW Pacific Hwy, Tigard; 503-639-2001.
- **Valley Lanes**, 9300 SW Beaverton-Hillsdale Hwy, Beaverton; 503-292-3523.
- **Wilsonville Lanes**, 29040 SW Town Center Loop E Wilsonville; 503-682-2346.

Carousels

If you are looking for an out-of-the-ordinary treat for your youngster, consider a ride on one of the following carousels. Parents and kids alike smile at the sound of the tinkly music and the chance to climb aboard a lovingly carved animal.

Carousel at Jantzen Beach SuperCenter

1405 Jantzen Beach Center, Portland
503-286-9103
www.jantzenbeachsupercenter.com

Hours: Mon–Sat 11 A.M.–8 P.M., Sun noon–5 P.M.

Tickets: $2/person, free/children ages 2 and under

This 1921 C. W. Parker carousel has been restored and is now the centerpiece of the Jantzen Beach SuperCenter's Food Court. Listed on the National Register of Historic Places, the carousel includes 72 elaborate, hand-carved, one-of-a-kind animals.

Herschell-Spillman Carousel

Oaks Amusement Park: foot of SE Spokane St, Portland
503-233-5777
www.oakspark.com

Season: Open the week of Spring Break, then weekends in June only until school's out; summer Tues–Sun; Sept weekends only; closed from Oct until Spring Break begins; check Web site for hours

Tickets: $2.25/person

The carousel at Oaks Amusement Park isn't exactly indoors, but it is covered. Nicknamed "Noah's Ark," it features brightly colored wooden animals. Choose from horses, roosters, frogs, pigs, dogs, cats, kangaroos, storks, lions, goats, dragons, and giraffes and climb aboard!

Salem Riverfront Carousel

101 Front St, Salem
503-540-0374
www.salemcarousel.org

Hours: Summer Mon–Thurs 10 A.M.–7 P.M., Fri–Sat 10 A.M.–7 P.M., Sun 11 A.M.–5 P.M.; winter Mon–Thurs 10 A.M.–7 P.M., Fri–Sat 10 A.M.–9 P.M., Sun 11 A.M.–6P.M., closed Thanksgiving Day

Tickets: $1.50/person

OK, Salem is a long drive for a couple of minutes of joy on a merry-go-round, but if you are in the area, this one is well worth a visit (see "Salem" in chapter 10, Out-of-Town Excursions). An old-world-style machine, it stands next to a playground (and within walking distance of A. C. Gilbert's Discovery Village) in a building on the banks of the Willamette River. This beauty features 42 horses and two "Oregon Trail" wagons, lovingly hand-carved by community artists.

Climbing Walls

Constructed from concrete, wood, and a variety of other materials and punctuated by bolted-on handholds, carabiners, and dangling ropes, climbing walls are a big hit with climbing enthusiasts who are forced indoors during inclement weather or can't head out to the mountains. And it's no surprise that kids are intrigued as well, especially those who were climbing (living-room bookcases, neighbors' fences, kitchen drawers . . .) before they could walk.

All these clubs have discount cards available for frequent climbers. Another option for beginners is to reserve a group session with several friends. Typically scheduled during off-hours, group parties include a brief instruction period and lots of practice time with a staff belayer.

Tip

Don't throw away old tennis shoes. An uncomfortably tight pair of sneakers worn without socks makes a decent substitute for rock-climbing shoes and saves a few dollars in rental fees. For bouldering (technical climbing without ropes), however, it's worth springing for the real climbing shoes.

ClubSport Adventure Center

18120 SW Lower Boones Ferry Rd, Tigard
503-968-4500
www.clubsports.com/oregon

Hours: Mon–Fri 10 A.M.–11 P.M., Sat–Sun 10 A.M.–10 P.M.

Fees: Nonmembers: $18/adults, $10/children ages 12 and under; plus $9/equipment rental (shoes and harness)

ClubSport is a large, well-equipped athletic center that offers a great assortment of classes and sports opportunities for kids as well as adults. The Adventure Center is the largest rock-climbing gym in Oregon, with 11,500 square feet of climbing space. Walls reach up to 45 feet high and feature top roping, leading, and bouldering. They encourage young climbers with special climbing times for kids several times a week as well as offering a junior climbing team (acceptance by tryout) that competes in regional competitions.

Mount Hood Aquatic and Rock Wall Center

Mount Hood Community College: 26000 SE Stark St, Gresham
503-491-7243

Hours: Mon–Fri 3 P.M.–8:30 P.M., Sat noon–4:30 P.M.

Fees: $6/adults, $4/children ages 12–17; $5/equipment rental

This facility boasts an 1,800-square-foot rock wall. To use the structure, young climbers must be at least 12 years old and accompanied by an adult.

Portland Rock Gym

21 NE 12th Ave, Portland
503-232-8310
www.portlandrockgym.com

Hours: Mon–Wed, Fri 11 A.M.–11 P.M., Tues, Thurs 7 A.M.–11 P.M., Sat 9 A.M.–
7 P.M., Sun 9 A.M.–6 P.M.

Fees: Nonmembers: $14/adults, $7/children 11 and under and seniors 62 and
older ($10 for weekends); plus equipment rental (shoes and harness)

Portland Rock Gym, open since 1989, features 8,000 square feet of climbing walls
and prides itself on variety. Equipped with a 4-foot lead wall, 35- and 20-foot top
ropes, and bouldering areas, including a "cave," the gym does its best to simulate
real-life outdoor experiences. The club makes a big effort to encourage young
climbers with a special kids' climbing time, climbing birthday parties, and a Kids
Klimb card that includes lessons as well as discounted climbing time. They also
offer a junior climbing team (applicants must try out) that trains for competitions.

Recreational Equipment Inc. (REI)

1405 NW Johnson St, Portland
503-221-1938
www.rei.com

Hours: Mon, Wed, Fri 5 P.M.–8:30 P.M., Sat 10 A.M.–6:30 P.M., Sun 10 A.M.–
5:30 P.M.

Fees: $3/members, $8/nonmembers

REI, the giant outdoor gear and clothing retailer, closed its Jantzen Beach
location in 2004 and opened a new one in downtown Portland's Pearl District. Like the Seattle flagship location, the dynamic store features a free-
standing climbing pinnacle that is a thrilling challenge for youngsters who
enjoy climbing. Store personnel are very helpful in guiding kids up the rock.
Shoes and harness are provided for the climbing fee. If you choose, you can
celebrate your child's climb by purchasing a cute "I climbed the rock" T-shirt
($16). Climbing the pinnacle is a popular activity, so if you go on a weekend or

expect to wait. REI is a cooperative; by paying a
.... nbers receive discounts as well as an annual cash

....

Stoneworks Inc. Climbing Gym

...... SW 11th Ave, Beaverton

503-...-....

www.belay.com

Hours: Mon–Thurs 4 P.M.–10 P.M., Fri 4 P.M.–8 P.M., Sat–Sun noon–8 P.M.

Fees: $10/person

Stoneworks caters to children with climbing camps, lessons, and climbing parties, as well as fielding a junior climbing team. The handholds here have been
purposely placed close together so kids don't have to stretch too far. Devoted
mostly to bouldering, the facility has more than 5,000 square feet of climbing
surface, including walls up to 30 feet high.

....

Family Dances

....

Family Country Dance
Multnomah Arts Center Gymnasium; 7688 SW Capitol Hwy, Portland
503-823-ARTS (2787)

Hours: Oct–Apr second Sat every month 5 P.M.–7 P.M.

Fees: $5/adults, $3/children ages 15 and under, free/infants; $15/family
maximum

The motto of the Portland Country Dance Community, which organizes Family
Country Dance potluck gatherings, is "If your kids can walk, they can dance. (So
can you.)" This family dance series is designed for beginners—both adults and

children. A caller offers instruction in a variety of American folk dances, and the steps are purposely kept rudimentary. Kids like best the live folk bands, with their fiddles, guitars, mandolins, and pianos. Wear comfortable clothes and shoes, bring a dish for the potluck that follows the dance, and expect to meet plenty of people; about 100 typically attend.

....

Indoor Play Parks

On a long, rainy winter day, there's nothing better than going to a place where the kids can play with other kids, running and romping with abandon while you relax with other parents—all for a minimal fee. The idea of the indoor park is simple and the need is great, so it is no surprise that many indoor parks exist all over the greater Portland area.

Following is a sample of indoor play parks in the metro area. Finding them is not always easy, however; they often are "beneath the radar," in church basements and community centers. Most are cooperative, which means that parents agree to pitch in and help with administrative tasks as well as park setup and cleanup. Below are several places we suggest you look, but also ask parents in your neighborhood for their recommendations.

....

Community Center Indoor Parks
503-823-2525
www.portlandonline.com/parks

Hours: Vary by season and location; check Web site under "Recreation/Activities Information/Parent & Child" for up-to-date information

Fees: Minimal

The Portland Parks and Recreation Department offers indoor park programs at several of its facilities. Typically these programs take place at a community center's gym that has been set up with balls, bikes, and portable play structures. Sometimes trampolines are available. Parents supervise their own children and help with setup and takedown of equipment.

Tigard Indoor Play Park
United Methodist Church: Walnut Pl, off Hwy 99, Tigard
503-524-8794

Hours: Mon, Wed, Thurs 9 A.M.–11:30 A.M.

Fees: $3/child, $5/family

Tigard Recreation Association's Indoor Play Park is a parent-supervised play area for children up to five years old. It includes crafts activities as well as a wide selection of age-appropriate toys, including riding toys, a climbing structure, and a playhouse, plus infant and toddler toys.

Tualatin Hills Athletic Center Indoor Play Group
15707 SW Walker Rd, Beaverton
503-629-6330
www.thprd.com/facilities/thr_ip.cfm

Hours: Mon, Wed, Fri 10 A.M.–11:30 A.M.

Fees: Annual: $25/in-district family, $43.75/out-of-district family; onetime $15 refundable deposit also required

The Tualatin Hills Parks and Recreation Department has an Athletic Center Indoor Play Group (ACIP) for babies and toddlers from newborn to six years. This is a safe, enclosed play area with riding toys, a playhouse, a tot-sized basketball setup, and more. ACIP is a cooperative, with parents sharing duties. For more information, visit the Web site.

Laser Tag Arenas

"Capture the Flag" meets *Star Wars*. This, in essence, is the concept behind the high-tech laser games that are so popular with kids and many adults. Equipped with laser "guns" and computerized vest packs, players are divided into opposing teams whose mission is to disable the enemy and claim their home base.

Disappearing into dark, mysterious, cavernlike mazes obscured by machine-made fog and illuminated by black lights and special lighting effects, players are immersed in a three-dimensional video game in which stealth, cunning, and quickness reap the biggest rewards. Games last about 25 minutes, and monitors on duty throughout the area ensure there is no running or physical contact among players. Still, arena owners do not recommend laser tag for children younger than six or seven years old.

The "regulars" at laser tag arenas tend to be young adult males dressed in black, and they leave drenched in sweat. Weekdays, when the arenas are less crowded, are best for families. Call ahead to reserve if you want to be assured a chance to play.

....

Family Fun Center LaserXtreme
29111 SW Town Center Loop W., Wilsonville (Exit 283 off I-5)
503-685-5000
www.fun-center.com

Hours: Vary seasonally

LaserXtreme is part of Family Fun Center, the 6-acre amusement park 20 miles south of Portland. See "Amusement and Action Parks" in chapter 5, Outside Fun & Learning, for details.

....

Laserport
6540 SW Fallbrook Pl, at the intersection of Allen Blvd and Scholls Ferry Rd, Beaverton
503-526-9501

Hours: Mon–Thurs noon–9 P.M., Fri noon–midnight, Sat 10 A.M.–midnight, Sun 11 A.M.–9 P.M.

Fees: $6.50/person

Since moving to its new location on Allen Boulevard, Laserport's sound system and equipment have gotten rave reviews. Laserport's computers keep a running tally of game scores and relay that information to voice chips in players' equipment vests. There's also a full-service restaurant, video and simulation games, and a party room. Reservations are recommended for groups of 10 or more.

....

Ultrazone

Holly Farm Shopping Center: 16074 SE McLoughlin Blvd, Milwaukie
503-652-1122
www.ultrazoneportland.com

Hours: School year: Tues–Thurs 4 P.M.–9 P.M., Fri 3 P.M.–midnight, Sat 10 A.M.–11 P.M., Sun 11 A.M.–8 P.M.; summer: Mon–Thurs noon–9 P.M., Fri noon–midnight, Sat 10 A.M.–11 P.M., Sun 11 A.M.–8 P.M.

Fees: Prices vary for groups, individuals, and parties; check Web site or call.

Ultrazone is located in the Holly Farm Shopping Center in Milwaukie, just 10 miles south of Portland on McLoughlin Boulevard, also known as Highway 99 E. Beyond a super sound system and a three-team format, Ultrazone has an added wild card: an enemy robot sentinel, programmed to fire randomly, that roves the upper level. Teens congregate here after school and on weekends to play laser tag and video and simulation games.

Ultrazone makes a point of maintaining a wholesome atmosphere. On report-card days students form a long line to cash in on discounts for As and Bs. Sunday is Family Day, when parents play free with paying children until closing. Prices are also good on Friday evenings ($18 to play all evening 8 P.M. to midnight), and on Saturday morning until noon children 11 and under get a deal ($5.50/game). Reservations are required only for parties or groups of 10 or more.

Museums

See also the Oregon Museum of Science and Industry (OMSI) in chapter 2, Exploring the Natural World.

Portland Children's Museum
4015 SW Canyon Rd, Portland
503-223-6500
www.portlandchildrensmuseum.org

Hours: Spring/Summer hours: daily 9 A.M.–5 P.M., Sun 11 A.M.–5 P.M.; Fall/Winter hours: Tues–Sat 9 A.M.–5 P.M., Sun 11 A.M.–5 P.M.

Admission: $8/person, $7/seniors ages 55 and up and military, free/children under 1

This is one of those places in Portland where you're likely to hear cries of "But when can we come back again?" as parents herd their children toward the exit. The oldest children's museum west of the Mississippi River, the Portland Children's Museum opened in 1949 in a downtown location. Since 2001 it has been situated in Washington Park, which harbors a number of other sites popular with kids, including the Oregon Zoo and the Rose Garden Children's Park. A popular spot with the younger set, the museum now draws some 200,000 visitors each year. Everything about this museum is geared to kids, from the hands-on exhibits—aimed especially at children from birth through age 10—to the tyke-sized facilities in the restrooms. Among kids' favorite permanent exhibits are these:

Water Works: This exhibit is hugely popular. Highlights include a 12-foot-high waterfall; a hand-cranked Rube Goldberg–type "conveyor belt" that carries water in such whimsical recycled objects as mugs, kitchen tools, and even an old shoe; a twirling bouquet of kitchen mops; an array of instruments that kids "play" by spraying water; and a table that allows kids to experiment with ways of altering water flow.

The Grasshopper Grocery & Butterfly Bistro: A child-size version of a grocery store, this hot spot bustles with kids filling miniature shopping carts with fabulous fake foods. And it's right next door to the cafe—complete with a drive-up window, booths, and a lunch counter—where kids do, indeed, play with their food, serving it up to parents and friends.

The Garage: In this art studio children select odds and ends from an ever-changing assortment of recycled objects, and with the help of such tools as a drill and a hot glue gun, they create amazing, colorful sculptures. (This area is just for children ages six and over, or five and over with a caregiver.)

Baby's Garden: Tucked away in a corner, this area is perfect for the museum's youngest visitors. Here an imaginary stream meanders through a forest of trees decorated with bright fabrics, sparkling jewels, and fanciful insects. And soft padding, low steps, tubes, and tunnels give babies from birth to age two the chance to explore in a safe space.

There's more fun to be had at other exhibits, such as the Kid's Clinic, wherein children explore what it's like to be a doctor, dentist, nurse, or patient in a doctor's office, dentist's chair, and neonatal unit; and the Clay Studio, wherein everyone can try sculpting and, for a small fee, have creations glazed and kiln-fired.

And the fun doesn't stop with the many permanent exhibits. The museum also offers an enticing lineup of special events and programs, such as story times for little ones, puppet shows, and visits from multicultural musicians and actors.

Chances are, you'll need to refuel sometime during the hours you spend here. You can bring your own snacks to eat at tables in a vending area near the museum entrance. Or, if the weather's nice, you may want to head outdoors for a picnic on the grassy area, to the left of the building.

There's so much to do here, and kids love it so, that many families wisely use the Portland Children's Museum as an "indoor park," purchasing a membership and then visiting weekly if not more often. So, although the children's museum is a sure bet for beating the rainy-day blues, know that it can get pretty busy (especially during the holidays and spring break).

Exploring History

End of the Oregon Trail Interpretive Center
1726 Washington St, Oregon City
503-657-9336
www.endoftheoregontrail.org

Hours: Mon–Sat 9:30 A.M.–5 P.M., Sun 10:30 A.M.–5 P.M.

Admission: Included in the Historic Oregon City Pass (see sidebar)

From I-205 you can't miss the Paul Bunyan–size covered wagons in conference on Abernethy Green. This is the End of the Oregon Trail Interpretive Center—not quite a museum, not quite a theater. The live 30-minute presentation inside helps enlighten visitors about the history, heritage, and spirit of the immigrants who arrived in Oregon via wagon train in the mid-19th century.

In the Missouri Provisioner's Depot you'll take a seat among barrels, flour sacks, and earthenware jugs to hear a living-history interpreter describe the shopping trips and other preparations required to survive the 2,000-mile trek. In the adjacent Cascades Theater you can take in *Bound for Oregon*, an original film that follows the travels of four pioneers—a child, a young man, a woman with eight children, and another man—in their words. Then visit the gallery, which features changing exhibits that focus on life on the Oregon Trail and historic Oregon City in the 1800s.

And last, stop in at the Willamette Trades and Crafts Building, which features ever-changing hands-on pioneer-living activities. Here kids can practice loading supplies for the trail into a life-size wagon bed, or they can learn how to grind wheat into flour, tinker with old-fashioned toys, or learn different sewing stitches.

A covered picnic area provides a great place to have lunch. If you're going with a group of 12 or more, ask about group rates and be sure to make reservations.

The Historic Oregon City Pass

The Historic Oregon City Pass highlights the fact that there is much to see in this, the oldest incorporated city west of the Rockies. Established in 1829 and made the capital of the Oregon Territory in 1849, Oregon City is rich in historical homes and buildings.

The Historic Oregon City Pass is good for several months, and it always includes free admission to the End of the Oregon Trail Interpretive Center and the Museum of the Oregon Territory. Admission and/or discounts to a variety of other sites are included as well. For instance, the inaugural pass gave purchasers a free day pass on the Historic Oregon City Trolley, $2 off the purchase of the Barlow Road Driving Guide CD, a 10 percent discount at Philip Foster Farm Store, and $3 off a cruise on the *Belle of the Falls* paddle wheeler (see "Boating" in chapter 5, Outside Fun & Learning).

Available at both the End of the Oregon Trail Interpretive Center and the Museum of the Oregon Territory, the pass costs $9/adults, $7/seniors ages 65 and up, and $5/children ages 5–17 (group rates available). Because so much is included on the pass, you are not expected to use it all in one day. Instead, you use the pass on different days anytime during the valid period. The card is punched at each site you visit.

Fort Vancouver
1501 E. Evergreen Blvd, Vancouver, WA
360-696-7655 ext. 10, 800-832-3599
www.nps.gov/fova

Hours: Spring–summer daily 9 A.M.–5 P.M., fall–winter daily 9 A.M.–4 P.M. (closed select holidays)

Admission: $3/person, $5/family, free with National Park Pass

Fort Vancouver's heyday was in the early 19th century. At that time it was the administrative headquarters and main supply depot for the Hudson's Bay Company's fur-trading operations in the region. Under the leadership of John McLoughlin (now known as the "Father of Oregon"), the fort became the center of political, cultural, and commercial activities in the Pacific Northwest. When American immigrants arrived in the Oregon Country during the 1830s and 1840s, the fort provided them with essential supplies to begin their new settlements.

Now a National Historic Site, Fort Vancouver is still busy, drawing between 75,000 and 80,000 visitors each year. And with all the ongoing research and reconstruction at this once politically pivotal site, the attraction is getting stronger all the time. Most recently, professional and student archaeologists from Portland State University and Washington State University unearthed the remains of the circa 1832 Powder Magazine, the only brick building at Fort Vancouver. The National Park Service is using the archaeological research conducted as part of the field school to aid in its reconstruction, and other artifacts will help interpret how the Powder Magazine was used and what other activities occurred in the southwestern portion of the fort's stockade.

In fact, the park has developed a public archaeology program that includes "Kid Digs" (held selected dates during summer and fall). During these digs children get to help out with the research. Working in a team, they not only "excavate" but also take part in screening, taking notes, and describing the artifacts found in their unit.

The National Park Service has reconstructed much of this fort. Before entering the stockade, you wander through a well-tended period garden planted with the same vegetables and grains once consumed at the fort. Inside are a half-dozen buildings, including the chief factor's residence, a blacksmith's shop, a bakery, a trade shop, a fur store, a washhouse, a kitchen, a carpenter shop, and a jail.

One of the fort's additions is the Counting House, and here—in the fort's first exhibit designed specifically for children—young visitors can explore what it was like to be a clerk for the Hudson's Bay Company. Through "Growing Up at Fort Vancouver," kids can also explore the lives of three children who were actually at the fort in the 1840s—Cecilia Douglas, the daughter of one of the post's officers; Simon Guille, the son of a fur trapper and a Native American woman; and Rebecca Newell, who traveled over the Oregon Trail with her parents and married another settler.

Kids also like climbing to the top of the three-story bastion to touch a cannon and spy on "enemies." Elsewhere within the fort, you can watch blacksmithing and baking demonstrations and visit the carpenter shop to see furniture being made. Through the park service's Junior Ranger Program, children can complete a series of activities that help them learn about the fort's history and professions of Hudson's Bay Company employees to earn a Junior Ranger badge and certificate. This program is free and can be completed in one or two hours, depending on the activities pursued. (Check at the visitors center or the office at the stockade entrance for details and a Junior Ranger booklet.)

The Fort also now includes a playground for kids near the visitors center. It's not old-fashioned like most of what the fort has to offer, but it's sure old-fashioned fun.

History really does come to life at Fort Vancouver through a variety of special events and presentations, including a brigade encampment, a soldier's bivouac, and 1860s-style vintage baseball games. Check the Fort Vancouver Web site for a complete listing before you go.

And if a visit here sparks your interest in John McLoughlin, the fort's chief factor and the man who helped so many Oregon Trail immigrants survive, plan a visit to his home in Oregon City (see "Restored Homes" later in this section).

....

Museum of the Oregon Territory

211 Tumwater Dr, Oregon City
503-655-5574
www.orcity.com/museum

Hours: May 23–Sept 1 daily 11 A.M.–4 P.M.

Admission: Included in the Historic Oregon City Pass (see earlier sidebar)

Opened in 1990, this museum is a striking contemporary structure on the bluffs above Willamette Falls. It provides a thorough overview of the inhabitants of Clackamas County, from prehistory to the present day. Arrowheads and stone tools are among the artifacts on display from early settlements. A covered wagon sits packed and ready for adventure. The shelves of a replica pharmacy are stacked with hundreds of colorful, tiny bottles. And display cases reveal the tools used by practitioners of various trades. Children are asked not to touch these and other artifacts, many of which are not under glass.

Oregon Historical Society Museum

1200 SW Park Ave, Portland
503-222-1741
www.ohs.org

Hours: Mon–Sat 10 A.M.–5 P.M., Sun noon–5 P.M.

Admission: Nonmembers: $10/adults, $8/students ages 18 and older and seniors ages 60 and older, $5/children ages 6–18, free/children 5 and under. Free to the public the third Saturday of every month.

At the heart of this museum in downtown Portland is "Oregon My Oregon," an award-winning exhibit that occupies an entire 7,000-square-foot floor. More than 50 separate displays here tell the Oregon story from the earliest settlements to current issues with artifacts, artwork, photographs, documents, audiovisual presentations, and hands-on displays.

Children, of course, seem to gravitate to the most kid-friendly exhibits. They seek out the otter pelt for petting; test out the kid-size bunks in the hull of a Hudson's Bay Company ship, where sea chanteys and the creaking of the ship can be heard; and peer into the riverside tent to see the sketches and flower presses of David Douglas, a Scottish naturalist who explored the Oregon Country in the early 1800s.

But the behind-glass exhibits are appealing, too. It's fun to choose favorites in a display of shoes and hats worn by a variety of different Oregonians through the years and then admire a pair of 9,300-year-old sandals found at Fort Rock. In a section on the Oregon Trail a real covered wagon stands packed and ready to go, and displays show a few of the items—from delicate china plates to children's toys—that pioneers managed to bring with them on the long journey.

Two small theaters within the exhibit show short films that focus on early exploration and on Oregon's natural resources. And near the end of "Oregon My Oregon," youngsters and adults alike perch on the red and green stools at an old lunch counter salvaged from a Newberry's that closed in the 1990s to push jukebox buttons, selecting short films about such issues as education, racism, fish, and urban growth.

Prime time for families to visit the museum is every other month or so, when the museum's education department hosts a program, often on a Sunday afternoon, that includes hands-on activities for kids, storytelling, and music. Look for details on the museum Web site, and while you're there, look for information about occasional museum workshops for kids that focus on such topics as making postcards or pressing flowers.

(Bonus: The Oregon History Project, found through a link on the museum's Web site, offers a wealth of historical information online. With maps, biographies of noteworthy Oregonians, and research on such issues as women's history in Oregon, Lewis and Clark in Oregon, and reservation life in Oregon, it's a great resource for students and teachers.)

....

Oregon Maritime Center and Museum

On the steamer *Portland,* in Tom McCall Waterfront Park: foot of Pine St between Morrison and Burnside bridges, Portland
503-224-7724
www.oregonmaritimemuseum.org

Hours: Wed–Sun 11 A.M.–4 P.M. (call to verify schedule)

Admission: $5/adults, $4/seniors, $3/children ages 6–17, free/children 6 and under

This museum is located on the *Portland,* a restored stern-wheeler steam tugboat built in 1947 to help ships navigate the Willamette River. The main deck (the wheelchair accessible part of the boat) holds abundant artifacts of Portland's shipbuilding industry. It also has dozens of model ships, including those of sailing vessels and early stern-wheelers that plied the Columbia and Willamette Rivers.

Children especially enjoy inspecting the ships in bottles, testing out the horns from various ships, and peeking inside the Navy diving helmet. They find adventure, too, in climbing down the ladder to visit the boat's engine room and then, from the main deck, climbing up steep stairs to check out the pilot house.

The *Portland* itself is something of a celebrity: It was used in the filming of the 1994 movie *Maverick* (rated PG), which featured James Garner, Mel Gibson, and Jodie Foster.

Pearson Air Museum

1115 E. Fifth St, Vancouver, WA
360-694-7026
www.pearsonairmuseum.org

Hours: Wed–Sat 10 A.M.–5 P.M.; summer: Sun 11 A.M.–4 P.M.

Admission: $6/adults, $5/seniors ages 55 and up, $3/students ages 6–12, free/children 5 and under; group tours available

Located at the nation's oldest operating airfield (it dates to 1905), the Pearson Air Museum is dedicated to preserving the airfield and its rich aviation heritage. Visitors can view more than a dozen fully restored planes that predate World War II and see the oldest wooden hangar in the United States, a structure that dates to 1918 and, during WWII, housed Italian prisoners of war. In the museum's theater you can watch footage of the Soviet transpolar flight that touched down at Pearson in 1937 and learn of the accomplished career of Lieutenant Alexander Pearson, for whom the airfield was named in 1925.

A multimillion-dollar project has resulted in two restored buildings, one that was part of a barracks and another that was a munitions building. These buildings now hold offices and museum archives. Interactive exhibits teach the principles of flight, such as gravity and lift. For the true aviation fan the museum also offers popular aviation summer camps that teach children about flight and actually give them a chance to take the controls during a real flight.

Washington County Museum

Portland Community College's Rock Creek Campus: 17677 NW Springville Rd, Portland

503-645-5353

www.washingtoncountymuseum.org/

Hours: Mon–Sat 10 A.M.–4:30 P.M., closed on major holidays

Admission: $3/adults, $2/seniors and children ages 6–17; free every Mon

You can learn about all of Washington County's history—from the early Atfalati Indians to the influx of today's high-technology companies—through this museum's rotating exhibits. For a quick overview, check out a single-wall exhibit titled "The History of Washington County in a Nutshell." Then take some time with "Whipsaws to Chainsaws," which details the importance of the logging and timber industry to the county.

Kids tend to gravitate toward one of the museum's newest additions, the old county jail, which is featured in the exhibit "Doing Time: Then and Now." One of the original five buildings that made up Hillsboro, the log jail was built in 1853. Recently moved from the local fairgrounds, it has been completely restored.

One of the museum's highlight events is the "Draft Horse Plowing Exhibition," which is always the third Saturday of May. (In 2006 this family-friendly event marked its 40th anniversary.) Thousands turn out for this free living-history event that celebrates the region's close ties to agriculture. The big attraction here—and we do mean big—is the 40 to 60 draft horses that take up residence for the day. Some of the horses get a bit of a workout plowing a nearby field, while others are hitched up to provide popular wagon rides. The event also features trade and crafts booths where kids can learn such skills as how to churn butter, crank out some homemade ice cream, clean grain, and weave fabric.

(If your child is involved in scouting, you'll be interested in the museum's popular "Scout Saturdays," which makes history fun and helps both Boy Scouts and Girl Scouts of various ages earn badges and patches. For more information, visit the museum's Web site.)

This small museum has completed phase one of an ambitious building expansion. Visiting the museum gets them that much closer to completion of their goal.

Restored Homes

If yours is a child who loves reading books like the ones in Scholastic's Dear America series, you might want to put a trip to one of the Portland area's lovingly restored homes on your "Must See" list. After all, these homes provide vivid snapshots of family life at distinct periods in Oregon history. You'll find that many volunteers at these homes are willing to tailor their talks to suit the ages and interests of young visitors, especially when they're given a little advance notice. So call first if you have questions or want to arrange a special tour.

....

McLoughlin House
713 Center St, Oregon City
503-656-5146
www.nps.gov/mcho

Hours: Wed–Sat 10 A.M.–4 P.M., Sun 1 P.M.–4 P.M. (closed on major holidays, for nearly two weeks at end of calendar year, and in Jan)

Admission: Free

Dr. John McLoughlin was chief factor, or superintendent, of the British Hudson's Bay Company, and he established Fort Vancouver on the Columbia River in 1825. Forced into retirement in 1846, he and his family settled into this home by the Willamette Falls in Oregon City. The home was moved to its present location in 1909 and was added to the National Park System in 2003 as a unit of the Fort Vancouver National Historic Site.

....

Philip Foster Farm
29912 SE Hwy 211, Eagle Creek
503-637-6324
www.philipfosterfarm.com

Hours: Father's Day–Labor Day daily 11 A.M.–4 P.M.; Sept Sat–Sun 11 A.M.–4 P.M.; Oct–Father's Day grounds open daily, buildings closed; Apr–Oct group tours may be scheduled

Admission: $3/person donation suggested

The Philip Foster farm was a prominent stopover on the Barlow Road during the 1840s through the 1860s. Now a National Historic Site, the farm is the only authentic location along the Oregon Trail to showcase and actively interpret the original use of the site. It includes an 1860 barn, 1883 farmhouse, pioneer store, blacksmith, covered wagons, antique carriages, vegetable gardens, historic apple orchard, and possibly the oldest lilac tree in Oregon. Period-dressed volunteers are often on hand to tell stories of the past, demonstrate pioneer skills, and offer hands-on activities for the whole family.

Annual events include a Mother's Day brunch; Mary Charlotte's Garden Party, on the third Sunday in July, with a fashion show, tea, and antiques appraisal; the Cider Squeeze on the last Saturday in September; and Christmas at the Country Store, the first weekend in December, with Santa in the parlor, hot cider, and traditional carols. Check the Web site for current activities.

Pittock Mansion
3229 NW Pittock Dr, Portland
503-823-3623
www.pittockmansion.com

Hours: Feb 1–June 30 daily 11 A.M.–4 P.M.; July 1–Aug 31 daily 10 A.M.–4 P.M., Sept 1–Dec 31 daily 11 A.M.–4 P.M. (closed Jan)

Admission: Nonmembers: $7/adults, $4/children ages 6–18

The Pittock Mansion is a turn-of-the-20th-century architectural treasure. Once home to Portland pioneers Georgiana and Henry Pittock, former owner of *The Oregonian*, the fully furnished mansion offers a sweeping view of the surrounding Cascade Mountains and the city. Tours of the renovated Gate Lodge—once home to the family of James Skene, the Pittock estate's steward—began in spring 2005. There is no charge for just viewing the grounds, picnicking there, or using the wilderness trails. Parking is free.

Rose Farm
Holmes Ln at Rilance St, Oregon City
503-656-5146
www.mcloughlinhouse.org/rosefarm.html

Hours: July 5–Sept 6 Sat 2–4 P.M.

Admission: $3/adults, $2/children ages 6–17, free/children 6 and under

The oldest American home in Oregon City, this house was originally owned by William and Louisa Holmes. Nicknamed Rose Farm because of the many roses Louisa planted in the yard, it is known as the site where the first Oregon Territorial Legislature met, in July 1849.

....

Simon Benson House
1803 SW Park Ave Portland
503-725-4948
www.pdx.edu/alumni

Hours: Advance arrangements must be made for tours of the home; call ahead Mon–Fri 9 A.M.–5 P.M. Closed major holidays.

Admission: Free. $2/person donation requested for groups of 8 or more.

The Simon Benson House, a landmark in PSU's South Park Blocks, may look like it has been there for years. However, this beautiful, century-old Queen Anne–style home was moved in January 2000 from 11th and Clay to its current location and lovingly restored. It is now the home of the PSU Alumni Association and the University Visitor's Center. It also serves as a meeting place and resource center for the campus and the community.

....

Stevens-Crawford Museum
603 Sixth St, Oregon City
503-655-2866
www.endoftheoregontrail.org/stevns.html

Hours: Wed–Fri noon–4 P.M., Sat–Sun 1 P.M.–4 P.M.

Admission: Included in the Historic Oregon City Pass (see earlier sidebar)

The Stevens-Crawford house was built in 1907–1908 for the Harley Stevens family. A textbook example of the Foursquare or Classical Box architectural style, the house remained in the hands of the family that built it and still has most of its original furniture.

Fire and Police Museums

....

Jeff Morris Fire Museum
55 SW Ash, Portland
503-823-3615
http://jeffmorrisfoundation.org

Operated by the Jeff Morris Foundation, this walk-by museum (with viewing from the Naito Parkway sidewalk only) is adjacent to the Portland Fire Bureau building on SW Ash. It's dedicated to the memory of Jeff Morris, a loyal firefighter who pioneered the bureau's safety-education program and died of cancer in 1974 at age 46. Signage describes the historic equipment inside, much of which tells its own story of the past—from hand-drawn hand pumpers and ladder trucks (1860s–1870s) to a horse-drawn steam pumper from 1911.

....

Portland Police Museum
Justice Center: 1111 SW Second Ave, 16th fl, Portland
503-823-0019
www.portlandpolicemuseum.com

Hours: Tues–Fri 10 A.M.–3 P.M.

Admission: Free

Tucked away on an upper story of the Justice Center, the Portland Police Museum occupies three rooms. Children like dressing up in the museum's various police uniforms, and they clamor to sit atop the vintage Harley-Davidson motorcycle and in its sidecar. Dozens of display cases hold such items as bulletproof vests, firearms and other confiscated weapons, badges, arrest logs, and historical photographs. An officer is often on hand to talk to visitors and answer questions.

Safety Learning Center and Fire Museum

Historic Belmont Firehouse: 900 SE 35th St (at Belmont), Portland
503-823-3616 (event hotline), 503-823-3615 (tours and appointments)
http://jeffmorrisfoundation.org

Hours: Safety Saturdays: second Sat each month 10 A.M.–3 P.M.; group tours by appointment. Closed some summer Saturdays, call ahead.

Admission: Free

Working together, Portland Fire and Rescue and the Jeff Morris Foundation have developed the Historic Belmont Firehouse, where you can see a variety of fire equipment dating from 1879 to modern days. Since September 2004, the firehouse has been open to the public on Safety Saturdays, the second Saturday of each month. During these events you can slide down a fire pole, sit in the driver's seat of a fire truck, learn how firefighters live, visit "Hazard House" to learn how to make your home safer, and learn about the history and heritage of firefighting in Portland.

The center also offers free educational programs on seasonally appropriate topics, such as fireworks safety in July, and on other topics such as fire safety, poison prevention, and car-seat safety.

Skating

Skating—whether rollerblading on a sunny day, swaying to the music in an indoor roller rink, or gliding on ice—is a good activity when the whole family wants to get some exercise and have fun together. Often it is the parents who worry (for good reason) about hard falls. Wear protective gear (helmets, wrist and knee guards), don't be shy about getting lessons, and if you do go skating outside, bring along a baby in a stroller that you can push for added stability!

Ice

Right after your children have watched the Winter Olympics figure-skating championship, they will likely want to go ice skating—and expect to glide and twirl with ease. Remember to give them a reality check and be sure to bring gloves and padded clothing for all of you. Also, don't forget the glacially cool rink during the hottest days of summer. The rinks listed below offer lessons as well as party packages. Call ahead to check on public skate times.

Ice Chalet at Lloyd Center

953 Lloyd Center, Portland
503-288-6073

Fees: $6.25/adults, $5.25/children ages 17 and under; $3/skate rental, $3.50/hockey skate rental

Mountain View Ice Arena

14313 SE Mill Plain, Vancouver, WA
360-896-8700
www.mtviewice.com

Fees: $7.50/person ages 6 and up, $4.50/children ages 5 and under; $2.25/skate rental

Valley Ice Arena

9250 Beaverton–Hillsdale Hwy, Beaverton
503-297-2521
www.valleyicearena.com

Fees: $8/person, skates included; free/children ages 6 and under with paid adult

Roller and In-Line

Who could have predicted that roller-skating would become so hip? The advent of in-line skates brought skating back, and roller rinks couldn't be happier. Easier than ice skating and a lot warmer, roller-skating is fun for the whole family. Skaters may bring their own skates (in-line are usually allowed as long as they don't have back brakes) or rent them (be sure to bring socks). Call for information about family skate times and rates (rates often vary by day and time). All the places listed below have classes and host parties.

Mount Scott Community Center

5530 SE 72nd Ave, Portland
503-823-3183
www.portlandonline.com/parks

Hours: Vary

Fees: $1/person; $1/skate rental

Opportunities for skaters of all ages to learn to skate abound here. They even offer a Roller Hockey for Families class.

Oaks Park Skating Rink

Foot of SE Spokane St, Portland
503-233-5777
www.oakspark.com

Hours: Vary; check Web site

Fees: ; $5.75–$6.75/person; $1 skate rental

This rink is one of the largest on the West Coast. It has a well-maintained wooden rotunda floor and is equipped with a genuine Wurlitzer organ. The rink offers special morning skating sessions each week for children ages six and under. These sessions include a short lesson. Parents can go on the floor with their street shoes to help their youngsters practice new skills. Call for the Skating Club and family night at the rink.

Skate World

1220 NE Kelly, Gresham; 503-667-6543
4395 SE Witch Hazel Rd, Hillsboro; 503-640-1333

Hours: Daily noon–5 P.M.; Tues–Thurs 7 P.M.–9:30 P.M. Fri–Sat 7 P.M.–10 P.M. Sun, 7 P.M.–9:30 P.M.

Fees: $3–$5.50/person, skates included; $3 extra for in-line skate rental

A special session for homeschoolers ($3/person, skate rental included) takes place every Thursday during the school year. The rinks also offer a Tiny Tots program for preschoolers and caregivers on Thursdays in Gresham and on Saturdays in Hillsboro during the school year, with 30 minutes of instruction plus games and playtime. Parents are welcome on the rink in street shoes during this session, as are strollers. Also, there's the occasional Midnight Roller Disco, if you dare!

Swimming—Indoor Pools

It's true that Oregon may not be blessed with many months that invite swimming outside. But as the list below indicates, it's not hard to find a pool close to you where your family can get good exercise and soothe frayed nerves with some hydrotherapy—no matter the cold and wet weather outside.

North Clackamas Aquatic Park
7300 SE Harmony Rd, Milwaukie
503-557-7873
www.clackamas.us/ncprd/aquatic

Hours: Year-round (call for hours)

Fees: $6.99/adults, $4.99/children ages 9–17, $3.99 children ages 3–8, free/children under 3 with paying adult (limit 2 kids to 1 adult)

A Disneyland of swimming pools, this beautiful county facility has it all: a wave pool, lap pool, shallow wading pool, diving pool, whirlpool, and three water slides. Children under eight years old must be accompanied in the water by a responsible person age 13 or older. Snack foods are available from the on-site cafe; food and beverages from home are not allowed. To save dollars at the admission desk, check out the different rates on the Web site. There is a discount for swimming the last hour of open swim, as well as a special family rate on certain days.

Portland Parks and Recreation

503-823-PLAY (7529)
www.portlandonline.com/parks

Portland Parks and Recreation and Portland Public Schools together manage five indoor pools as well as eight outdoor pools (see "Swimming—Outdoor Pools" in chapter 5, Outside Fun & Learning). Suited to all skill levels—from waders and nonswimmers to swim-team members—most of these pools have shallow ends that begin at 1.5 feet. Indoor pools are available year-round, with closures for holidays and sometimes lengthy seasonal maintenance: always call first. (Check the Web site for hours.) All pools offer an excellent program of lessons, water-exercise classes, lap swims, and open swims. Pools are also available for parties—a great idea for a get-together of high-energy and exuberant kids.

Buckman Pool

320 SE 16th Ave
503-823-3668

This 20-yard pool, located at Buckman Elementary School, is heated to 85 degrees.

Columbia Swim Pool

7701 N. Chautauqua, Portland
503-823-3669

Located in Columbia Park, this 25-yard indoor pool has water depths from 1.5 feet to 8 feet. The pool offers lap swim, lessons, and recreational swims.

East Portland Community Aquatic Center
740 SE 106th Ave
503-823-3450

This facility, which includes an indoor pool, has been under construction since summer of 2007 and is slated to open its doors in early 2009. Check with the center for current status.

Matt Dishman Community Center and Indoor Pool
77 NE Knott, Portland
503-823-3673

Located two blocks west of Martin Luther King Jr. Boulevard, this 25-yard, L-shaped indoor pool facility is part of a community center and includes a 1-meter diving board as well as a whirlpool spa.

Metropolitan Learning Center Swim Pool
2033 NW Glisan, Portland
503-823-5130

Located in the basement of a public school right in the middle of downtown Portland, this public pool is one of the city's best-kept secrets. You'll find open swim hours, lap swim sessions, aquaerobics classes, and weekly swim lessons. Plus, you can rent the pool on weekday evenings. Check for extended closures.

Mount Scott Community Center and Swim Pool
5530 SE 72nd, Portland
503-823-3183

The Mount Scott Community Center, where this pool is located, also has a small roller rink available for rental. What a place for a birthday party!

Southwest Community Center and Swim Pool
6820 SW 45th, Portland
503-823-2840

With a popular interactive play structure and slide, this 25-yard, six-lane lap pool is popular with families. Water depths range from a zero-depth entry (a nice feature for very young children) to 9 feet. A variety of party packages are available.

Tualatin Hills Parks and Recreation
503-645-7454
www.thprd.com

Fees: $2/adults, $1.50/children ages 3–17

The Tualatin Hills Parks and Recreation District manages six indoor pools, where swimming and diving lessons and family open-swim sessions are offered year-round.

- **Aloha Swim Center**, 18650 SW Kinnaman Rd, Aloha; 503-629-6311.

- **Beaverton Swim Center**, 12850 SW Third, Beaverton; 503-629-6312.

- **Conestoga Recreation–Aquatic Center**, 9985 SW 125th, Beaverton; 503-629-6313. The Conestoga Aquatic Center has both a lap pool (78 degrees) and a leisure pool (88 degrees) as well as a water slide and water features.

- **Harman Swim Center**, 7300 Scholls Ferry Rd, Portland; 503-629-6314.

- **Sunset Swim Center**, 13707 NW Science Park Dr, Portland; 503-629-6315.

- **Tualatin Hills Aquatic Center**, 15707 SW Walker Rd, Beaverton; 503-629-6310.

Tours

Their questions begin almost as soon as they can talk: "Why?" "How come?" At first you dutifully try to answer, but before long these queries don't even register. And that's OK. Like the involuntary jerk of the lower leg after the doctor taps that tender spot just below the kneecap, kids can't help themselves; their questioning is reflexive.

Not for long. As they grow, the kind of questions changes. Your ears prick up; this could get interesting: "Where does the mail come from?" "Why is cheese different colors when milk's white?" "Where do the police officers' horses go at night?" "Who decides what's news?"

Schoolteachers have long known that one of the best ways to motivate children is not to explain, but to show. Most of the places listed here expect a large group to tour, not a couple of people. But why wait for a teacher to work a field trip or group tour into the curriculum? Gather together the neighborhood kids and head for fun and learning. The locations below open their back doors to the general public for a peek at what really goes on.

The Candy Basket

1924 NE 181st Ave, Portland

503-666-2000

Hours: Mon–Sat 9 A.M.–5 P.M., Sun noon-5 P.M.; tour reservations required

Fees: $3/person

Right out of *Charlie and the Chocolate Factory*, the 45-minute tour of this 60-plus-year-old, family-run operation begins next to the 20-foot chocolate waterfall. Watch the candy-making process up close, then taste the results. Learn about fudge, peanut brittle, chocolate molds, how creams are dipped, and how to package boxed candy. Open to ages five and up; the maximum group size is 10.

Chevy's Mexican Restaurant

Various metro-area locations

Hours: Vary from store to store

You have to like a restaurant that's willing to let you in the kitchen. Follow a patron's order to the kitchen and back out to the table. The famous El Machino tortilla press turns out 900 tortillas an hour—that's one every 53 seconds! Leave with a goodie bag full of fun stuff, including a coupon for a free kid's meal. This tour is recommended for ages three and up; some locations ask for a minimum group size of 10; plan to have at least one adult for every five children.

Franz Bakery
340 NE 11th Ave, Portland
503-232-2191 ext. 365
http://usbakery.com

Hours: Mid-Sept–June Mon, Wed–Sat (times vary)

Visitors see it all—from sifting flour to packaging loaves of bread to loading them on delivery trucks—during this 90-minute tour. Try samples as you go. Sandals and jewelry are not allowed. This tour is recommended for ages seven and up; group size is 10 minimum, 40 maximum.

Mounted Police Horse Stables
1362 NW Naito Pkwy, Portland
503-823-2100

Hours: Winter–spring Tues–Fri 10:30 A.M.; summer–fall Tues–Fri 2:30 P.M.

Follow an officer through the stables and learn about the care and training of the horses in the Portland police force on this tour lasting 30 to 45 minutes.

Oregon Candy Farm
48620 SE Hwy 26, Sandy
503-668-5066

Hours: Candy-making: Mon–Tues 9 A.M.–3 P.M.; store: Mon–Fri 9 A.M.–5 P.M., Sat noon–5 P.M. (closed Sun)

While the Oregon Candy Farm doesn't actually offer a tour, it does offer a behind-the-scenes view of the candy-making process to visitors of all ages who line up at big windows to watch and receive a free sample.

....

Portland Center for the Performing Arts
1111 SW Broadway, Portland
503-248-4335
www.pcpa.com

Hours: Wed 11 A.M., Sat 11 A.M.–1 P.M. (every half hour); first Thurs each month 6 P.M.

Visit the regal Arlene Schnitzer Concert Hall, built in the 1920s, and the Newmark and Dolores Winningstad theaters in the contemporary New Theatre Building next door. Together with the Keller Auditorium, these buildings make up the Portland Center for the Performing Arts, one of the largest in the nation. Learn about the theaters' histories, art, and architecture, and—if you're lucky—get a peek at a dress rehearsal. The one-hour tour is recommended for ages four and up; there's no restriction on group size.

....

Tillamook Cheese Factory
4175 Hwy 101, Tillamook
503-815-1300
www.tillamookcheese.com

Hours: Fall–spring daily 8 A.M.–6 P.M.; June–Labor Day daily 8 A.M.–8 P.M. (closed Thanksgiving and Christmas)

Located on the Oregon Coast, this place is too far to travel just to come to the museum, but if you are in the area, the kids will like the self-guided tour. Begin in the exhibit hall. Here a mechanical cow demonstrates the milking process, and a short video provides a history of the Tillamook factory. Then move upstairs, where three videos help explain the cheese-making process that is on view on the factory floor below. End the tour with a complimentary sample of cheese. (You may not be able to resist buying an ice-cream cone, though it's hard to choose from among the 40 flavors.) This tour is recommended for all ages; there's no limit on group size.

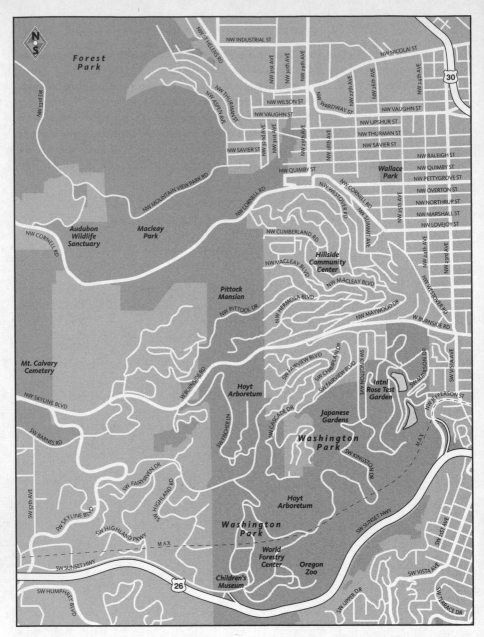

Forest Park &
Washington Park

Chapter 7

Parks & Gardens

Portland is known for its parks, and for good reason. Here you'll find the nation's largest forested city park (the aptly named Forest Park), the world's smallest park (Mill Ends Park), and a park that sits atop an extinct volcano (Mount Tabor Park). It's impressive to note that the city's Parks and Recreation Department manages 10,000 acres of land at more than 250 locations. This includes natural areas, recreational facilities, gardens, trails, and, of course, scores of neighborhood parks. So next time your child angles for a trip to a park, check out our suggestions and then have a new adventure! Unless otherwise indicated, park admission is free.

Portland and Environs

Audubon Wildlife Sanctuary

5151 NW Cornell Rd, Portland

503-292-6855

www.audubonportland.org

Hours: Nature center: daily 10 A.M.–6 P.M.; Nature Night: Sept–June second Tues each month 7 P.M.; trails open year-round, dawn–dusk

The Audubon Wildlife Sanctuary, nestled against Forest Park's southwestern flank, provides a tranquil escape from city life. The 150-acre park consists of lush native forest and more than 4 miles of trails that weave over bridges and boardwalks, past a pond, below a rough-hewn picnic hideout, alongside Balch Creek, and up and down steep hillsides. Two longer loops begin south of Cornell (be alert when crossing this busy road).

The Wildlife Care Center, where volunteers tend to injured birds and other forest creatures, is located at the trailhead. The Nature Center gives an up-close look at the backyard birds and squirrels that come to feast at a large platform feeder; there's also a display of birds, nests, and eggs (see "Wildlife Viewing" in chapter 2, Exploring the Natural World). Walk down Cornell Road to Macleay Park, which features green grass, picnic tables, and additional restrooms. (The Nature Center is wheelchair accessible, but trails are not.) The Audubon Society of Portland hosts a regular selection of nature programs for families and children. Call for a program guide or check the Web site, which is frequently updated.

Beverly Cleary Sculpture Garden for Children

Grant Park: NE 33rd Ave and Brazee, Portland

www.multcolib.org/kids/cleary

Oregon native and award-winning children's author Beverly Cleary mastered reading at a grammar school in Northeast Portland, not far from the Klickitat Street she made famous in *Henry Huggins* and her many other books about childhood—and not far from Grant Park, site of this monument. Dedicated in October 1996, the Beverly Cleary Sculpture Garden for Children features a central fountain surrounded by bronze statues of Ramona, Henry, and his dog, Ribsy. Local sculptor Lee Hunt took pains to make the sculptures accessible to children (even toddlers can sit on Ribsy's back) and realistic, though whimsical: Henry is wearing a Band-Aid and Ramona has on rain boots. In the summer months the fountain is a great place for young kids to cool off. Restrooms are adjacent to the nearby playground. To check out the garden before you go, visit the Multnomah County Library Web site.

Blue Lake Regional Park

Off Sandy Blvd and NE 223rd Ave, Portland

503-797-1850, 503-665-4995 (shuttle)

www.metro-region.org

Hours: Daily 8 A.M.–sunset

Admission: $4/car, $7/bus; pets not allowed

Operated by Metro Regional Parks and Greenspaces, Blue Lake Park is a 185-acre recreational paradise. The big draw is the 64-acre natural lake fed by underground springs. Older children can wade and splash at the swim park (no lifeguards); kids under five years old aren't allowed in the lake, but they can take advantage of the water-play area, which is open to all ages. You can also rent a paddleboat, canoe, or rowboat.

There's more to do than get wet at Blue Lake. Bring bikes to tour the interior or to explore the scenic 40-Mile Loop, which runs adjacent to the park. Fish for largemouth bass, bluegill, green sunfish, and catfish from the docks. Hang from the jungle gym or slurp on a Popsicle. Then try horseshoes or archery, or visit the wetlands and wildlife viewing area, and take a hike around the perimeter trail. (Most sports gear is provided on loan; bring your own fishing and archery equipment.) Picnic tables and shelters abound, as do restrooms. Bring a lunch or purchase hot dogs or other snack foods at the concession stand. In the summer of 2005, Blue Lake Park added a shuttle bus from the Gresham Transit Center to the park on summer weekends and holidays. Call for availability.

....

Cedaroak Park
4515 S. Cedaroak Dr, West Linn
503-673-7100

Hours: Sat–Sun, holidays dawn–dusk; school days 3:05 P.M.–dusk

At this park you'll find a wooden fantasy castle designed, with the input of schoolchildren, by noted playground architect Robert Leathers of New York (see also Columbia Park and Hallinan Park, later in this section). Parents, children, and staff members on the grounds of Cedaroak Park Primary School built the play structure in 1988. Twice a year, volunteers from the community return to refurbish and repair the structure, which is surrounded by gravel. You'll find playing fields, a tennis court, and a few picnic tables here, but not much shade and no restrooms. Park in the school parking lot, not on the street.

Columbia Park

1600 SW Cherry Park Rd, Troutdale

503-665-5175 (Troutdale Parks and Facilities Dept)

503-674-7262 (reservations)

www.ci.troutdale.or.us/parks-facilities/documents/columbiapark.html

Hours: Daily dawn–dusk

Columbia Park is famous for its community-built wooden play structure, yet another Robert Leathers design (see also Cedaroak Park and Hallinan Park in this section). Erected in 1994 behind Reynolds High School, Imagination Station is a circular, castlelike construction on a springy ground-cover cushion. The park itself, with its extensive playing fields, benefits from continued improvement. It now features walking trails, a picnic shelter, and restrooms.

Cook Park

South of Durham Rd at end of 92nd Ave, Tigard

503-639-4171 (city of Tigard)

Hours: Daily dawn–dusk

At 79 acres Cook Park—Tigard's prized play park—has long attracted metro-area families with its expansive playground, well-groomed fields, and clusters of shaded picnic tables. Toddlers are content on the swings and slides, while older children get involved in games of volleyball, basketball, and horseshoes. Adults tend to venture toward the Tualatin River, where there's a fishing dock, a boat ramp, and a paved, mile-long trail that is wheelchair accessible. The park recently added a wetlands-viewing gazebo and a butterfly garden. Reservations for the large picnic shelter go fast in summer, so call early.

Forest Park

3339 NW Skyline to St Helens Rd, Portland
503-823-PLAY (7529)
www.portlandonline.com/parks

Hours: Daily 5 A.M.–midnight

Some 50 miles of trails crisscross 5,000-acre Forest Park in the West Hills—the largest natural area in any U.S. city. Navigating this expansive tangle of firs, alders, and maples with children takes some forethought, though, because few of the paths make loops. Hoyt Arboretum (see entry under "Parks with Gardens") has free Forest Park trail maps and staff who can offer suggestions for family walks. See also "Biking" and "Hiking and Walking" in chapter 5, Outside Fun & Learning.

Hallinan Park

16800 Hawthorne Dr, Lake Oswego
503-635-0353

Hours: Summer daily dawn–dusk; school days 4 P.M.–dusk, Sat–Sun, holidays dawn–dusk

Erected by the Hallinan Elementary School community following an ambitious fund-raising campaign in 1988, the extensive play structures here were designed by New York playground architect Robert Leathers (see also Cedaroak Park and Columbia Park, earlier in this section). Tucked away in a quiet suburban neighborhood, the park is largely unknown outside its immediate environs. Facilities include picnic tables, playing fields, a running track, and portable toilets.

Ibach Park
10455 SW Ibach St, Tualatin
503-691-3061

Hours: Daily dawn–dusk

Surrounded by suburban sprawl, award-winning Ibach (pronounced "I-back") Park's play area is a 19-acre oasis that translates history into an interactive educational play area for children of all abilities. Young children rush to explore the dinosaur bones, splash in the water-play stream, scale the meteor, and ride the trolley. Older children are no less inspired; they've never imagined a play-ground quite like this. Adults talk about it the way they would a work of art, and there are intriguing and varied sculptural references to many of the fixtures.

Learn of the Atfalati tribe, natives of the Tualatin River Valley, from interpretive signs posted along a paved pathway. Bring baseball equipment and tennis racquets. Spread a picnic blanket on the vast lawn or a tablecloth in the picnic shelter and stay all day. There's little shade, so wear sunscreen and hats in summer.

A teen play area, requiring a bit more strength and dexterity, gives older kids a place to hang out while younger siblings play nearby. Parents can sit in between the themed area and the teen area and keep an eye on both.

Jurgens Park
17255 SW Jurgens Ave, Tualatin
503-691-3061

Hours: Daily dawn–dusk

Opened in 2000, this 12-acre park has been completed in phases. The park now includes a unique farm-themed playground, sand play, picnic areas, ball fields, open grass play areas, a wetlands restoration area, walking trails, and tennis and basketball courts. Using a theme of agriculture and history, the park offers kids the opportunity to race up a wagon ramp to a covered bridge, search for "vegetables" embedded in the wall of the sand-play area, and "feed" the pig sculpture that stands in the middle of the area above a water trough.

Kelley Point Park

N. Marine Dr and Lombard, Portland
503-823-PLAY (7529) 503-823-2525 (picnic area reservations)
www.portlandonline.com/parks

Hours: Daily 6 A.M.–9 P.M.

Located on the tip of the peninsula where the Columbia and Willamette Rivers meet, Kelley Point Park is a great place to pick blackberries and cool your feet on summer's hottest days. This 95-acre park features picnic tables, hiking trails, restrooms, a natural area, and sandy beaches. Kids enjoy watching large ships navigate the waters and osprey hovering, then diving, for fish.

Mount Tabor Park

SE 60th Ave and Salmon, Portland
503-823-PLAY (7529)
www.portlandonline.com/parks

Hours: Daily 5 A.M.–midnight

At first description, one might consider a visit to Mount Tabor a daring adventure. It is a volcano, after all. While actually an extinct volcano, this peak is one of only two found in cities in the continental United States (Bend has one also). Climb or bike the cone for a view (on a clear day) of downtown Portland and Mount Hood. Below are basketball and tennis courts, a playground, picnic shelters, and restrooms. An area near the reservoir is popular with dog walkers. Cinders discovered in the park were used to surface its roads. Send the children off to hunt for volcanic rocks.

Oxbow Regional Park

3010 SE Oxbow Pkwy, Gresham
503-797-1850, 503-663-4708
www.metro-region.org/parks/oxbowpage.html

Hours: Daily 6:30 A.M.–sunset

Admission: $4/car, $7/bus; Salmon Festival: $8/vehicle ($7 in advance); pets not allowed

Evidence indicates Native Americans inhabited the Oxbow Regional Park area 9000 years ago, and it's easy to see what drew them here. Oxbow's 1,000 acres encompass an ancient old-growth forest and an oxbow in the Sandy River, one of the state's most scenic. Owned and managed by Metro Regional Parks and Greenspaces, Oxbow has been left relatively undeveloped.

Come to hike, bike, or ride horseback on the 15 miles of trails throughout the park. Please leave your pets at home; they're not allowed, in or out of your vehicle, due to conflicts with resident wildlife. Motorized boats are not allowed, but canoes, kayaks, and rafts are welcome, as are anglers (consult park staff regarding regulations). In season, several small, rocky beaches provide access to the river for swimmers (*brrr!*).

Recently upgraded picnic tables and shelters dot the park, and there are two playgrounds. The campground, open year-round, features 66 campsites available on a first-come, first-served basis. The campground has two restroom buildings that boast hot and cold running water, coin-operated showers, heated-air hand dryers, radiant floor heating, and Oxbow's first flush toilets. The newer restroom facilities and two of the newer campsites are accessible by wheelchair.

The park hosts regular nature programs for families throughout the year, but in summertime it's especially busy. Schoolchildren investigate park ecosystems and animal habitats in "Oxbow Adventures," a series of four hourlong sessions (June–mid-July; check for days and times). Campfire programs (Fri–Sat nights July–Labor Day) spotlight history lessons, storytellers, and birds of prey. Call for a schedule of these and other special events or check online at the Web site.

Oxbow Park is also the site of the annual Salmon Festival (mid-Oct), which coincides with the return of spawning chinook salmon to the Sandy River. Tiptoe beside the river for a chance viewing and learn about the life cycle of these anadromous fish from park guides. Stay for a salmon-bake lunch, live entertainment, and children's crafts activities.

Tualatin Hills Nature Park

15655 SW Millikan Blvd, Beaverton
503-629-6350
www.thprd.com

Hours: Daily dawn–dusk

The Tualatin Hills Nature Park, a 222-acre wildlife reserve in the heart of Beaverton, is made up of evergreen and deciduous forests, creeks, wetlands, ponds, and meadows; the park encompasses the area where Cedar Mill Creek and Beaverton Creek merge. The park has 5 miles of trails (one of them wheelchair accessible), a visitors center, and covered shelter. Bicycles are allowed on two paved trails, each 0.75 mile in length. Picnic tables are located near the interpretive center.

The park offers a Nature Kids Preschool for four- and five-year-olds three mornings a week, as well as school field trips, summer camps, and a winter-break camp for kids of all ages. They also have family programs throughout the year, including Nuts About Newts and Bat Night. Check the Web site for details about days and times.

Vancouver Lake Park

6801 NW Lower River Rd, Vancouver, WA
360-619-1111
www.ci.vancouver.wa.us/parks-recreation

Hours: Daily 7 A.M.–dusk

Located just a few miles north of Portland, Vancouver's 234-acre park stretches for 2.5 miles along the lake, with 35 developed acres. Picnic tables, play equipment, and sand volleyball pits are available. Swimming is allowed in a cordoned-off water contact area with a sand beach, but *no* lifeguards are on duty.

Vancouver Lake is the site of many college and professional rowing (sculling) competitions during the year. The lake is also great for beginning windsurfing, kayaking, and canoeing. Views of Mount Hood, Mount Adams, and

Useful Contact Information

- **City of Tualatin Parks and Recreation Department**, 503-692-2000; *www.ci.tualatin.or.us/*

- **Gresham Parks and Recreation**, 503-618-3000; *www.ci.gresham. or.us/departments/des/parksandrec*

- **Hillsboro Parks and Recreation**, 503-681-6120; *www.ci.hillsboro. or.us/ParksRec/*

- **Lake Oswego Parks and Recreation District**, 503-697-6500; *www. ci.oswego.or.us/parksrec*

- **Metro Regional Parks and Greenspaces**, 503-797-1700; *www. metro-region.org/parks*

- **Oregon State Parks Information Center**, 800-551-6949; *www.prd. state.or.us/*

- **Portland Parks and Recreation**, 503-823-PLAY (7529; information hotline), 503-823-2525 (reservations); *www.portlandparks.org*

- **Reservations Northwest**, 800-452-5687 (state-park campgrounds in Oregon and Washington)

- **Tigard Public Works Department**, 503-639-4171; *www.ci.tigard.or. us/community/parks*

- **Tualatin Hills Park and Recreation District**, 503-645-6433; *www. thprd.org/*

- **Vancouver Parks and Recreation**, 360-619-1111; *www.ci.vancouver. wa.us/parks-recreation*

Mount St. Helens abound; the park is also a wetlands haven for wildlife and migratory waterfowl. A 2.5-mile multi-use trail connects Vancouver Lake Park to Frenchman's Bar Riverfront Park.

Willamette Park

SW Macadam and Nebraska, Portland

503-823-PLAY (7529)

Hours: Daily 5 A.M.–10 P.M.

Admission: Memorial Day–Labor Day: $3/vehicle, $4/vehicle plus trailer; free rest of year

Relatively flat and smooth, the park's Willamette Greenway Trail traces the west side of the river from the Fremont Bridge to the Sellwood Bridge, and on the east side—though a bit fragmented—has sections between most of the bridges and a lovely stretch in St. Johns. Though there are gaps that sometimes send you winding through a neighborhood, the path is generally great for strollers, toddlers, and still-wobbly bicyclists. More experienced bicyclists can follow the trail even further on both sides.

Popular with runners and cyclists, the path gets crowded on sunny weekend afternoons; give your kids a wide berth if their steering and braking are uncertain. Take time to skip stones and watch the boats at one of the rocky "beaches," and then retrace your steps to a playground for a picnic.

When you're ready, follow the path south from Willamette Park, through the adjoining neighborhood, and emerge in Butterfly Park. In spring and summer the native shrubs, trees, and meadowlands here are particularly attractive to butterflies and other colorful flying insects.

Parks with Gardens

Classical Chinese Garden

121 NW Everett and Third, Portland

503-228-8131

www.portlandchinesegarden.org

Hours: Daily Nov 1–Mar 31 10 A.M.–5 P.M.; Apr 1–Oct 31 9 A.M.–6 P.M.

Admission: $8.50/adults, $7.50/seniors, $6.50/students, free/children ages 5 and under

Located within Chinatown, this walled Ming Dynasty–style garden occupies an entire city block between NW Everett–NW Flanders and NW Second–NW Third. Built by artisans from Portland's sister city, Suzhou, the garden features ponds, bridges, and serpentine walkways, as well as a meticulously arranged landscape of rock groupings, delicate trees and shrubs, lattice screens, and pavilions. While it is a wonderful place to introduce a child to the Chinese culture, the garden is not a playground. Older children might enjoy tea and a light meal at the teahouse on the grounds of the garden. Or you can round out the experience with dim sum at one of several nearby Chinese restaurants, such as House of Louie on NW Davis, or Fong Chong at NW Fourth and Everett.

....

Crystal Springs Rhododendron Garden
SE 28th Ave, 1 block north of Woodstock, Portland
503-771-8386
www.portlandonline.com/parks

Hours: Apr 1–Sept 30 6 A.M.–10 P.M.; Oct 1–Mar 31 6 A.M.–6 P.M.

Admission: Labor Day–Feb free; rest of year $3/adults, free/children ages 12 and under; free Tues–Wed and before 10 A.M. or after 6 P.M.

Operated by the Rhododendron Society on land owned by Portland Parks and Recreation, this 6.5-acre enclave is a paradise of birds. All manner of ducks and other waterfowl flock here, and local bird-watching groups regularly visit to take a new census. Bring binoculars, cracked corn, and a notebook to keep tally of the wood ducks, domestic ducks, wigeons, buffleheads, pie-billed grebes, and coots. The wooden boxes nailed to tree trunks are for wood ducks (with round door openings) and bats (without).

Surrounded by the Eastmoreland Golf Course and fed by 13 springs, the peaceful gardens are planted with hundreds of rhododendron species and azaleas, which generally reach their peak blooming season in late April and early May. Winding, paved trails loop around lakes, over bridges, past waterfalls and fountains, and along a lagoon. There are no tables or any shelter, but picnicking is allowed on the lawn. Be aware that while the garden is wheelchair accessible, the park's restrooms are not.

And by the way, leave your stale bread at home when you come. Ducks prefer cracked corn, and park supervisors prefer that you feed them that. You can buy cracked corn at the park's entrance booth, or pick up a bag at a local bird shop or at the nearby produce stand.

....

Hoyt Arboretum

4000 SW Fairview Blvd, Portland
503-865-8733
www.hoytarboretum.org

Hours: Visitors center: Mon–Fri 9 A.M.–4 P.M., Sat 9 A.M.–3 P.M. Grounds: daily 6 A.M.–10 P.M.

Established in 1928, Hoyt Arboretum boasts one of the nation's largest collections of conifers, including Brewer's weeping spruce, Himalayan spruce, dawn redwood, Chinese lacebark pine, and a maturing grove of coast and giant redwoods. This 175-acre city-owned garden of trees is adjacent to Washington Park, and many of its 10 miles of trails dip into its neighbor and link with Forest Park byways beyond. When you arrive in Hoyt Arboretum, stop first at the visitors center to get oriented. The restrooms are here, and a large picnic shelter is directly across the street. Trail maps are available.

International Rose Test Garden

In Washington Park at 400 SW Kingston Ave, Portland
503-823-3636

Hours: Daily 7 A.M.–9 P.M.

From its terraced hillside above the city, the International Rose Test Garden is more to Portland than a botany laboratory. To serious rose hybridizers, this idyllic spot represents a confluence of conditions too good to be true. Since 1917 the 5-acre rose garden, one of only 25 such sites in the country, has been methodically conducting research into the performance levels of new rose varieties. Best Rose winners are exhibited chronologically in the Gold Medal Garden. Roses still in the guinea-pig stage are designated by numeral only.

Tourists visit all the time, but Portlanders prefer to come on lazy Sunday afternoons after church or for wedding portraits against the scenic skyline backdrop. (Blooms are at their best early June to early November.) Whether locals or not, visitors to the International Rose Test Garden bring their cameras.

Children may quickly lose interest in row upon row of flowers (8,000 plants, 532 varieties). Encourage them to study just a few closely and soon they'll initiate a hunt for a family favorite—be sure to factor in aroma, as well as color, shape, and texture. Enjoy a giggle at the roses' funny "celebrity" names, then ask your children to select the varieties by which they would choose to be immortalized.

The adjoining 2-acre amphitheater, which hosts summer concerts, is a great place to run and romp. Restrooms and picnic shelters are located near the tennis courts and parking lots up above on Kingston Avenue, as are a seasonal concession stand, a gift shop featuring all things rose, and the zoo train depot. The Rose Garden Children's Park (see entry later in this section) is an easy walk farther down Kingston.

Japanese Garden

In Washington Park at 611 SW Kingston, Portland
503-223-1321
www.japanesegarden.com

Hours: Apr 1–Sept 30 Mon noon–7 P.M., Tues–Sun 10 A.M.–7 P.M.; Oct 1–Mar 31 Mon noon–4 P.M., Tues–Sun 10 A.M.–4 P.M. (last admission half hour before closing)

Admission: $8/adults, $6.25/seniors 62 and up and college students with ID, $5.25/children ages 6–17, free/children ages 5 and under

In 1990, at the 25th anniversary of the Japanese Garden, the Japanese ambassador to the United States proclaimed this "the most beautiful and authentic Japanese garden in the world outside of Japan." Ambassador Matsunaga was merely confirming what loyal visitors have long suspected: The Japanese Garden is a spiritual oasis. The feeling is serene, quiet, and meditative on this Washington Park promontory, with views out over downtown Portland and on to Mount Hood. Among the pristinely manicured shrubs, deftly raked pebbles, and artfully designed bamboo fences, children may subconsciously sense an indefinable otherness.

Within the 5.5-acre spread are representations of five separate formal garden styles: Strolling Pond Garden, Tea Garden, Natural Garden, Dry Landscape Garden, and Flat Garden. Ask your kids to identify them (without reading the plaques!). There is much that appeals to children here: peekaboo pathways along a cascading stream, creaky boardwalks through a marsh, and mysteriously intriguing koi. But parents should be aware that this is not a place for a free-for-all: Adults and children alike must stay on the pathways.

If you have a particularly rambunctious child, perhaps the best time to visit is Children's Day, celebrated each year in early May. Bring the kids then, and they'll be caught up in origami workshops, tea ceremonies, dancing, and martial arts demonstrations.

···

Jenkins Estate
8005 SW Grabhorn Rd, Aloha
503-629-6355
www.thprd.org/Facilities/Jenkins/.cfm

Hours: Winter daily 8 A.M.–4 P.M.; Memorial Day–Sept daily 8 A.M.–8 P.M.

Originally owned by heiress Belle Ainsworth Jenkins, the 68-acre Jenkins Estate was purchased by the Tualatin Hills Park and Recreation District in 1975. The main house—built to resemble an English hunting lodge—and stable and gatehouse have been restored and are available by reservation for private receptions and business functions.

With winding, hide-and-seek gravel paths, a rockery, and a koi pool, the gardens were designed in the traditional English picturesque style. Rhododendrons and wildflowers are at their best in spring; the perennial gardens peak in summer. Bring a picnic to spread out on a lawn, park bench, or covered table. But be mindful that there are no public restrooms, save one portable toilet in Camp Rivendale.

If the Jenkins Estate's lush landscaping isn't reward enough for your children, entice them with images of a pot of gold at trail's end. Walk south past the teahouse to Camp Rivendale (in use mid-June–end Aug Mon–Fri until 4 P.M.), a clearing where outdoor sessions for youths with physical and learning disabilities are held each summer. There's a fine play structure here, an ample lawn, and a picnic shelter. Best of all, well away from the peaceful estate, kids are free to shake their sillies out.

Tip

A fun time to visit the Jenkins Estate is the annual Spooktacular held each year (last Sat of October 11 A.M.–5 P.M.; $7/adults, free/children). This not-so-spooky event is geared for children 10 and under and features carnival games, a spooky snack shack, pictures in the scarecrow garden, and cookie decorating. Costumes are welcome.

The Oregon Garden
879 W. Main St. on south side of Silverton
503-874-8100, 877-ORGARDEN (674-2733)
www.oregongarden.org

Hours: May–Sept daily 10 a.m.–6 p.m.; Oct–Apr daily 10 a.m.–4 p.m.

Admission: May–Sept $10/adults, $9/seniors, $8/students, free/children ages 7 and under; Oct and Apr $8/adults, $7/seniors, $6/students, free/children ages 7 and under; Nov–Mar $5/adults, $4/seniors and students, free/children ages 7 and under

Officially dedicated in 1999, the Oregon Garden has sprouted from a glimmer in the eyes of a few nurserymen to a mature and diverse display garden. Located in Silverton, 40 miles south of Portland, the garden encompasses 80 acres, with more than 100 acres yet to be developed.

While adults will marvel at the diversity of plants found throughout the garden, kids will probably be most enthusiastic about a specially designed Children's Garden that features funny Dr. Seuss–style plantings, an *Alice in Wonderland*–like archway tunnel that grows smaller the farther you walk into it, and the sandbox where careful digging reveals dinosaur bones.

Other specialty gardens include the Lewis and Clark Garden, with plants that the two explorers recorded seeing on their journey west, from the plains to the high desert to the Pacific Coast; the Pet-Friendly Garden, which is filled with plants that the family dog can eat without getting sick; and the Oregon Market Garden, where kids can help water and tend growing fruits and vegetables that are later donated to the Silverton Food Bank.

Concerts and educational programs are scheduled throughout the year. Every Saturday in the summer, kids can participate in the children's program; there's no start or end time—just show up and a garden employee will help with the day's activity, which could be making leaf rubbings, planting seeds, or studying bugs. For up-to-date information on both concerts and other educational programs for kids, check the garden's Web site.

....

Peninsula Park and Rose Garden
700 N. Rosa Parks Wy, Portland
503-823-PLAY (7529)
www.portlandonline.com/parks

Hours: Daily 5 A.M.–midnight

Peninsula Park is considered one of the foremost examples of a formally designed neighborhood park, typical of the early 1900s. Completed in 1913, it includes the city's first public rose garden and the city's first community center. Much remains of the original features, including the lantern-style streetlights, the stone pillars, vast brickwork, and the nearly 100-year-old fountain in the center of the rose garden.

Rose Garden Children's Park

In Washington Park at SW Kingston Blvd (adjacent to the International Rose Test Garden), Portland

503-823-PLAY (7529)

www.portlandonline.com/parks

Hours: Daily 5 A.M.—10 P.M.

Originally envisioned by the Rotary Club of Portland as the nation's first park designed to fulfill the specific needs of children with disabilities, the Rose Garden Children's Park has been wildly successful with children of all abilities. So inconspicuous are the special handicapped aids—handrails, armrests on benches, Braille instructions—that one scarcely notices them. But, then, it's hard to concentrate on much of anything amid the hustle and bustle of children here.

Themed "pods" feature a castle, spaceship, clock tower, and tree house. In addition, the park offers a sand-play area, tube slides, a variety of swings, and shaded lawns for picnicking. Nearby, the old zoo's elephant house is now a picnic shelter with restroom facilities. Be warned: On sunny weekends this place is a beehive of activity and parking is scarce.

State Parks

Champoeg State Heritage Area

7679 Champoeg Rd, St Paul

503-678-1251

www.oregonstateparks.org

Hours: Daily dawn—dusk

Admission: $3/vehicle

In 615-acre Champoeg (pronounced "sham-POO-ee") State Park, the Willamette River is slow and wide and the environs are tranquil. But Champoeg wasn't always so serene. On this site on May 2, 1843, farmers who had settled the area voted 52 to 50 to establish a provisional government, the region's first. With its strategic location on the river, Champoeg became a regular stop for stagecoaches and steamboats and was a thriving village (population 200) until a record flood washed out the town in 1861. Visitors today can peek in at the Manson Barn, which was salvaged from the flood. Two other structures are open to the public in season: the Pioneer Mothers Cabin Museum (503-633-2237), a massive log structure built in 1931; and the Robert Newell House Museum (503-678-5537), which was reconstructed by the Daughters of the American Revolution.

Many are content instead to enjoy the setting, to hike in the woods near the river, or to ride bikes along the 4-mile paved trail. There are three picnic shelters along the river and expansive meadows and lawns on which to spread out. The campground features 57 electric hookup sites, six walk-in tent sites, six yurts, and six camper cabins. To reserve, call Reservations Northwest (800-452-5687).

If you're a Frisbee fan, don't miss the 12-hole disc (Frisbee) golf course. Located near the Oak Grove Day-Use Area, the field is equipped with 12 baskets into which players try to launch their flying discs. There is no fee to play, but you must bring your own equipment. Pick up a course map at the visitors center on entering the park.

Also, between Memorial Day and Labor Day, the park runs special Junior Ranger programs on the weekends for ages 6 to 12 in the campground program area. Check flyers in the park for details.

....

Silver Falls State Park
20024 Silver Falls Hwy, Sublimity
503-873-8681, 800-551-6949
www.oregonstateparks.org

Hours: Daily dawn–dusk

Admission: $3/vehicle

Washington Park

In 1871, when forest, hills, and the Willamette River surrounded Portland and the city's population stood at 8,000, the city purchased more woods—41 acres—from a private citizen for the then-steep price of $32,624. The 1901 Park Commission's report reads: "The purchase was at first regarded by most citizens with disapprobation or contempt." Fortunately, nothing came of this general dissatisfaction, and Washington Park (503-823-PLAY, *www.portlandonline.com/parks*) is now among Portland's best-loved and most-used parks. At the head of SW Park Place, the park is open daily from 5 A.M. to midnight.

Many special sites are located within or adjacent to Washington Park's 130 acres, including Hoyt Arboretum, the International Rose Test Garden, the Oregon Zoo, the Portland Children's Museum, the World Forestry Center, and the Japanese Garden. See "Animals Up Close" in chapter 2, Exploring the Natural World, for details on the Oregon Zoo; see the Portland Children's Museum under "Museums" in chapter 6, Inside Fun & Learning; and see the World Forestry Center Discovery Museum under "Museums That Teach Natural Science" in chapter 2, Exploring the Natural World.

At 8,700 acres, Silver Falls State Park, the largest of Oregon's state parks, is aptly named. From the main day-use parking lot it's just a short, flat walk to a viewpoint that looks directly down on the 177-foot South Falls. But the park has nine other hidden treasures, which are visible from the popular 7-mile Trail of Ten Falls. (This hike is arduous, so think twice about embarking on it with small children.) Stop by the visitors center for trail maps and advice. The lodge also features a snack bar, a fireplace (a great place to warm up), nature displays, and a small gift shop.

Few children (or adults) can pass up an opportunity to stand behind a waterfall, so you'll likely want to descend into the canyon and slog through the mud and mist to crouch under the massive rock outcropping, sheltered from the spray and deafening rush. Bring bikes for the paved, 4-mile loop trail, or rent horses or ponies (Memorial Day–Labor Day: $27/hour per person) and explore 14 miles of equestrian trails. Picnic tables and shelters are scattered throughout the park, as are restrooms.

In summer the river is dammed south of the parking lot for swimmers. The beach is rocky, not sandy, and the water is cold—but that doesn't seem to discourage children. The Silver Falls campground is outfitted with 46 tent sites and 54 sites with electrical hookups. To reserve, call Reservations Northwest (800-452-5687).

....

Tryon Creek State Park

11321 SW Terwilliger Blvd, Portland
503-636-4398
www.tryonfriends.org, www.oregonstateparks.org

Hours: Park: daily 7 A.M.–8 P.M., Nature Center: daily 9 A.M.–5 P.M.

Nestled in a shady canyon between Lewis and Clark College and Lake Oswego, Tryon Creek State Park is a 645-acre forest with 14 miles of trails for hikers, bikers, runners, and equestrians. Restrooms are found in the nature center. At the nature center ask for a trail map and for advice on activities appropriate for your family's stamina. Shorter legs are happy enough with the 0.35-mile Trillium Trail, a paved, all-abilities loop. Older children may prefer to venture farther into the wilderness to explore the creek and its bridges. Look for rough-skinned newts in the water and pileated woodpeckers, barred owls, and Cooper's hawks in the trees. Bicyclists stay on a 3-mile paved path that runs parallel to Terwilliger Boulevard (this is not a loop trail). Horseback riders have two packed-gravel loops to choose from, for a total of 5.2 miles. A large pavilion shelter is equipped with benches.

The park is known for its Winter Solstice celebration and for the Trillium Festival, which occurs in spring. In summer, watch for details on the park's concert series, Forest Music. And if you haven't heard about them already, check out the park's popular after-school programs, as well as its summer day camp and winter- and spring-break camps. The park has also become a hit as a birthday party site.

A Bit Farther Afield

Wildwood Recreation Site
Just east of milepost 39 off Hwy 26, 39 miles east of Portland
503-622-3696

Hours: May–Oct 8 A.M.–sunset; walk-in visitors are welcome during the closed season

Admission: $3/vehicle

Nearly 600 acres in size, Wildwood is a day-use recreation site tucked in the forested foothills of Mount Hood, along the Salmon National Wild and Scenic River. Wildwood is managed by the Bureau of Land Management and offers family and group picnic facilities, ball fields, and a play area. The park also features miles of trails, including the wheelchair-accessible Cascade Streamwatch Interpretive Trail and the Wildwood Wetland Boardwalk Trail.

Chapter 8

Spectator Sports

When it comes to sports, there's plenty to cheer about in Portland. For many parents sharing the thrill of an exciting sports event is a great opportunity to establish common ground with their children. While Portland is home to various professional-level teams, don't overlook local high school or college sports teams. Often, these put on the best show. And sitting just 10 feet from the action can be a terrific way to observe lessons in fair play, cooperation, and persistence. The athletes may not be superstars, but they're role models you can feel good about. And besides, the price is right!

Professional Teams

Portland Beavers
PGE Park: 1844 SW Morrison, Portland
503-553-5555
www.pgepark.com/beavers

Season: Mid-June–early Sept

Tickets: $8–$15/person, free/children ages 2 and under

Portland General Electric Park is home to the triple-A baseball Portland Beavers, a farm team of the San Diego Padres, as well as the A-league soccer Portland Timbers, both of which are owned and operated by Portland Family Entertainment.

The sideshow antics during the game (costumed characters, prizes delivered with a slingshot) as well as a visit to the Fred Meyer Family Deck, with the vintage soda fountain, will help kids get through the slow parts of the game. If your child is a real fan, arrive early: A couple of players usually offer autographs prior to each game.

Portland Timbers
PGE Park: 1844 SW Morrison, Portland
503-553-5555
www.portlandtimbers.com

Season: Late Apr–Sept

Tickets: $5–$25/person, free/children ages 2 and under

If your children play soccer, they'll likely learn from and enjoy watching a professional match. Portland is a city of serious soccer fans. The team gives them much to yell about, so crowd enthusiasm runs high at Timbers games.

Portland Trail Blazers

Rose Quarter: 1 Center Ct, Portland
503-797-9600
www.nba.com/blazers or *www.rosequarter.com*

Season: Oct–May

Tickets: $10–$131/person; discounts for quarter-, half-, and full-season ticket packages; also family nights

The Portland Trail Blazers, a National Basketball Association franchise, are the town's big ticket. The team plays in one of the league's glitziest arenas, the Rose Garden. And with all the activities that go on in addition to the game—the BlazerDancers strutting their stuff on the floor, the remote-control blimp cruising the arena while dropping fast-food coupons—each game is truly a spectacle.

Consult with a ticket agent and ask about special family discounts and ticket packages. If your child is a big fan, ask any Rose Garden employee to direct you after the game to the autograph sections that exist both for the Blazers and the visiting team.

Portland Winter Hawks

Memorial Coliseum: 300 N. Winning Wy, Portland
Rose Arena: Rose Quarter, 1 Center Ct, Portland
503-238-6366
www.winterhawks.com

Season: Sept–Mar

Tickets: $5–$23.75/person

A fast-paced, rough game (yes, there might be brawls), hockey draws capacity crowds in the northeastern United States and Canada. On the West Coast, where kids are less apt to have grown up on ice skates, it's an acquired taste. Nevertheless, the Winter Hawks, a Portland fixture since 1976, have developed a loyal following.

Nonprofessional Leagues

Alpenrose Little League Softball World Series

Alpenrose Dairy: 6149 Shattuck Rd, Portland
www.softballworldseries.com

Season: Aug

Admission: Free

No longer a working dairy farm, Alpenrose Dairy remains a local fixture, known as much for its sprawling sports complexes and special holiday events as for its milk and ice cream (see "Farm Visits" in chapter 4, Agricultural Adventures). Developed to accommodate the activities of the children and grandchildren of the founding Cadonau family, the athletic facility includes a 3,000-seat baseball stadium that each August since 1994 has hosted the Little League Softball World Series, home to more than 100 of the world's female youth players competing to be crowned the world champions.

Spectators are admitted free but are encouraged to purchase food and souvenirs from the concession stand to support the tournament. Food from home is allowed.

Alpenrose Velodrome

Alpenrose Dairy: 6149 Shattuck Rd, Portland
503-246-0330
www.obra.org/track

Season: May–Sept

Admission: Free, membership costs vary

Oregon Sports Hall of Fame and Museum

321 SW Salmon, Portland
503-227-7466
www.oregonsportshall.org

Hours: Tue–Sat noon–5 P.M.

Admission: $10/family (min 5 people), $4/adults, $3/students and seniors, free/children ages 7 and under

This 7,000-square-foot facility is full of interactive exhibits that center on great Oregon athletes, including runners Steve Prefontaine and Mary Decker Slaney, basketball star Clyde Drexler, baseball's Dale Murphy, golf's Peter Jacobsen, and many more. Youngsters get a kick out of climbing up on a rodeo saddle, testing their mettle in a racing wheelchair, powering out of the starting blocks, lifting a full-size shot and discus, and trying out full hockey goalie gear. Special visiting exhibits highlight such sports events as the 1936 Berlin Olympics. Other presentations have included displays about baseball in Japanese internment camps, exhibits from the National Basketball Hall of Fame, and special pieces of sports art.

A banked, 268-meter concrete track that resembles a giant cereal bowl, this 500-seat track velodrome is specifically designed for technical, Olympic-style events that feature fixed-gear bikes without brakes. Check the Web site for scheduled events and classes.

Spectators are admitted free to the races, where they can picnic in the bleachers (no concession stands). Children are encouraged to bring their own bikes, trikes, and bikes on training wheels for noncompetitive, 1-kilometer races on the infield track that take place before Thursday events. All participants receive ribbons.

Alpenrose Quarter-Midget Racing
Alpenrose Dairy: 6149 Shattuck Rd, Portland
503-649-2404

Hours: Mar–Oct Sat 9 A.M., Sun noon

Admission: Free

The vast Alpenrose Dairy athletic facilities are also home to the competitive races among child drivers (ages 5 to 16) sponsored by the Portland Quarter-Midget Racing Association (PQMRA). Seated at the wheel of a gas- or alcohol-powered miniature racecar equipped with a one-cylinder engine, drivers can reach up to about 30 miles an hour on the banked, oval racetrack. To race, you must be a member of the PQMRA and bring your own vehicle and safety equipment, so this is not an event that you just drop by and try on a whim. However, it makes for a highly entertaining show, and spectators are admitted free to the bleachers. A snack bar is available; food from home is also allowed.

College Teams

Portland State University
506 SW Mill St, Portland
503-725-3307, 888-VIK-TIKS (845-8457)
http://goviks.com/info/tickets

Football
PGE Park: 1844 SW Morrison, Portland
Season: Sept–Nov
Tickets: $12–$25/person

Playing at the Division 1–AA level, PSU offers the best bet for family football watching. A crisp autumn Saturday afternoon in the open-air stadium, low-price tickets, and a well-behaved crowd there to have fun—what more does a fan need? The team plays six home games.

Basketball
Peter Stott Center, 903 SW Hall St, Portland
Season: Nov–Mar
Tickets: Men's games: $12–$25/person; women's games: $4–$6/person

The university's men's and women's basketball teams play primarily at Stott Center but usually have a few games at the Rose Garden.

....

University of Portland
5000 N. Willamette Blvd, Portland
503-943-7525
www.portlandpilots.com
www.ticketswest.com

Baseball
Pilot Stadium: N. Willamette Blvd and N. Portsmouth Ave
Season: Feb–May
Tickets: $3–$5/person

The UP baseball games are another good family event. Your aspiring baseball player will enjoy impressive displays of athleticism up close in a low-key (and low-cost) setting. Tickets are general admission. There are concessions, but food from home is also allowed.

Basketball
Chiles Center: N. Willamette Blvd and N. Portsmouth Ave
Season: Nov–Feb
Tickets: Men's games: $8–$15/person; women's games: $4–$6/person; group and youth team discounts

University of Portland basketball is also a popular spectator sport with families. The women's team regularly competes in the National Collegiate Athletics Association postseason tournament.

Soccer
Merlo Field: N. Willamette Blvd and N. Portsmouth Ave
Season: Sept–Nov
Tickets: $3–$4/person; youth team discounts

If your children really like soccer, taking them to a Pilots game is a must. Soccer is the big fall sport at the University of Portland. The east-side school consistently fields nationally ranked soccer teams. If you arrange group tickets with your child's soccer team, you'll get a discount. Coolers with food from home are allowed, but not glass bottles.

Volleyball
Chiles Center: N. Willamette Blvd and N. Portsmouth Ave
Season: Sept–Nov
Tickets: $3–$4/person; youth team discounts

Also in the fall, women's volleyball (there is no men's volleyball team) competes in the 5,000-seat Chiles Center gymnasium. Seating is general admission.

Support Your Local High School

Deafening brass bands and highly energetic crowds of teens compete with the sports teams for attention at high school games, and it can be great fun to follow the athletic career of a babysitter or other teen friend or to play talent scout and try to spot incipient star power.

Call your local high school in the fall for a schedule of home games in your sport of choice, or check the public school district Web site. If you prefer to be more selective, plan to attend one of the state's all-star games. Held in June and July at venues throughout Oregon, these contests provide an opportunity to see the year's best crop of athletes. Each year Portland hosts various girls' and boys' all-star games. For this year's schedule, check the Oregon Coaches Association Web site (*www.oregoncoach.org*).

Introduced in 1997, the Great Northwest Shootout hosts the regional rivalry between Oregon and Washington high schools with two seniors-only basketball games for boys, one for girls. Selected by the coaches' associations, most of the team's 12 graduating seniors have, met as rivals on opposing teams prior to this night. Here, they must forget feuds to work together as a team. Games are held in mid-June at the Chiles Center at the University of Portland and are televised locally; call for tickets to the double-header (503-223-6251).

Chapter 9

Eating Out

When it comes to dining out, Portland offers a smorgasbord of options. So how did we decide what to recommend? Well, we looked not just for good food but also for places that not only say they are kid-friendly but actually are, with speedy service and a variety of price ranges to fit a variety of budgets. And because you want to have fun when you go out, we also sought out spots that have that certain something—a particular appeal for kids and families, as in the handy play space, the live music, a fountain to frolic in, or an out-of-the-ordinary kids' menu.

Bon appétit!

Pricing Guide (adult meals, per person)

Inexpensive:	$	Less than $8
Moderate:	$$	$8–$15
Expensive:	$$$	More than $15

Aztec Willie & Joey Rose Taqueria
1501 NE Broadway, Portland
503-280-8900
$$, kids' meals ~$3

Hours: Daily 11 A.M.–2 A.M.

There aren't too many restaurants where you can monitor the kids' playroom from your table while sipping a frosty margarita. Aztec Willie & Joey Rose Taqueria is a parents' oasis in the heart of the bustling Broadway shopping district, offering families convenient, casual Mexican dining and an unobstructed view of the glass-enclosed playroom from virtually every table.

Diners may choose from several traditionally prepared dishes: Options range from an authentic taco pequeño to a delectable prawn fajita dinner featuring spicy tiger prawns grilled to order. The children's menu is simple and affordable; among other choices, the ever-popular quesadilla comes with a side of chips. Or, a full roster of generous sides on the adult menu makes it easy to please finicky eaters. If you're lucky, you will find flan (baked custard) for dessert. An assortment of Mexican beverages including the delicious *horchata* (sweet Mexican rice milk) is also available. ¡Salud!

—Kirsten Kaufman

Bob's Whole Grain Kitchen
Bob's Red Mill Natural Foods: 5000 SE International Wy, Milwaukie
503-607-6455
www.bobsredmill.com
$$, kids' meals ~$3

Hours: Mon–Fri 6 A.M.–3 P.M., Sat 7 A.M.–3 P.M.

The wholesome folks at Bob's Red Mill aspire to help their customers become "physically enriched and fully satisfied." You too may find yourself in such a state of nutritional bliss when you treat your family to breakfast or lunch at Bob's Whole Grain Kitchen. A major attraction for youngsters is the 8-foot waterwheel and the giant millstones out front, which represent the old-world technology Bob's utilizes to mill hundreds of whole-grain products.

Breakfast is served all day Saturday with a menu that features assorted omelets and eggs served with garden sausage or turkey ham, organic corn grits, flapjacks, waffles, or French toast. All come with scratch biscuits or "the best toast in the world"—a tough choice. For porridge fans, there are freshly milled whole-grain cereals, including organic Scottish oatmeal and Swiss-style muesli with yogurt. The kids' breakfast is a stack of dollar-sized pancakes and eggs, enough to feed two preschoolers. When weather permits, children love sitting outdoors next to the millpond, which is filled with colorful koi.

—K.K.

. . . .

Bread and Ink Café
3610 SE Hawthorne Blvd, Portland
503-239-4756
www.breadandinkcafe.com
$$–$$$, kids' menu $4–$8

Hours: Daily 8 A.M.–10 P.M.

Long before Hawthorne became hip and Portland became known for its great restaurants, the Bread and Ink was serving up innovative and consistently delicious meals. Just celebrating its 25th anniversary, the cafe (open for breakfast, lunch, and dinner) uses as many locally sourced ingredients as possible and serves only natural meats, poultry, and wild seafood. Their baked goods and yummy pastries are made fresh daily in the on-site bakery.

The evening menu, which changes frequently, always includes specials, pasta, poultry, something for the red-meat lovers in your family, and at least one creative vegetarian choice. On any given night you can expect entrées like Vera Cruz–style spaghetti with house-smoked salmon, Parmigiano-Reggiano–crusted chicken, or a spicy flatiron steak diavola. The popular Bread and Ink burger is a staple, and all the salad dressings, sauces, and even the catsup, mayo, and mustard, are housemade.

Kids will love the Bread and Ink for their butcher-paper-topped tables, just waiting to be decorated with the waiting cup of crayons (parents often can't resist, as well). Parents will love what may be the only kids' menu in town that includes risotto and beef tenderloin. The ricotta-filled blintzes, with jam on the side, are always a hit with little ones, as are the kid-sized burger and the hummus plate.

The Bread and Ink is a tried-and-true, cozy place to settle in to one of those comfy green armchairs, gaze out the big picture windows, and watch the world go by. There's a full bar, beer, and wine.

Also: A more recent addition, the Bread and Ink Waffle Window, has quickly become a bona-fide Portland attraction. After a trip to Brussels, the owners' sons came home raving about the waffles they'd had there. Mom re-created them and now sells them out a window on the side of the cafe. The waffles come topped with bananas and Nutella; housemade granola, fresh fruit, and yogurt; ham and Gruyére; or seasonal specialties like apple pie with caramel sauce, lavender-poached pears, or roasted pears. Take yours to go, or set yourself down at one of the outdoor tables and dig in.

—*Shawn Jones*

Caro Amico
3606 SW Barbur Blvd, Portland
503-223-6895
www.caroamicoitaliancafe.com
$$–$$$, kids' meals ~$4

Hours: Mon–Thurs 4:30–9:30 P.M., Fri–Sat 4:30–10:30 P.M., Sun 4–9 P.M.

With all the swanky Italian places Portland now boasts, Caro Amico, established in 1949, is one of those great old-fashioned, family-friendly joints. Specializing in pasta and pizza, the menu also includes some great fish and meat choices, like steak florentina, chicken picatta, and pan-seared scallops.

For kids, there are simple Italian offerings—spaghetti and meatballs, noodles with butter and parmesan—but also the choice of ordering their very own kid-sized pizza (cheese, pepperoni, or Hawaiian). Kids' meals include dessert.

There is a deck, open in nice weather, and an upstairs room with a lovely view of the river and Mount. Hood, which can be reserved for parties. There's also a full bar, a good wine list, and a very friendly waitstaff.

—*S.J.*

Chang's Mongolian Grill

12055 N. Center Ave, Jantzen Beach, Portland; 503-240-0205
1600 NE 122nd Ave, San Rafael Shopping Center, Portland; 503-253-3535
18925 SE McLoughlin Blvd, Milwaukie; 503-655-2323
2502 E. Powell Blvd, Gresham; 503-665-8998
1935 NW 167th Pl, Beaverton; 503-645-7718
www.changsgrill.com
$$, kids' meals $2–$6

Hours: Mon–Thurs 11:30 A.M.–2:30 P.M. and 5–9 P.M., Fri 11 A.M.–2:30 P.M. and 5–10:30 P.M., Sat–Sun noon–3 P.M. and 5–10 P.M.

If you're looking for a little action in your dining experience, take your hungry horde to Chang's Mongolian Grill. It's the perfect place for restless little diners because there is no waiting at the table—you just head straight for the food and get busy. At Chang's, you get to mix and match thinly sliced meats, fresh veggies, noodles, sauces, and condiments to create a custom stir-fried meal. Once you've selected all your ingredients, you hand off your bowl to a chef armed with a long metal spatula, who sizzles up your meal on a huge round iron grill while you watch the fiery show. Within minutes you'll be back at your table. Be sure to bring a few dollar bills to stuff in the tip jar of these hardworking chefs. Each all-you-can-eat meal includes soup, rice, wraps, and dessert.

—K.K.

Courtyard Restaurant at Kennedy School

5736 NE 33rd Ave, Portland
503-288-2192, 888-249-3983
www.mcmenamins.com
$$, kids' meals $3–$6

Hours: Daily 7 A.M.–1 A.M.

If school cafeteria food isn't high on your list of favorites, you probably haven't been to Northeast Portland's Kennedy School. Originally opened in 1915, the elementary school was closed in the mid-1970s when the district declared it too far gone to repair. In 1997 Portland restaurateurs Mike and Brian McMenamin transformed the abandoned building into a bed-and-breakfast complete with movie house, soaking pool, bars, event spaces, and a popular restaurant.

Open for breakfast, lunch, and dinner, the Courtyard Restaurant features contemporary pub fare, including natural Oregon Country Beef burgers, veggie burgers, salads, sandwiches, individual- and family-sized pizzas, pasta, ribs, steak, seafood, and more. The children's menu is limited to standards such as noodles and cheese, grilled cheese, and peanut butter and jelly sandwiches, but the regular menu includes kid-friendly options such as pizza, quesadillas, and burgers. Breakfast includes a nice selection of traditional favorites. Desserts and milkshakes provide the perfect end to a hearty family meal, and a full bar serves, among the typical offerings, McMenamins' signature ales, wines, and spirits.

Locals take advantage of sunny days by dining in the outdoor courtyard, although shade is limited. There's usually a wait for dinner on weekends, but the building and artwork provide ample opportunity for exploring. You'll find other family-friendly McMenamins' pubs with similar atmospheres and menus throughout the region.

—Emily Puro

....

Grand Central Café—Sellwood
7987 SE 13th Ave, Portland
503-546-3036
www.grandcentralbakery.com
Check Web site for other Portland locations
$

Hours: Daily 7 A.M.–6 P.M.

Grand Central Baking Company has numerous cafes around Portland offering some of the city's best hearth baked artisan breads and hand-formed pastries. The cafe menu features homemade soups, entrée salads, and sandwiches on rustic bread, with seasonal specials made from fresh local ingredients. The kids' menu is basic—peanut butter and jelly or a grilled cheese sandwich; the sack lunch comes with chips and a giant cookie. Breakfast is served all day on weekends and until noon weekdays. The location nearest you may even have a playroom for the kids.

—K.K.

Sit, Sip, and Knit

Portland is all tangled up in the knitting craze, and several shops in recent years have created cozy cafes where stitchers enjoy sitting, sipping, knitting—or crocheting—and visiting. These two spots in Southeast Portland help make handicrafts a family affair.

The Busy Bee Café at Abundant Yarn & Dyeworks
8524 SE 17th, Portland
503-258-9276
www.abundantyarn.com
$ (beverages and light meals)

Launched by a Waldorf handwork teacher, this Sellwood-area store and cafe opened in late summer 2005. As the name implies, the store features an abundance of beautiful yarns. At the Busy Bee Café the calendar includes times for knit clubs for new and expectant moms as well as teens who want to connect with other like-minded crafters. The cafe serves up sandwiches (about $5) as well as kid-

Grandma Leeth's
10122 SW Park Wy, Portland
503-291-7800
www.grandmaleeths.com
$$–$$$, kids' meals $6

Hours: Summer, Thurs –Sat 10:30 A.M., last seating at 8:30 P.M., Tues, Wed, and Sun 10:30 A.M., last seating at 7:30 P.M. Other than summer, Tues–Sun 10:30 A.M., call for last seating times. Closed Mon.

Grandma Leeth's is one of only a handful of restaurants in Portland with a full-fledged play area for kids, and this one is even supervised! Children ages two to nine can join staff in fun, imaginative projects. Call the restaurant for the current fee.

The kids' menu offers some great alternatives to the often deep-fried dishes you're used to seeing (the restaurant doesn't even have a deep-fat fryer).

size snacks ($3) and other goodies. At press time, plans called for the shop to offer seasonal classes for kids and summertime knitting camps. Also in the works were birthday parties featuring fiber arts for children, and for expectant moms, baby showers during which partygoers would join forces to create a specially handcrafted baby blanket.

The Sipperie at Yarn Garden

1413 SE Hawthorne Blvd, Portland
503-239-7950
www.yarngarden.net
$ (beverages and snacks)

After feasting on this shop's spectacular variety of patterns and yarns, you can sink into a comfy chair in the little brightly colored cafe, sip a cup of delicious Earl Grey tea, and nibble a chocolate chip cookie while your little one delves into the toy bin. Some mornings, the room bustles with a group of expectant moms and moms with babes who meet in an informal club. At other times, like-minded sock-knitters or those who want to knit for charity gather to confer.

The creatively named meals—like Worms 'n' Veggies (shredded, diced, and julienned veggies with Yakisoba noodles) and Krusty Kakes (fluffy fish cakes with a side of fresh veggies)—help you to help them make healthy choices. There's even a dish for the really wee ones: Smash Mash, a small, pureed version of any dish, with homemade applesauce or any seasonal vegetable mash.

The restaurant offers fare from 12 countries and is focused on creating food that is both healthy and delicious. They cater to special diets and use icons to designate foods that are, for example, vegan, vegetarian, or gluten free. They also point out spicy dishes, like the South Indian–style green beans, and when they say spicy they mean it.

Many diners elect to dine tapas-style, choosing from many appetizer options on the Start-up Menu. Begin with Clent's bruschetta, with basil, tomatoes, and olive oil on house-baked sourdough—all breads and pastries are baked in-house—a slice of quiche, and maybe a Northwestern quesadilla filled with house-smoked salmon. (Many of these appetizers, served as a meal in themselves, will also satisfy an adolescent's hunger.) If you're still hungry choose a variety of great entrees: coconut milk curry and rice, Althea's biriyana, the Carnivore's Grill, or a variety of pasta options. The restaurant also offers a dish that will appeal to those who can never find a place that suits their diet: Tell your server what your restrictions or preferences are and then trust the kitchen to cook up a plate of four delicious dishes for you. Wow! It's not very often that you can say accurately that a restaurant is unique, but Grandma Leeth's is one such place.

—Melissa Moore

....

Hopworks Urban Brewery
2944 SE Powell Blvd, Portland
503-201-8957
www.hopworksbeer.com
$$, kids' meals ~$5

Hours: Sun–Thurs 11 A.M.–11 P.M., Fri–Sat 11 A.M.–midnight

Hopworks will make everyone in your family happy with local, organic, healthy food, award-winning craft beer, and a playroom for the kids in a unique sustainable building decorated with recycled bicycle parts. Sit outside on the deck, upstairs in the crow's nest, or in the main dining room. Make sure to ask your server for some pizza dough for the kids to play with while the kitchen makes your order. Offering bar food you won't feel guilty eating, the Hopworks menu lists healthy kids' meals, pub appetizers, soups, salads, sandwiches and burgers, pizza made to order, desserts, wine, beer, and a full bar.

—Nate Angell

....

Juan Colorado
10075 SW Barbur Blvd, Portland
503-244-4360
$$, kids' meals ~$4

Hours: Mon–Thurs 11 A.M.–9 P.M., Fri–Sat 10 A.M.–10 P.M., Sun 10 A.M.–9 P.M.

Parents know that almost all Mexican restaurants are a great choice when dining out with kids. Chances are there's a place much like Juan Colorado's right in your neighborhood with the same features that make you feel so comfortable taking your brood: bright, colorful decor, comfy booths, cheerful music, friendly staff, and most importantly, those chips and salsa to munch on straight away.

This especially congenial spot offers a relatively extensive kids' menu, including typical Mexican choices—cheese nachos, quesadillas, and the like, most served with beans and rice—as well as grilled cheese, chicken strips, hamburgers, and fries.

The main menu includes everything you'd expect, with some good, authentic additions like *tacos al pastor*—tacos with grilled, marinated pork—and *pollo a la crema*, a rich, wonderful Oaxacan dish of sautéed chicken breast and Mexican cream. ¡Delicioso!

They also make a mean margarita . . .

—*S.J.*

....

The Laughing Planet Café
3320 SE Belmont St, Portland
503-235-6472
www.laughingplanetcafe.com
Check Web site for other locations around Portland

Hours: Daily 11 A.M.–10 P.M.

Thanks to the Laughing Planet Café, healthy fast food is no longer an oxymoron. With an emphasis on local and organic ingredients, the menu features burritos ranging from Southwestern green chile to Thai peanut to Jamaican jerk as well as quesadillas, vegetarian soups and chili, salads, and more. The kids' menu includes burritos, quesadillas, mashed potatoes, and rice and beans with options to add meat, tofu, or vegetables to any item. Freshly squeezed juice, smoothies, natural soda, beer, and wine—as well as surprisingly tasty vegan baked goods—complete the menu.

This casual neighborhood favorite is stocked with plastic dinosaurs, books, and other toys that kids are welcome to play with while you dine, and an outdoor area with picnic tables is perfect for warm weather.

—*E. P.*

Laurelwood Public House & Brewery

5115 NE Sandy Blvd, Portland
503-282-0622
www.laurelwoodbrewpub.com
Check Web site for other locations around Portland
$$, kids' meals ~ $5

Hours: Mon–Fri 11 A.M.–midnight, Sat–Sun 10 A.M.–midnight

Located in the historic Hollywood District, Laurelwood Public House & Brewery offers a family-friendly atmosphere with a menu that ventures beyond standard pub grub and an impressive list of handcrafted beers—including root beer—all brewed on site. The highlight for kids is a playroom with a fascinating bird's-eye view of the brew house where workers clad in white coveralls and big rubber boots tend to huge shiny vats.

The kids' menu offers a variety of favorites, such as mac and cheese with a drink and dessert. Adults will find an extensive menu with an emphasis on regional ingredients. Happy hour (3–6 P.M.) presents some real bargains, including an Oregon Country Beef burger and brewery fries. Although it is a relatively roomy establishment, the Laurelwood can become quite crowded during peak dining hours, especially after work on Friday. Plan to arrive early to beat the crowds—or have a pint and join the fray.

—K. K.

Macaroni Grill

9073 SE Sunnyside Rd, Clackamas; 503-496-5571
2290 NW Allie Ave, Hillsboro; 503-352-0963
17003 SW 72nd Ave, Tigard; 503-783-0550
300 SW Yamhill St, Portland; 503-546-3040
www.macaronigrill.com
$$, kids' meals ~$5

Hours: Sun–Thurs 11 A.M.–10 P.M., Fri–Sat 11 A.M.–11 P.M.

Like the other Italian-fare chains that have popped up, the Macaroni Grill offers good food at a good price. It's a big menu, including, of course, many traditional Italian and pasta choices. But they've rounded out the menu with plenty of meat and fish choices as well. Diners can tuck into Chianti steak, honey balsamic chicken, or parmesan-crusted sole. The kids' menu includes the usual fare—mac and cheese, chicken fingers—with a couple of nice additions: a boneless, skinless grilled chicken breast and steamed broccoli served with pasta (granted, a meal that parents will want for their kids, but not what most kids clamor for), or an individual kid-sized cheese or pepperoni Mona Lisa Masterpizza. There's full bar, wine list.

—S.J.

....

Me Too
16755 SW Baseline #102, Beaverton
503-439-6586
metoobeaverton.com
$–$$, kids' meals ~$3

Hours: Mon–Fri 9 A.M.–8 P.M., Sat 10 A.M.–8 P.M. (they stay open later if need be), closed Sun for special events

Play area fees: $5/ first child in a family, $4/2nd child, $3/3rd child, $2/4th child, 5+ kids are $1 each

Like the now-closed, much-loved Peanut Butter & Ellie's, Me Too is a place that is all about bringing the kids. But this café goes even further than most: Me Too provides an actual day-care play space—complete with caregivers and fun and/or educational toys. There's a quick registration process the first time you come, then after that you'll be greeted like long-lost friends, as the kids run off to the play room. You can peek in on them at any time, but the windows are high enough for you to be discreet. The whole space is designed with both kids' and parents' needs in mind, down to bathrooms with extra diapers and baby wipes at the changing table, a stool for little people to reach the sink, and a lock too high for most little hands to reach.

The space is spare, and the breakfast and lunch menu is limited but tasty and very reasonable. There are just a few breakfast options; lunch fare is mostly soup, sandwiches, and salads—with all of the standard kids' choices (presented in a divided dish so none of the different foods touch each other. Smart.) Dinner is more ambitious, offering specials like baked salmon with chipotle or raspberry dill glaze and comfort foods like meat loaf and chicken pot pie. The waitstaff and owner are as friendly as they come.

The cafe also hosts lessons, presentations, and discussion forums: Finances for the Family, Sign Language for special needs children, and Knitting with Amy are just a few examples of recent offerings. It can be a little tricky to find, tucked away in the back of a newer strip mall. Consult their well-done, very informative Web site—chock-full of information—for directions, the event calendar, and to sign up for their newsletter.

A great spot to relax, have a business meeting, host a birthday party or shower, or have an easy, inexpensive grown-up date—all without hiring a baby-sitter. At press time, the café was in the process of obtaining a liquor license.

—S.J.

....

Mississippi Pizza Pub

3552 N. Mississippi Ave, Portland
503-288-3231
www.mississippipizza.com
$

Hours: Fri–Sat 11:30 A.M.–1 A.M., Sun–Thurs 11:30 A.M.–midnight

The Mississippi Pizza Pub serves tasty slices and frosty cold ones at fair prices, but the real attraction here is live music in a family-friendly environment, virtually every night of the week. Dinner at Mississippi is fast and easy with several varieties of pizza available by the slice, or pizzas can be made to order. Round out your meal with a Caesar or spinach salad, a flavorful combination of red onion, feta, pine nuts, Roma tomato, and balsamic vinaigrette. Microbrews are available by the pint or pitcher with happy-hour specials daily.

While you eat, you can watch live performances in the music room, where the decor is comfy and the music is a mixed bag, with multiple acts playing various genres on any given night. Early performances begin around 6–7 P.M., and minors are allowed to stay in the music room until 9 P.M. Some nights there is a cover charge or donation requested by the artists. Special kids' shows are scheduled on a monthly basis. For the current schedule, check the restaurant's Web site.

—K. K.

Mother's Bistro & Bar
212 SW Stark St, Portland
503-464-1122
www.mothersbistro.com
$$, kids' meals $3–$5

Hours: Tues–Thurs 7 A.M.–2:30 P.M. and 5:30–9 P.M., Fri 7 A.M.–2:30 P.M. and 5–
10 P.M., Sat 9 A.M.–2:30 P.M. and 5–10 P.M., Sun 9 A.M.–2:30 P.M. (brunch only).
Closed Mon.

Mother's Bistro & Bar, serving breakfast, lunch, and dinner, is an especially
wonderful place for brunch with the kids. Plan ahead and make reservations, or
you may find yourself waiting in a line that extends well onto the sidewalk. Once
you're seated, the servers provide children with a kids' menu that is also a col-
oring page. Parents need to read about the mini breakfast plate, kids' pancake,
PB&J, mac and cheese, and small portions of pot roast, chicken-n-dumplings,
and meat loaf before the words are colored over.

There is a very small play area near the women's restroom just large enough
for one parent and child to explore a few toys left in the window bench. But with
the lively environment, children could find all the entertainment they need by
watching nearby tables. With great food and a friendly, familial atmosphere,
this restaurant certainly lives up to its name. As they say at Mother's, "You
should eat so good!"

—M.M.

The Old Spaghetti Factory
0715 SW Bancroft St, Portland; 503-222-5375
12725 SE 93rd Ave, Clackamas; 503-653-7949
730 SE 160th, Vancouver, WA; 360-253-9030
18925 NW Tanasbourne Dr, Hillsboro; 503-617-7614
www.osf.com
$$, kids' meals ~$4

Hours: Mon–Thurs 4:30–9:30 P.M., Fri 5–10:30 P.M., Sat 4–10:30 P.M., Sun 4–
9:30 P.M.

Restaurants with a great view tend to be a bad fit for kids because of their fancy atmosphere, fancy patrons, and correspondingly fancy prices. But Portland families are lucky to have one big, beautiful exception—the Old Spaghetti Factory on the Willamette River. This is not just any Old Spaghetti Factory, but the flagship of the family-friendly nationwide chain, which was founded here in 1969. Located just south of downtown, in the burgeoning South River District, the grand old building with its purple-tiled roof looks, from afar, like a grand castle. Inside, diners can watch the river roll by, surrounded by old world charm of polished wood, leaded glass, Victorian lampshades, and whimsical decor.

While waiting for a table, check out the kids' corner upstairs, where you will find pinball machines, video games, and a VCR playing G-rated movies. At the table, crayons are presented with utensils and followed promptly by applesauce for kids. The classics are complete spaghetti dinners with the choice of tomato, mushroom, clam, meat sauce, or browned butter and mizithra cheese—or combinations of two or three of these options. All entrées come with soup or salad; fresh-baked bread; coffee, tea, or milk; and ice cream—a super value. Kids' meals include mini versions of the classics or mac and cheese, plus a drink and dessert.

—K. K.

....

Old Wives' Tales Restaurant
1300 E. Burnside St, Portland
503-238-0470
www.oldwivesrestaurant.com
$$, kids' meals ~$3

Hours: Fri–Sat 8 A.M.–10 P.M., Sun–Thurs 8 A.M.–9 P.M.

Old Wives' Tales is a local family favorite with good reason. The menu offers plenty of healthy choices for all ages, and families are strategically seated together near the playroom. So chances are you will find yourself surrounded by sympathetic diners. Inside the playroom, children can climb aboard a colorful circus train or set sail in tiny sailboats while you order and await your meal.

Old Wives' Tales' extensive menu is eclectic and healthful, with many options for people with special dietary needs, including gluten free, dairy free, and refined-sugar free. Each day there are several special entrées, including vegan, vegetarian, chicken, and seafood dishes drawn from various ethnic cuisines. The kids' menu covers all the favorites, with a particularly yummy twist on the old mac and cheese: noodles, Asiago cheese, and cream. Breakfast is served all day, meaning the kids can have pancakes or oatmeal for lunch or dinner while you have something more exotic, such as an Indian burrito. The soup and salad bar are popular choices—a pint bowl of soup and salad. If you go this route, be sure to try the Hungarian mushroom soup, a memorable house specialty.

—K. K.

....

Pastini Pastaria

1426 NE Broadway, Portland; 503-288-4300
1506 NW 23rd Ave, Portland; 503-595-1205
2027 SE Division, Portland; 503-595-6400
911 SW Taylor, Portland; 503-863-5188
7307 SW Bridgeport Rd, Ste B-105, Tigard; 503-718-2300
www.pastini.biz
$$, kids' meals ~$4

Hours: Mon–Thurs 11:30 A.M.–9 P.M., Fri–Sat 11:30 A.M.–10 P.M., Sun 4–9 P.M. (Tigard location: Sun 11:30 A.M.–10 P.M.)

With five locations in the area, Pastini Pastaria serves up Italian fare at remarkably reasonable prices in an atmosphere that welcomes even the youngest diners. As the name implies, the focus is on pasta, but with a wide variety of sauces, an impressive selection of sandwiches and salads, and a wine list that pairs quality with affordability, dining here is a pleasure for the whole family. Thanks to a steady stream of families with young children, the restaurants bustle with activity, but they're light and open and handle the noise well.

Flavorful pasta dishes range from a simple olive oil and garlic sauce to more elaborate recipes featuring fresh vegetables, chicken, sausages, and seafood. Options are plentiful for vegetarians and meat-eaters alike. The kids' menu includes standards such as spaghetti, plain buttered noodles, macaroni and cheese, and pizza, and the waitstaff cheerfully accommodates special requests. Don't forget to save room for the chocolate *tartufo*, a dense and gooey chocolate truffle cake served warm and topped with whipped cream. It's rich enough to share.

—E. P.

Pine State Biscuits

3640 SE Belmont St, Portland
503-236-3346
www.pinestatebiscuits.com
$

Hours: Tues–Sun 7 A.M.–2 P.M.

This little eatery, which originated at and still has a spot at the downtown Saturday Market, is the cool kind of place that makes you happy to be a Portlander. The three owners, all from North Carolina, have now branched out to the Southeast, up a couple of blocks from the Belmont Dairy.

Pine State does one thing, and does it really well: biscuits. From the standard biscuit with gravy—sausage or mushroom—to the Reggie (fried chicken, bacon, and cheese topped with gravy) or a biscuit sandwich of a housemade sausage patty, an egg, and cheddar, there's something for everyone to love. Other toppings include jam, butter and honey, Pine State pimento spread, or fruit with whipped cream. Add a side of grits or hash browns, a glass of fresh-squeezed orange juice, and a steaming mug of Stumptown coffee, and you're in Pine State bliss.

Seating is limited, though you can park yourselves at a picnic table at neighboring Triple Nickel until 10:30 A.M.

—*S.J.*

Salvador Molly's

1523 SW Sunset Blvd, Hillsdale
503-293-1790
www.salvadormollys.com
$$, kids' meals ~$5

Hours: Fri–Sat 11 A.M.–10 P.M., Sun–Thurs 11 A.M.–9 P.M.

If "pirate cookin' " sounds intriguing to your crew, then take your little mateys to Salvador Molly's for flavorful cuisine and a cheerful Caribbean atmosphere. You can find many delicious items to choose from, all prepared with island flair.

Lunch and dinner menus are extensive, so look or ask for the "Pirate's Picks." The Famous Mojo Kalua Pork with "dirty" mashers is a tasty meal—a Hawaiian-Cuban fusion doused with garlicky mojo sauce—that makes you feel as though you are in an exotic port o' call. Kids love the complimentary bowl of peanuts in the shell, Crayons are also available. Kids' meals are reasonable, and if you have food allergies, the servers and chefs are very accommodating. The variety of specialty drinks is cool and tasty. Adults and children feel welcome to sit back, relax, and soak up the tropics.

—Diana Sticker

Sip & Kranz, A Coffee Lounge

901 NW 10th Ave, Portland
503-336-1335
www.sipandkranz.com
$, kids' meals ~ $3-$5

Hours: Mon–Thurs 6:30 A.M.–7 P.M., Fri 6:30 A.M.–8 P.M., Sat 7 A.M.–8 P.M., Sun 7 A.M.–7 P.M.

Kids in tow but still want to feel civilized? Bring the tots to the Pearl's chic Sip & Kranz and relax in the clean European cafe with a cappuccino and pain au chocolat or local craft beer and cheese platter while the kids romp in the glass-walled fun room. Suit them up during summer and sit outside, watching the kids wade in the Jamison Square fountain next door. Open for breakfast, lunch and early, light dinners, Sip & Kranz offers light, unusual kids' meals like grilled cheese panini or Nutella sandwiches with fruit, Goldfish crackers, milk, and a Tootsie Roll; for you there's sandwiches, soups, salads, ice cream, desserts, espresso drinks, wine, and beer.

—N.A.

Stickers Asian Café

6806 SE Milwaukie Ave, Portland
503-239-8739
www.stickersasiancafe.com
$$, kids' meals ~$4

Hours: Mon–Thurs 11:30 A.M.–9 P.M., Fri and Sat 11:30 A.M.–10 P.M., Sun 11:30 A.M.–9 P.M.

At first glance, this wee Sellwood Asian eatery doesn't say kid-friendly, but indeed it is. The cafe menu includes a wonderful variety of offerings from Chinese, Thai, East Indian, Korean, Malaysian, Vietnamese cuisines and, of course, several choices of pot stickers. There are many vegetarian options, and the dishes are all made from scratch without MSG.

Many kids will be happy just munching on pot stickers, but there is also a kids' menu with simple Asian choices: chicken and rice, noodles either plain or with pork shreds or tofu, and a white rice or noodle plate with sliced cucumbers for your pickiest little diners. Some nice additions are smaller-sized drinks just for kids, soy milk options, and some fancy kids' drinks from the bar. Kids' meals also include ice cream with coconut and fried banana. Delicious. Full bar, beer and wine.

—Katie Gourley

Sweet Tomatoes Restaurant

13011 SE 84th Ave, Clackamas; 503-794-2921
6600 SW Cardinal Ln, Tigard; 503-443-6161
1225 NW Waterhouse Ave, Beaverton; 503-439-0850
12601 SE Second Circle, Vancouver, WA; 360-891-0240
www.sweettomatoes.com
$, kids' meals ~$3–$5, free/children 2 and under

Hours: Fri–Sat 11 A.M.–10 P.M., Sun–Thurs 11 A.M.–9 P.M.

Like other buffets, Sweet Tomatoes is inherently kid-friendly—you get your food right away, pay up front, and get to run around the restaurant with legitimate purpose. However, despite these obvious advantages, some parents may still steer clear of any buffet they find in a strip mall, based on childhood memories of going out to dinner with their grandparents. Don't worry; you won't find any warmed-over mashed potatoes or anemic iceberg lettuce masquerading as "salad" at this suburban buffet, which is part of a California-based chain of health-conscious restaurants.

Instead, at Sweet Tomatoes, families are greeted by a 55-foot-long salad bar, brimming with a colorful array of veggies, prepared and tossed salads, and a diverse selection of dressings and toppings. For the main course there are soups, chowders, and chilis, all made from scratch; an assortment of fresh-baked muffins and breads; plus pizza, focaccia, a baked potato bar, and three varieties of hot pasta. There are many vegetarian offerings, all clearly marked, as well as featured seasonal items. For dessert the kids always make a beeline for the frozen yogurt bar, where you can pull a cone or create your own sundae with a choice of syrups and toppings. For a special treat be on the lookout for servers roaming the dining room with baskets full of warm chocolate chip cookies.

—K. K.

Chapter 10

Out-of-Town Excursions

No doubt there's plenty in Portland to keep your family busy, but sometimes you just need a change of scenery. When the open road calls and the kids seem willing, don't hesitate: Pack up the car and go. Numerous destinations within just a few hours' drive of downtown Portland will provide your family with a deeper understanding of the region's culture and history. And you'll know your own neighborhood better for having gotten away.

Astoria

"O! how Tremendous is the day."

So wrote William Clark as the Corps of Discovery made its way west along the Columbia River 200 years ago. Today travelers who venture to Astoria, just 99 miles west of Portland, in search of their own adventures just might want to write that same entry, or something like it, in their own journals.

Astoria Column (503-325-2963; *www.astoriacolumn.org*; dawn–dusk; $1/car donation requested) is a great place to begin a visit. On a clear day you'll have a fantastic panoramic view of the city as well as the surrounding rivers, bay, forest, mountains, and the Pacific Ocean. Follow the signs up 16th or 14th Streets, and in a wooded park at the top of the hill, you'll find the column, which commemorates the westward sweep of discovery and migration. Built in 1926, the column is 125 feet high and has 164 steps winding to the top.

Once you recover from ascending the column's winding staircase, head back down the hill into Astoria for a visit to the **Columbia River Maritime Museum** (17th and Marine Dr; 503-325-2323; *www.crmm.org*; daily 9:30 A.M.–5 P.M., except Thanksgiving and Christmas; $8/adults, $7/seniors, $4/children ages 6–17, free/children under 6, $24/family). Here you can learn about all kinds of marine transportation from the days of dugout canoes to the present. Catch a dramatic 12-minute film that introduces the history of life and commerce on the Columbia River, then walk the bridge of a World War II warship, take the helm in a tugboat wheelhouse, and participate in a simulated Coast Guard rescue on the river. You can also board the *Lightship Columbia*, a floating lighthouse and a National Historic Landmark. This beautiful, newly renovated museum has been designated the official Oregon State Maritime Museum in recognition of its quality.

At a stop in front of the museum, it's easy to catch the **Astoria Trolley** (503-325-6311, 800-875-6807; *http://webpages.charter.net/astoriatrolley*; Memorial Day–Labor Day Fri–Sun noon–9 P.M., Mon–Thurs 3–9 P.M., weather permitting; $1/person per boarding to ride as long as you like, $2/person to ride all day). As you ride the trolley, which runs from the Port of Astoria through downtown along Astoria's historic working waterfront to the East End Mooring Basin, you'll see Astoria's historic Victorian homes on the hillside as well as fishing boats unloading their daily catches. The average round-trip takes 40 to 45 minutes.

For a little climb, jump, swing, and dig time, head over to the **Tapiola Playground** (take Hwy 202 south approximately 1 mile from Astoria roundabout on

Hwy 101 at west end of town). This 15,000-square-foot play structure features uniquely Astorian components such as replicas of the Astoria-Megler Bridge, Astoria Column, Flavel House, and Liberty Theater Stage.

And then, it's essential to visit the **Lewis & Clark National Historical Park** (503-861-2471 ext. 214; *www.nps.gov/focl*; hours: mid-June–Labor Day daily 9 A.M.–6 P.M., Sept–mid-June daily 9 A.M.–5 P.M.; admission: mid-June–Labor Day $5/adults 17 and older, $2.50/children 16 and younger; after Labor Day–mid-June $3/adults 17 and older, free/children 16 and under. Located about 5 miles south of Astoria, this park was created by incorporating state parks in Washington and Oregon along with the current Fort Clatsop National Memorial Park. In October 2005 a fire destroyed a 1955 community-built replica of the explorers' fort. But volunteers and National Park Service employees have since rebuilt a rustic and rough-hewn replica. During summer the park offers interpretive programs with rangers in costume; schedules are posted in the visitors center daily.

Check out, too, the **Fort-To-Sea Trail** (*www.forttosea.org*), a 6-mile trail that replicates the route members of Lewis and Clark's Corps of Discovery may have taken from the original site of Fort Clatsop to the Pacific Ocean.

Tip

Want to know more about Lewis and Clark? Cross the Columbia River at Astoria and head for Washington's Cape Disappointment State Park, two miles south of Ilwaco, to explore the Lewis and Clark Interpretive Center. Here a series of mural-size timeline panels guide visitors through the Corps of Discovery's westward journey. You can learn still more by watching several short films. And don't miss the chance to admire the view of the river, headlands, and sea from the center's glassed-in observation deck.

The Lewis and Clark Interpretive Center (*www.parks.wa.gov/lcinterpctr.asp*) is open year-round. Admission is $3/adult, $1/children ages 7–17, free/children ages 6 and under. For specific seasonal operating hours, call the park office at 360-642-3078.

Resources

- **Astoria-Warrenton Area Chamber of Commerce**, 111 W. Marine Dr, Astoria; 503-325-6311; *www.oldoregon.com*
- **Oregon Coast Visitors Association**, 137 NE First St, Newport; 541-574-2679, 888-OCVA (6282)-101; *www.visittheoregoncoast.com*

....

Columbia River Gorge

Though Portland straddles the Willamette River, the Columbia River attracts a lot of attention. And well it should. Just 40 miles east of the city lies some of the state's most spectacular scenery: fir-speckled basalt cliffs and granite outcrop-pings, bubbling brooks, cascading waterfalls, and peaceful pastureland.

From Portland, take Interstate 84 east and then follow signs for the **Historic Columbia River Highway** (Exit 17 at Troutdale). A masterpiece of engineer-ing know-how, this scenic roadway—constructed between 1913 and 1922—winds along a high bluff past many beautiful waterfalls and several state parks. Look for original Italian stonework walls that still line sections of the route, and stop for a panoramic view at the **Portland Women's Forum** overlook at Chanticleer Point. From here you can see Crown Point, the site of Vista House, one of the most photographed spots in the Columbia River Gorge.

Built between 1916 and 1918 as a memorial to Oregon pioneers and a rest stop for those traveling the highway, **Vista House** (503-695-2230; *www.vista house.com*; daily 9 A.M.–6 P.M.) has undergone an extensive restoration, reopen-ing in April 2006. The octagonal stone structure, which towers 733 feet above the Columbia River, is home to an interpretive center and a gift shop. Vista House is listed on the National Register of Historic Places and in the National Geographic Society's 2001 book *Save America's Treasures*. Check online for information about special events at Vista House.

After you leave Crown Point, plan to get out of the car to explore at least one waterfall up close. The gently sloping lower trail at **Latourell Falls** is ideal for younger kids. Wear hiking boots or other sturdy shoes, and tote rain gear. The trails are often muddy and damp from rain and mist, and the dense forest keeps the sun at bay. For trail maps and other information, contact the **Columbia Gorge National Scenic Area Forest Service** (503-308-1700; *www.fs.fed.us*).

Don't miss a stop at **Multnomah Falls**. Some 2.5 million visitors stop each year to see this magnificent falls. At 620 feet, the falls is Oregon's tallest and America's second highest year-round waterfall. And it is spectacular. Volunteers like Max and Maxine Wilkins are there to answer questions, and you can pick up a brochure about the falls at the visitors center in the **Multnomah Falls Lodge** (503-695-2376; *www.multnomahfallslodge.com*), which is operated by the U.S. Forest Service (503-695-2372). Then walk the 0.25-mile up to the bridge to feel the cooling mist from the falls, or, if you're feeling more adventurous, hike to the top of the falls—a total of 1.25 miles—on the paved trail. You'll want to explore the lodge, too. Built in 1925, this historic building features a cozy restaurant, restrooms, snack bar, and gift shop.

Rejoin I-84 at Exit 35 and continue east to Cascade Locks (Exit 44), a great town in which to break for a meal or snack. The **Charburger** (745 WaNaPa St; 541-374-8477) grills made-to-order hamburgers to go with its great view of the river and Bridge of the Gods, and the gift shop sells delicious home-baked cookies. Just down the street at the **East Wind Drive-in** (541-374-8380), indulge in a chocolate, vanilla, or swirl soft-serve ice-cream cone.

Cross the Bridge of the Gods into Washington, then head east on Highway 14 to Stevenson, home of **Skamania Lodge** (800-221-7117; www.*skamania.com*). Open since 1993, the lodge sits regally on a rolling meadow facing the Columbia River. Constructed of heavy timbers, with a massive stone fireplace in the lobby and Mission-style furnishings throughout, this grand place is reminiscent of Timberline Lodge at Mount Hood.

Come on a Sunday to indulge in the sumptuous brunch buffet at Skamania Lodge (9 A.M.–2:30 P.M.; $24.95/adults, $15.95/children ages 7–12, $10.95/children ages 4–6, free/children 3 and under; reservations recommended). Then stay to work off the meal by wandering the 3-mile-long nature trails that meander past the golf course and ponds. The fitness center and pool are open daily (non-lodge guests: $10/adults, $5/children 12 and under). The rock-pool hot tub outside is fun for kids in nice weather. On a rainy day they can splash instead in the indoor whirlpool and lap pool. Locker rooms are equipped with saunas, hot tubs, showers, and towels.

Don't return home before visiting the **Columbia Gorge Interpretive Center** (990 SW Rock Creek Dr, Stevenson; 800-991-2338; *www.columbiagorge.org*; daily 10 A.M.–5 P.M., except Thanksgiving, Christmas, and New Year's Day; $7/adults, $6/seniors and students, $5/children ages 6–12, free/children 5 and under). Designed to resemble the sawmills that sat here earlier in the century, this gem of a museum is located just below Skamania Lodge. Its manageable size and engaging exhibits, which trace the history of the gorge by underscoring its resources and inhabitants, make it particularly suitable for families. Children are intrigued by the basalt cliff adornments, indoor waterfall, replica fish wheel, and Corliss steam engine and logging truck. A short slide presentation examines the geologic formation of the gorge.

On the drive back to Portland on I-84 westbound, turn in at the **Bonneville Locks and Dam** and stop at the **Bradford Island Visitors Center** (541-374-8820; *www.nwp.usace.army.mil/op/b/*; year-round daily 9 A.M.–5 P.M., except Thanksgiving, Christmas, and New Year's Day). The glass-walled visitors center features an observation deck, historical displays, and underwater windows that look out on fish ladders. Chinook, coho, and sockeye salmon and steelhead migrate upriver to spawn in spring, summer, and fall. The best viewing is June through September. Check the Web site before you go to coordinate your visit with one of the dam's special events. And be sure to call ahead for reservations to take a guided tour of the dam powerhouse. As you head for the highway to leave, stop to examine the navigation lock.

Adjacent to the dam is the **Bonneville Fish Hatchery** (541-374-8393), where approximately 20 million salmon fingerlings are raised for release into neighboring Tanner Creek each spring. The parklike setting features ponds, picnic tables, and a gift shop (closed in winter). Learn about what happens at the hatchery through a 13-minute informational video shown at the visitors center. Then wander the grounds, where you can buy a handful of pellets to feed the rainbow trout that teem in the natural-style rock ponds. And don't miss seeing the underwater view of a 10-foot-long, 60-year-old sturgeon named Herman.

Note: Security measures closing areas of the Bonneville Dam or restricting access are subject to change on a daily basis, and closures or restrictions may apply to visitor facilities, fishing access areas, roadways, and scheduled tours. Call (541-374-8820) to determine current public accessibility.

Resources

- **Columbia River Gorge Visitors Association**, 800-98-GORGE (46743); *www.crgva.org/*

- **Historic Columbia River Highway**, 503-731-8200; *www.oregon.gov/ODOT/HWY/HCRH*

Hood River

Located 60 miles east of Portland, just off Interstate 84, Hood River is known as the sailboarding capital of the Northwest. A walk down Oak Street reveals shops that hawk every device necessary to equip a board and sailor—as well as the requisite souvenirs. Even so, the town is quaint with pretty bungalows, rolling lawns, and views of the Columbia River, and there's plenty to do here even if you're not a windsurfer.

Start your visit with a stop at the **Hood River Visitors Center** and the local Chamber of Commerce, located off I-84 at Exit 63 (720 E. Port Marina Dr; 541-386-2000, 800-366-3530; *www.hoodriver.org*). Nearby, you can get an up-close view of windsurfers at play at the **Columbia Gorge Sail Park** at the Hood River Marina. Marina Park also has a public beach, grassy park areas, windsurfing schools, picnic areas, and restrooms with public showers.

Before there was windsurfing, of course, Hood River was renowned for its orchards. A large percentage of the nation's pears—Anjou, Bosc, Comice, and Bartlett—are grown here, as are the world's preeminent Newton Pippen apples. Pick up a copy of the **Hood River Valley Fruit Loop** map, an annual guide to local farm stands, which is available at the visitors center and various shops and restaurants around town or online (*www.hoodriverfruitloop.com*). The Fruit Loop is approximately 45 miles long, leading visitors through the valley's orchards, forests, farmlands, and friendly communities. Pick and choose where you want to go—it's easy to tour all or just part of the loop. And for the most fun, plan your visit around one of the many seasonal festivals, which include the Blossom Festival (third weekend in Apr), the Gravenstein Apple Days (late Aug), the Annual Pear Celebration (mid-Sept), and the Harvest Fest (mid-Oct).

See the orchards from a different perspective by catching a ride on the historic **Mount Hood Railroad** (110 Railroad Ave; 541-386-3556, 800-872-4661; *www.mthoodrr.com*; times and prices vary). From the open-air car, luscious fruit can seem close enough to pluck as the train makes the leisurely 22-mile run through some of Hood River County's 14,000 acres of orchards to the tiny town of Parkdale. (Parents of Thomas the Tank Engine fans will want to watch for this train's annual summertime visit to the railroad.)

Back in Hood River, if you're a carousel lover, you won't want to miss the **International Museum of Carousel Art** (304 Oak St; 541-387-4622; *www.carousel museum.com*; check for current hours and admission). Dedicated to restoring antique carousels and preserving their history, the museum is home to what's reputed to be the world's largest and most comprehensive collection of antique carousel art.

From Hood River, if time and stamina allow, get back on I-84 and head 15 miles or so east to the Chenowith exit, where you'll find the **Columbia Gorge Discovery Center** and **Wasco County Historical Museum** (541-296-8600; *www.gorge discovery.org*; year-round daily 9 A.M.–5 P.M., except Thanksgiving, Christmas, and New Year's Day; $8/adults, $7/seniors, $4/children ages 6–16, free/children 5 and under). Located on a beautiful bluff in the town of The Dalles, the museum's kid-friendly exhibits are largely devoted to the geology of the gorge and the early inhabitants of the region. Children scramble through a marmot tunnel, try on old-fashioned pioneer clothing, and even clamber onto a sailboard to give windsurfing a try. You can also purchase snacks (including espresso drinks) at the museum's own cafe. Or, if you've brought your own food, picnic outside in the **Oregon Trail Living History Park**, where you might get to visit with a living-history interpreter portraying an Oregon Trail pioneer.

For a scenic drive back to Portland from Hood River, take Highway 35 south. The 44-mile route begins in flat fruit orchards, then climbs steadily and winds past mountainous, glacial terrain. From this vantage point, Mount Hood looms gracefully to fill the windshield. Continue to **Timberline Lodge** (see "Mount Hood," below) at the summit, then descend via Highway 26 and return to Portland.

Resources

- **The Dalles Area Chamber of Commerce**, 404 W. Second St, The Dalles; 541-296-2231, 800-255-3385; *www.thedalleschamber.com*

Mount Hood

Native Americans called it Wy'east, and at 11,235 feet, **Mount Hood** is the state's tallest peak. The mountain is famous for its summer skiing and offers the longest ski season in North America (see "Snow Sports" in chapter 5, Outside Fun & Learning). But even if you don't ski, the 62-mile trip to Timberline Lodge at 6,000 feet is rewarding.

Located east of Portland, off Highway 26, **Timberline Lodge** (503-272-3391; *www.timberlinelodge.com*) was built during the Depression in 1937 as a showcase for the talents of local craftsmen and artisans. Now a National Historic Landmark, it is truly a masterpiece of hewn logs and great stone fireplaces—the quintessential Northwest mountain lodge.

Tap into Tourist Info

The Oregon Tourism Department (800-547-7842; *www.travel oregon.com*) has made a real effort to encourage families to take their vacations close to home. You'll find great information on traveling the state in both the *Travel Oregon* magazine and at the Web site. You can also call for visitor information. And if you're planning to visit our neighbor to the north, Washington, you'll find help creating an itinerary from the Washington State Tourism Department (877-260-2731; *www.experiencewashington.com*).

The lodge interior manages to feel at once massive and cozy. You can see a 27-minute video that highlights the handiwork and graphic themes that are echoed throughout the lodge. The Forest Service also offers guided tours of the lodge from mid-June through Labor Day. Check in the lower lobby across from the front desk for information.

Inside the lodge, children with energy to burn after the drive have three lobby areas to explore. There's also a tabletop shuffleboard game (ask at the front desk for board games), a pub, and a formal dining room. Hungry kids might prefer the fast-food offerings at the adjacent Wy'east Day Lodge, which feeds crowds of skiers at lunchtime. Or you can eat outside on the deck at the Market Café, which serves barbecue fare.

Outside, the **Magic Mile Express Chairlift** (800-547-1406; spring daily 10 A.M.–1:30 P.M.; summer daily 10 A.M.–5 P.M., weather permitting; $15/adults, $9/children ages 7–12, free/children 6 and under, $42/family pass) to the base of the Palmer Snowfield is also open to nonskiers. Purchase a sightseer pass for a view of the Oregon Trail's Barlow Road and south toward Mount Jefferson and the Cascades (bring quarters for the telescope). Then, if you're game, return to the lodge on foot. A free trail map, available at the lodge's front desk, highlights points of interest along the 1-mile trail down.

Keep in mind that during ski season, special Sno-Park permits are required of lodge guests and visitors, and parking spaces may be limited. You can purchase a **Sno-Park permit** ($3/one day, $7/three days, $15/year; service fee may be charged in addition) at a state Department of Motor Vehicles office, as well as at resorts, sporting goods stores, and various other retail locations.

If it's summer and you (or, more likely, the kids) are seeking more excitement, head to the **Mount Hood SkiBowl Action Park** (503-272-3206; *www.ski bowl.com*; summer Mon–Fri 11 A.M.–6 P.M., Sat–Sun 10 A.M.–7 P.M., some attractions open one hour later; ticket prices vary, check Web site for details) in Government Camp. Here you'll find the region's only alpine slide—a half-mile, side-by-side model—and more than a dozen other amusement-park activities such as the Scenic Sky Chair, Indy Karts, the Kids Super Play Zone (for the youngest kids), and the 100-foot bungee tower. Or you can mountain bike on 40 miles of well-marked trails designed to accommodate all levels of bikers, tee up for a round of miniature or Frisbee golf, or take an exciting ride on a 500-foot-high zip line.

On the way back to Portland, near Welches, stop at **Cascade Streamwatch** to walk the lovely 0.75-mile loop that lets you learn about the salmon's life cycle and see the fish from a streamside, underwater window. This Bureau of Land Management site requires a day-use fee ($3).

Put a sweet finish on the day by stopping at the **Oregon Candy Farm** (5.5 miles east of Sandy on Hwy 26; 503-668-5066; Mon–Fri 9 A.M.–5 P.M., Sat–Sun noon–5 P.M., closed around Christmas). In business for more than 70 years, the Oregon Candy Farm is known for making more than 140 kinds of chocolate (including some that are sugar free). Visitors line up to receive a free sample and see candy being made (Mon–Thurs 9 A.M.– 3:30 P.M.) through large windows in the retail area.

Resources

- **Mount Hood Information Center**, 65000 E. Hwy 26, Welches; 503-622-4822, 888-622-4822; *www.mthood.info, www.mthoodterritory.com*

- **Sandy Area Chamber of Commerce**, 39345 Pioneer Blvd, Sandy; 503-668-4006; *www.sandyoregonchamber.org*

Mount St. Helens

Like Mount Hood, **Mount St. Helens** is visible from many parts of Portland, even though it is north, in Washington state. And on May 18, 1980, the mountain gave the city's residents a dramatic show, erupting with the force of several atomic bombs. More than 50 people were killed, and the landscape was changed drastically for miles in all directions. Nearly 230 square miles of forest was blown over or left dead but still standing. In 1982 the president and Congress created the 110,000-acre Mount St. Helens National Volcanic Monument for research, recreation, and education.

Mount St. Helens National Volcanic Monument (360-449-7800; *www.fs.fed. us/gpnf/mshnvm*) features five interpretive centers lining Spirit Lake Memorial Highway (Hwy 504), east of Interstate 5 near Castle Rock, Washington. Visitors here are treated to a panoramic view of the mountain, video and slide presentations, and educational, interactive displays and exhibits that document the 1980 eruption and its aftermath as well as updates on what's currently happening on the mountain.

Pick and choose among the options; to visit each one may cause sensory overload. Avoid crowds of tourists in general by avoiding summer weekends, but pray for a clear day for the best view. Then carry lightweight jackets and rain gear—along with your sunscreen and water—just in case!

If you pack a picnic, you'll find plenty of places to spread it out at one of the visitors centers or at Seaquest State Park near Silver Lake. Or you can lunch in the Hoffstadt Bluffs restaurant (see listing below) or at the Coldwater Ridge cafeteria.

The U.S. Forest Service requires visitors to purchase a Monument Pass ($3/ adults for single-site pass, $6/adults for multisite pass, free/children ages 15 and under); this per-person pass is good for one day at the following recreational fee sites: Mount St. Helens Visitors Center (at Silver Lake), Coldwater Ridge Visitors Center Complex (including Coldwater Lake Recreation Area), and Johnston Ridge Observatory. Passes may be purchased at Monument Visitor Centers and Apes' Headquarters through the Northwest Interpretive Association.

The sites detailed below are listed in order of distance from Interstate 5, starting in Castle Rock and ending at Johnston Ridge.

The Cinedome Theater

1239 Mount St. Helens Wy, Castle Rock, WA
360-274-9844, 360-274-8000
www.thecinedome.com

Hours: May–Oct daily 9 A.M.–6 P.M.

Admission: $6/adults, $5/seniors and children ages 6–12, free/children 5 and under

Mount St. Helens erupts every 45 minutes in season on the giant 70-mm screen at the 174-seat Cinedome. An Academy Award–nominated 28-minute documentary, *The Eruption of Mount St. Helens* is more experience than a movie. The screen is three stories high, and five rows of special seats at the rear vibrate with the roar of the volcano. Children under five years old may be overwhelmed by the sound system; older kids will surely be enthralled. Photos of more recent activity at the mountain are featured in the theater lobby.

Mount St. Helens Visitors Center at Silver Lake

Hwy 504, 5 miles east of Castle Rock, WA
360-274-0962
www.parks.wa.gov/mountsthelens.asp

Hours: Late Oct–Mar daily 9 A.M.–4 P.M., Apr–late Oct daily 9 A.M.–5 P.M., closed Thanksgiving, Christmas, and New Year's Day

Exhibits at this U.S. Forest Service facility on the shores of Silver Lake provide an introduction to the eruption with a walk-through volcano mock-up, a 16-minute film, a check of the two seismographs, plus views of the mountain (on a clear day) through telescopes. You can also wander along the mile-long Silver Lake Wetlands Trail to discover how the lake was formed by a previous eruption and how the aquatic life continues to change the lake today.

Hoffstadt Bluffs Visitors Center

Hwy 504, 27 miles east of Castle Rock, WA

360-274-7750

Hours: Shop: summer daily 9 A.M.–7 P.M., winter Thurs–Mon 10 A.M.–4 P.M.; restaurant: summer daily 11 A.M.–7 P.M., winter hours vary

Built and owned by Cowlitz County, this post-and-beam, alpine-style building houses a gift shop and a full-service family restaurant with a view of the Toutle River Valley. In summer there are glassblowing demonstrations every day, with artists making ornaments from Mount St. Helens ash. Helicopter tours ($114 plus tax/person) depart regularly from the parking lot.

Charles W. Bingham Forest Learning Center

Hwy 504, 33 miles east of Castle Rock, WA

360-414-3439

www.weyerhaeuser.com/sthelens

Hours: Mid-May–mid-Oct daily 10 A.M.–6 P.M.; Oct daily 10 A.M.–5 P.M.

If you have smaller children, the "volcano" playground at the entrance to the Forest Learning Center will probably lure you into this free attraction. After you play, walk the 0.5-mile trail and try to spot elk through the telescopes. Inside, you can walk through a lifelike forest, experience the "eruption chamber," and learn about forest recovery and reforestation and conservation of forest resources. Weyerhaeuser, the Rocky Mountain Elk Foundation, and the Washington State Department of Transportation collaborated on this facility.

Coldwater Ridge Visitors Center

Hwy 504, 43 miles east of Castle Rock, WA
360-274-2114

Hours: Early May–late Oct daily 10 A.M.–6 P.M.; late Oct–early May Thurs–Mon
10 A.M.–4 P.M.

On a bluff directly opposite the mountain's lopsided crater, the U.S. Forest Service's Coldwater Ridge Visitors Center underscores the region's recovery process with interactive exhibits that detail native life-forms before, during, and after the eruption. Take a walk along the paved trails beside Coldwater Lake (once a river) and scout for hummocks—the rocky mounds that were blasted from the volcano.

Johnston Ridge Observatory

Hwy 504, 52 miles east of Castle Rock, WA
360-274-2140

Hours: Summer daily 10 A.M.–6 P.M.; opening date depends on snowpack

This is the end of the road and probably as close as you'll want to get to the crater. Opened in May 1997, Johnston Ridge Observatory represents Mount St. Helens National Monument's crowning glory. The observatory features a large, formal theater; a 15-minute, wide-screen, computer-animated video program; and a jaw-dropping view right down the throat of the mountain. The engaging exhibits examine the geologic events surrounding the big eruption and subsequent eruptions, techniques used by scientists to monitor active volcanoes, and eyewitness accounts from eruption survivors. Take the half-mile walk on the Eruption Trail to learn how the eruption shaped the surrounding landscape. Forest interpreters share their insight into the events surrounding the 1980 eruption through a variety of formal talks and guided walks.

Resources

- **Cowlitz County Tourism Department**, 360-577-3137; *www.co.cowlitz.wa.us/tourism/*
- **Washington State Tourism**, 877-260-2731; *www.experiencewashington.com*

Salem

If you're interested in exploring Oregon's roots, a trip to Salem—just 47 miles from Portland—is, so to speak, a capital idea.

Start your trip with a stop at the **State Capitol** (900 Court St NE; 503-986-1388; *www.leg.state.or.us/capinfo/*; Mon–Fri 8 A.M.–5 P.M.), where the legislature convenes every two years in regular session, beginning the second Monday in January in odd-numbered years. Guides offer free top-to-bottom tours of the awe-inspiring, four-story structure, pointing out everything from the bronze replica of the Oregon state seal embedded in the rotunda's marble floor to the massive wooden desk—and squeaky chair—in the Governor's Suite, where bills are often ceremoniously signed into law. Starting in spring break and throughout the summer, you can join a guide to hike the 121 steps to the tower (generally every 30 minutes 9 A.M.–3:30 P.M.), where you'll have an up-close look at the shining *Oregon Pioneer* statue that tops the building.

There is a lot to discover just outside the capitol building as well. Wandering the "walk of trivia" in the **Capitol Mall** becomes like an Easter egg hunt as kids discover the fun facts—such as the state bird (western meadowlark) and insect (swallowtail butterfly)—etched into the walkway. Just west of the capitol, explore **Wilson Park**, where you'll find the comical and much-loved *Parade of Animals* sculpture. Wander south to the Willamette University campus and gaze up at the **Star Trees**, five lush sequoias planted so that they create a star-shaped opening to the sky. (The view is especially beautiful when the trees are decorated in winter with holiday lights.)

After exploring this area, head for Salem's waterfront. Here, situated next to the Willamette River, you'll find **A. C. Gilbert's Discovery Village** (116 Marion St NE; 503-371-3631; *www.acgilbert.org*; Mon–Sat 10 A.M.–5 P.M., Sun noon–5 P.M., closed holidays; $5.50/ages 3–59, $4/seniors 60 and up, free/children 2 and under). Named for the Salem-born inventor of the Erector Set, this hands-on museum features a bubble room as well as the La"ball"atory, where balls go flying. In A. C.'s Backyard, a 20,000-square-foot outdoor discovery center, kids can scale a three-story Erector Set tower, swoosh down a curvy slide, plink out tunes on a marimba or xylophone on a musical ensemble deck, and take the helm of a play wooden paddle wheeler.

A real paddle wheeler is docked just a short walk upstream from the museum. If you venture out on a relaxing 50-minute excursion on the *Willamette Queen* (503-371-1103; *www.willamettequeen.com*; $12/adults, $5/children ages 4–10), you'll learn tantalizing bits of river history, and the kids can pick up a junior captain's license after taking a turn at the ship's wheel.

Back ashore, the grassy lawn and vast play structure of **Riverfront Park** await. A wide, paved path—popular with skaters, bicyclists, joggers, and walkers—leads to **Eco Earth** at the park's southern tip. This giant colorful globe—tiled with icons created by local artists and schoolchildren—doubles as a tribute to the world's diversity. The path then loops around to the **Salem Carousel** (101 Front St NE; 503-540-0374; *www.salemcarousel.org*; $1.50/person). Riders young and old line up for a spin on one of the beautiful hand-carved, hand-painted steeds. Each horse bears a name—look for Westwind, Billiebom, the General, and Maudie Ann—and no doubt the kids will have to ride more than once to be able to choose a favorite.

Just a few blocks southeast of the capitol, spinning of another sort is in the spotlight at **Mission Mill Museum** (1313 Mill St SE; 503-585-7012; *www.missionmill.org*; Mon–Sat 10 A.M.–5 P.M., closed some holidays; $8/adults, $7/seniors 55 and up, $4/children ages 6–18, free/children under 6). The only woolen-mill museum west of Missouri, this site has one of the few water-powered turbines in the Pacific Northwest that still generates electricity from a millrace. Hands-on exhibits tell of Thomas Kay's Woolen Mill, which launched Oregon's famous textile tradition in the 1800s. Historic homes dotting the grounds give a glimpse into the lives of Salem's missionary founders.

For a great place to picnic, head to **Bush's Pasture Park** (600 Mission St SE; 503-363-4714; *www.salemart.org*). Formerly a 100-acre estate, the park features a historic home and an art center. Visit in midsummer and you might catch the Salem Art Fair and Festival. For kids, though, the real treasure lies simply in exploring the park and discovering four different children's play areas that are tucked away in the peaceful, wooded landscape.

Wrap up your trip with a visit to an Oregon original, the **Enchanted Forest** (503-363-3060, 503-371-4242; *www.enchantedforest.com*; Mar 15–31 and May 1–Labor Day daily 9:30 A.M.–6 P.M., Apr and Sept Sat–Sun 9:30 A.M.–6 P.M.; $9.50/adults, $8.50/seniors 62 and children ages 3–12; free/children 2 and under). This theme park has been lovingly constructed on a wooded hillside about 7 miles south of Salem, just off Interstate 5 at Exit 248 in Turner. And younger kids love it. Preschoolers romp along the twisty trails, peering into the Seven Dwarfs' cottage and slipping down a bumpy slide at the Old Woman's Shoe. There are several kiddie rides as well (tickets cost extra), and for the older kids the biggest thrill comes from the Big Timber Log Ride, reportedly the biggest log ride in the Northwest, which ends in a spectacular 40-foot plunge.

Resources

- **Salem Convention and Visitors Association**, 800-874-7012; *www.travel salem.com*

See also:

- "John Day Fossil Beds National Monument," chapter 2, Exploring the Natural World
- "Oregon Coast Aquarium," chapter 2, Exploring the Natural World.

Quick Index

Educational field trips

FREE Free

🐓 Playgrounds

🚼 Wheelchair/stroller accessible

Index

Exploring the Emerald City with kids? You'll discover plenty of ideas in this updated guidebook to make your adventures memorable. From finding birthday party locations to excursions outside the city, there are plenty of tips to make your outings with family easy and fun.

OUT & ABOUT WITH KIDS: SEATTLE

Ann Bergman

paperback, 288 pages
$16.95

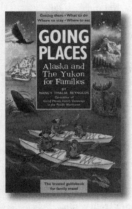

Now you can get away from it all—and still bring the kids! Discover Alaska and Canada's Yukon Territory with family-friendly attractions and travel resources. No matter the season, Nancy Thalia Reynolds and her crew of parent reviewers share the joys of a northern adventure on any budget.

GOING PLACES: ALASKA AND THE YUKON FOR FAMILIES

Nancy Thalia Reynolds

paperback, 448 pages
$21.95

Declared one of the most livable big cities in the nation, the difficult question when visiting Portland is not "what is there to do?" but "how am I going to do it all?" There is no shortage of amazing restaurants, unique attractions, growing local music and art scenes, and fine hotels. *Best Places Portland* lets you in on local favorites and the very best that Portland has to offer.

BEST PLACES PORTLAND

Edited by John Gottberg
and Elizabeth Lopeman
paperback, 400 pages
$19.95